To John Cammett

with best regards,

Carter Jefferson

ANATOLE FRANCE: *The Politics of Skepticism*

Anatole France:
The Politics of Skepticism

by Carter Jefferson

RUTGERS UNIVERSITY PRESS
NEW BRUNSWICK, NEW JERSEY

To Lucy and Laura

Preface

Fifty years ago Anatole France was world famous. Critics praised his books and readers bought them by the thousands. He was a member of the French Academy, and in 1921 he won the Nobel Prize for literature. Even now his works are widely read, but his literary reputation has suffered a steady decline.

Tastes change, of course, but literary reputations seldom rest on purely literary merits. Reviewing the various biographies of Anatole France and the volume of criticism concerning his works, one finds that most of France's detractors and almost all his admirers base their opinions of his writings not on literary values but on philosophical or straightforward political grounds. France is attacked, or praised, as a skeptic; his stylistic elegance, once the subject of panegyrics, is called a cloak for superficiality. Less subtle critics simply scold him for his alleged lack of morality. Since this is the case, it might be expected that his philosophy would be quite well known, and that his political position would be obvious. In fact, however, these things are quite obscure.

When I began to study France's career (in a graduate

history seminar in 1956), I quickly found that it was very difficult to discover what his philosophy really was, or even what his political attitudes had been. Communists called him a Communist; socialists called him a socialist; some Rightists called him a degenerated aristocrat; all sorts of writers berated him for being nothing at all. Literary critics, unfamiliar with his political life, tried to distill his philosophy from his literary works, only to find themselves disagreeing violently. Most serious biographers deprecated his political activities as unimportant. Other biographers were so studiously biased that their works were suspect. Only two obvious facts emerged: first, France was most certainly a skeptic (but what that meant was not quite clear); second, he had called himself a socialist for an undetermined period (but what kind of socialist he was, or how long he used the label, was a mystery).

In recent years the publication of three volumes of France's political speeches and letters has shed a certain amount of light on his political activities, but these materials have not by any means cleared up the confusion that surrounds his career. Letters and speeches do not always mean what they say, and the circumstances in which they are written or delivered always influence them heavily; besides, the collection is far from complete. Much of the evidence that would explain France's political development is still buried in files of old journals available only in Paris, and that which has been published has not been adequately studied.

This book is intended to show what France was politically, and how he came to that position; only by understanding these things can one understand his philosophical growth. Yet a proper evaluation of his philosophy is vital to a proper understanding of his works. Moreover, this book should help to explain why he has been attacked with such bitterness or dismissed with such condescension. It also should explain something about the intellectual climate of France's day and that of our own, for if opinions of his works have changed, the works themselves remain the same.

In dealing with France's political development I have, of course, had to take account of influences exerted by his parents, his schools, his friends and his enemies. This is not, however, a full-dress biography, so I have left out many things that seemed to me to have no political significance. I have also ignored certain episodes that are significant only in that they show again certain attitudes France revealed better on other occasions. Many of the facts I have recounted, particularly in the first two chapters, will be familiar to scholars. Much of the material on France's relations with the Socialist party is new, however, and the chapter on his dealings with the Communists is based largely on data not used by previous biographers. The interpretations, which differ in detail and in general with those of my predecessors in the study of Anatole France, are my own, though I have benefited by the insights of previous commentators and have tried to give credit where it is due. I have drawn heavily on the researches of others, most prominent among them Jacques Suffel, Edwin Preston Dargan, André Vandegans, Charles Braibant, and Micheline Tison-Braun, to all of whom I am greatly indebted. In the notes I have acknowledged my debt to scores of other scholars whose works I have used.

Many other people, both friends and friendly strangers, have helped me write this book. France's grandson, M.

Lucien Psichari, very kindly allowed me to examine France's travel notebooks, which, though deposited in the Bibliothèque Nationale, were not open for public inspection at the time I was in Paris. Mme Henriette Psichari allowed me to look over her notes for the forthcoming volumes of the collection of France's political writings that she and M. Claude Aveline are now editing. M. Suffel, Mme Jacques Lion, André Bay, the officers of the Société Anatole France, Mrs. Estrelle Vere Dargan, Professor William T. Starr of Northwestern University, Mr. William F. Dannemiller, and Mr. Phillips Brooks all gave me suggestions, introductions, information, or encouragement, or a combination of all four. Professors S. William Halperin, in whose seminar this work was begun, and Louis R. Gottschalk of the University of Chicago not only taught me a great deal about the methods of historical research but gave me valuable help by criticizing my manuscript. Professors Bernard L. Weisberger of the University of Rochester, Robert L. Peters of the University of California, William B. Willcox of the University of Michigan, and Herbert H. Rowen of Rutgers University also read the manuscript at various stages and made useful suggestions. Professor James Lea Cate of the University of Chicago first suggested that I write this book, and then continued to lend me his encouragement and assistance, as he has done ever since we met. Professors Donald F. Lach and Walter Johnson of the University of Chicago and Richard H. Powers of the University of Massachusetts all provided valuable moral support. The Committee on Scholarships and Fellowships of the University of Chicago helped to finance my research by awarding me the Albert Kunstadter Fellowship for 1956–57 and the Catherine Cleveland Fellowship for 1957–58. The staffs of the libraries of the University of Chicago, Wayne State University, and the University of Michigan all have been generous with their aid, as have the staffs of the Bibliothèque Nationale and the Bibliothèque Internationale de Documentation Contemporaine in Paris. To the *gardiens* of the Periodical Room of the Bibliothèque Nationale I owe special thanks—they were infinitely patient as they worked day after day, month after month, hauling bound volumes of newspapers from the stacks to my desk in the reading room. To all these I wish to express my heartfelt thanks.

My parents, who gave me their love and their support throughout the time that I worked on this book, contributed more than anyone can know to its completion. My wife has lived with this book for nearly eight years, and probably only another author's wife can appreciate her efforts; her confidence, her patience, and her criticism have lightened the burden of work and improved the quality of the final product, and her satisfaction as the job came to an end has made mine all the greater.

Carter Jefferson
Highland Park, New Jersey
January, 1965

Contents

PREFACE *vii*

1 *The Conservative (1844–1888)* *3*

2 *The Anarchist (1888–1898)* *43*

3 *The Crusader (1898–1906)* *92*

4 *The Socialist (1906–1917)* *150*

5 *The "Bolshevik" (1917–1924)* *198*

Conclusion *237*

NOTES *243*

BIBLIOGRAPHY *271*

INDEX *281*

ANATOLE FRANCE: *The Politics of Skepticism*

1
The Conservative
(1844–1888)

I

Some people seem to be born with political passions; others have politics thrust upon them. Anatole France was one of the latter. Born in 1844, he grew up in the days of the Second Empire, taking his political stance for the most banal of reasons and scarcely aware of political reality. Until he was twenty-seven years old he simply reflected the views of others. When his country went to war with Prussia in 1870, neither the outbreak of hostilities nor the defeat that followed seriously affected him. But the aftermath of that war, the Paris Commune of 1871, touched him deeply. It gave him the central tenet of the political philosophy he gradually developed over the years to come.

In 1871 France was just beginning to build a coherent philosophy of life. He was by then a thoroughgoing intellectual, desperately searching for a rational explanation of the art to which he was dedicated and the life he lived, but he was far from mature. So much is known of the circumstances of his childhood that his early development can be traced in considerable detail. His own memoirs, thinly disguised by a veneer of fiction, tell a great deal, and the work of a generation of scholars has bared much that he either neglected or suppressed. Here it will suffice to sketch France's background and to draw attention to certain factors that bore directly on his political growth.[1]

France grew up in a happy home. His mother, a woman of unusual strength but narrow intellect, was an example of the best that exists in the petite bourgeoisie.[2] She was an illegitimate child, born in 1811 to the unwed daughter of a relatively well-off peasant family of Beauce. Her feckless stepfather ran through her mother's dowry long before she grew up. She was a servant for a while, then a bride, and, at twenty-one, a widow. Eight years later she was married again, this time to Noël France.[3] Her second marriage was a solid success, though she seems to have grieved because she bore only a single child. She lavished her love on Anatole, teaching him thrift, enveloping him in her unsophisticated religion, and instilling in him a set of humanitarian beliefs that he never ceased to honor. She refused, for example, to let him play with the untutored children of certain poor neighbors, but she explained to him that those children could not be blamed for their rudeness.[4] She was plain, sensible, and charitable.

Unfortunately, Mme France loved her only child too well, and her protectiveness greatly irritated him in later years.[5] She praised him too much, and reproached him too harshly when he made mistakes. Her overwhelming affection probably was responsible for France's later failures in his dealings with women; he demanded that they mother him, then staged fits of pique when they became domineering.

France's father was a self-made man, all business, but he was still a romantic in a romantic generation. Reared as a peasant in Anjou, he joined the army during the reign of Charles X. There he won the attention and regard of his commanding officer, who set him up in business in Paris after he was discharged. Illiterate until he taught himself to read in his twenties, he became a respected bookseller and an expert on documents of the French Revolution. He and his wife were living above his bookshop on the Quai Malaquais when his son was born. There, and later in a similar shop on the Quai Voltaire, young Anatole played among his father's shelves, surrounded by the works of great men of the past and aware that among his father's customers were the literary giants of his own day.

Literature quickly became Anatole's passion. From his earliest childhood he lived in his dreams, reveled in his father's books, and disliked the mundane pleasures that suited his playmates. At school he never belonged: a dayboy among boarders, a poor boy among the rich, he found the Collège Stanislas intolerable. He read what he liked and ignored his assignments. He hated the "made Latin" he had to translate and rebelled when the strict schedule of studies took him too rapidly through the books he preferred. Throughout his school career he barely passed most of his courses, even though he occasionally won prizes in composition. He hated the prefects who kept him prisoner, the dirty tables and walls that surrounded him, the "horrible mixture of chalk and ink" that was everywhere.[6] Like a number of other future celebrities, he failed his first examination for the baccalaureate and had to spend a year readying himself to pass it on his second try. Naturally he grew to hate everything the school represented—including religion.

He left school with no idea what to do with himself.[7]

Working with his father compiling catalogues, doing odd jobs for his father's friends in the book trade, and trying fitfully to make some kind of career in the world of letters, he stumbled through these early years in a painful state of mild terror. He was shy; his attempts to find a place in the world of the salons foundered when he alternated between wooden idiocy and voluble gaucherie. Even when his literary efforts had earned him just enough of a welcome to allow him a modicum of assurance, people found him insincere and doubted that he believed the opinions he professed. His three or four love affairs ended badly; the one that seems to have been the most significant was no more than an infatuation with an actress he first saw in a play, then followed around at a distance, unable to hope for even a kind word. Through all this embarrassment, however, he remained ambitious. Underneath the mortified exterior there were intellect and power.

France's father despaired. All Anatole did was "scribble." He refused to become another "France, libraire." Yet gradually the scribbles began to amount to something. Finally, by 1868, he had carved a tiny place for himself in the literary avant-garde. In that year he published a short book, a brief biography of Alfred de Vigny, recently dead. He had, besides, a regular arrangement with two publishers, who gave him literary hackwork to do. One of them, Alphonse Lemerre, was to serve as the key to France's first real acceptance in the world of literature. A big room above Lemerre's bookshop in the Passage Choiseul, near the Bibliothèque Nationale, was the headquarters of a group of poets just becoming famous. Lemerre supported them—exploited might be a better word, since he made them pay their way by writing articles for encyclopedias and prefaces for his cheap editions of the classics. For some reason France weakened a little in 1869 and tried teaching school, but he botched the job.[8] His real life was his poetry, and his friends were the poets of Le Parnasse, so named after the series of anthologies of their poems, *Le Parnasse contemporain*, that Lemerre published for them.

To belong to that group France had to commit himself to an aesthetic gospel and a political attitude, for the Parnassians thought of themselves as militantly classical in style and fiercely republican in politics. Yet before 1871 France was far from sure of his aesthetic philosophy and utterly without serious political convictions.

During the decade after he left school, while he made his way as a critic and a poet, France built the basic personal philosophy within which all his later opinions were to fit. To be a poet, a littérateur, in nineteenth-century French society was to be a "philosopher" in the eighteenth-century sense: to live the examined life and to rationalize every move. Thus France was virtually forced to order his thoughts and attitudes. Much of the mental posture that had been unquestioned at home and at school he rejected. He considered alternatives. As a poet, he had to choose between the romanticism of his father's generation, which permeated the air in which he grew up, and the classicism represented by the Parnassians; he had also to consider the position of the "realists" typified by Flaubert and the devotees of the new religion of science, a cult that was rapidly gaining strength in the 1860s. As a human being, he had to find a religion or learn to do without one, and all the church seemed to offer in opposition to modern philosophy, and especially to science, was the flat condemnation of everything "modern" laid down by

Pius IX in the *Syllabus of Errors* of 1864. As a man of the world, he had to take a political position. All these conflicts overlapped. The romanticism France knew included a commitment to Catholicism and to a political conservatism usually expressed in a reverence for the traditions of the monarchy. Eighteenth-century classicism, at least as it was interpreted by the neoclassicists of the 1860s, was antireligious and anti-authoritarian but still basically aristocratic—one attacked Christianity and celebrated ancient paganism in measured accents hardly likely to appeal to avid followers of the adventures of romantic heroes like the Count of Monte Cristo.

When France began his philosophical apprenticeship, he was already committed to certain negatives. His father was a romantic and a supporter of the "legitimate" pretenders to the French throne.[9] From his earliest childhood France had quietly fought his father; this reflex action established his strong prejudice against romantics and Bourbons. He never struggled against his mother, for he respected her uncomplicated religious beliefs although he himself could not be satisfied with that kind of simplicity. His hatred of the priests of Stanislas prevented him from accepting anything the church taught that his mother might have neglected. These negatives were not guides for action, but they blocked some lines of thought and thereby forced France along other paths.

From the beginning of his career France gave himself out as a classicist.[10] In his first published article, in which he discussed newly published translations of *Werther* and *Tom Jones* by his father's patron, the Comte de la Bédoyère, he praised the translator's pure style and suggested that La Bédoyère had made it possible to see that Goethe, whatever his youthful accesses of feeling, really was close to classicism. In other words, he tried to kidnap Goethe from the romantic camp. His later criticism tended to follow the same pattern; as a critic, he was a classicist.

Literary forms are subtle, however, and when the classicist critic wrote poetry, he betrayed the romantic indoctrination he had undergone as an adolescent. All his early work, particularly the poetry he wrote for Elise Devoyod, his actress love, carries the stamp of Byron and Hugo. When he took his subjects from antiquity, he treated them in a manner that smells strongly of Chateaubriand rather than Racine. The boy who at seventeen had romantically rebelled in childish poems against the passing away of man and his works was too thoroughly steeped in romantic literature to become a classical poet overnight. Gradually, however, he began to reconcile his critical ideal and the style in which he wrote. By 1870 he had become a recognized satellite of Leconte de Lisle, a Parnassian committed to a doctrine that was consciously and systematically antiromantic.

The Parnassians saw beauty only in form, harmony, objectivity, impersonality. France the critic pointed out that "the beauty of the vases of classical Greece and the medals of Syracuse attest less to the genius of individuals than to the collective soul of cities living in familiarity with the beautiful." [11] The Parnassians deplored the "deformation" of nature by writers of the Middle Ages and felt, France said, that "every renaissance consists in the addition of an original link to the chain that comes out of the past." [12] Unlike Leconte de Lisle, however, France never went so far as to reject everything modern as bad. Influenced by the positivist doctrines that were coming into fashion, France maintained in 1870 that an author

could be individual and realistic without necessarily becoming offensively personal. Like the rest of the Parnassians, France argued for objectivity in literature, but he
kept his definition broad. In 1872 he praised Leconte de
Lisle for presenting human beings "in their true character, with nonessentials stripped away so that in the simplicity and intrinsic beauty of a type they are thereafter
endowed with superior and imperishable life." [13] He
could, however, appreciate Balzac, Flaubert, and Dickens, authors whose methods of immortalizing human traits
differed greatly from those of Leconte de Lisle; on the
other hand, the Goncourt brothers failed, he believed, because in their works they "deformed" life.[14] France built
this aesthetic between 1868 and 1874; afterward it never
really changed. He had a standard of taste, classical but
not narrow. The breadth of this doctrine gave him room
to be a tolerant critic and helped him avoid losing contact
with the readers of his day. He was a Parnassian, but he
was not dogmatic.

In 1871, however, that aesthetic was far from complete. France was still searching, and that search was forcing him to clarify his attitude toward religion. He had
lost his faith while still an adolescent, but he had not been
able to forget that faith existed or to follow the lead of
some of his eighteenth-century models by dismissing religion as a simple fraud—"damn'd stuff for the mob." [15]
He first reacted to his loss of faith with anger; he blamed
man's misery on God.[16] This was puerile, for he could no
more believe in an evil God than in a beneficent one. All
he believed in was an eternal flux. In 1869, musing on a
manuscript that carried the signature of Mary, Queen of
Scots, he breathed the perfume

Of fingers today mute, decomposed,
Changed, perhaps, into flowers in a solitary field.[17]

Nothing lasted, not even love; religion was false. But religion was still beautiful. Like Renan, for whom he developed a respect that lasted all his life, he could understand, even envy, people who were able to accept a faith that promised them life everlasting. He could not accept that faith, but neither could he face the prospect of annihilation. He sought assurance elsewhere.

For a short time he found serenity in the beautiful dreams of Camille Flammarion, a prophet of the 1860s who wrote book after book to spread his system of scientific spiritualism, a "nontheological refutation of contemporary materialism." [18] Flammarion argued that thought was more than a movement of nerves, force was more than a simple property of matter. God was not in the world, nor in heaven, but was the directing force that organized the world of atoms. France, following this doctrine, wrote several poems in 1870 and 1871 in which he spoke of a single soul, infinitely divided, shared by every living creature, finding its fullest expression only in the highest being, Man. He was able to merge this doctrine with Darwin's evolutionary theory, at least as that theory was interpreted by Darwin's French translator, Mme Clémence Royer. For Mme Royer evolution was progressive. It had direction. That directing force France could easily assimilate to the great soul that Flammarion described. For about two years France was a spiritualist.

Taine, Spencer, and Littré ruined that faith. Taine, the great determinist, convinced him that "with good experimental methods and well-made observations," men could soon create "universal rationalism." [19] In other words, no great soul is required. Spencer, the great theorist of progress through evolution, needed neither great soul nor determinism: he argued that man could never know anything of the absolute, the "essential world" Flammarion posited as the basis of the universe of matter; that knowledge was necessarily limited by the nature of man, and that perception was a matter of relation, difference and resemblance. Littré, the follower of Comte's positivism, applied that critique of knowledge to Darwin's theories and convinced France that no matter how obviously true evolutionary theory might seem, it was not proved. So in 1875, buffeted by the power of great thinkers he could not ignore, France wrote that "there are as many human truths as there are men and moments in the life of each of these men." [20] France had adopted the skepticism that was to remain the basis of his philosophy for the rest of his life.

Politically, France began as a harmless rebel.

"At twenty," he later recalled, "to the great dismay of my father, I was a republican, like all the young men of my class." [21] To be a republican meant to be revolutionary, for in 1864 Napoleon III, who like his greater uncle followed his star and ruled by force, was emperor of the French. By that time, however, the Empire was showing signs of strain. The emperor had promised peace and sent Frenchmen to fight in Russia and Italy; he had ruled as a friend of the church, then helped Italian patriots strip the pope of his Italian lands; he had promised plenty, and seen Frenchmen starve. Having lost his clerical support, he had begun to woo the rich liberals who lived by trade, but a great many people, remembering the bloody coup d'état that had put him in power, were unwilling to believe the emperor would ever change his ways. Anatole France was no convinced revolutionary; he rebelled because rebellion was fashionable. "We confusedly felt the breakdown," he later wrote. "We looked for alibis for the new regime. A lawyer entering practice would speculate on a censure, on a little prison. A political trial brought customers to his office." [22]

In 1867 France (speculating on a little prison?) wrote two poems, both quite Parnassian, attacking the Empire. One compared the emperor to "Denys, Tyrant of Syracuse" and forecast a bad end for the old gentleman. The other, heaping scorn on Napoleon III for making his ill-fated attempt to put a puppet emperor on the throne of republican Mexico, dilated on the misfortunes of Varus, the Roman general who committed suicide after his legions were destroyed by barbarian hordes in the Teutoburger Wald. France escaped punishment, as did *La Gazette rimée*, which published the two poems. *La Gazette* went bankrupt before the imperial police had time to close it. [23] On June 14, 1868, France carried his opposition further by joining La Démocratie, a republican group particularly dedicated to the prevention of war. [24] Later that year he and his friend Xavier de Ricard planned to bring out an *Encyclopédie de la Révolution* that, according to the prospectus they published, was to "bring . . . instruction that will not be useless to this and future generations." [25] One suspects that the emperor might have had a somewhat different view of the utility of the kind of information France and Ricard would have provided, but he never had to think about it, for the project did not attract enough subscribers to warrant its continuation. Undaunted by this failure, France kept on sniping. Hearing that a bas-relief of the emperor dressed in ancient Roman battle gear was to be executed, he took it on himself to state that Napoleon III had the right to raise up monuments to himself wearing the armor of Nero and Caligula but that such a costume would be ridiculous.[26] At about the same time he was reciting anti-Empire verses in one of the Parnassian salons.

People who knew him believed, however, that France's petty political activities were largely a matter of show. When he began to frequent the salon of Leconte de Lisle, a hotbed of violent republicanism, he was still timid, anxious, and, thanks to the manner he had acquired during his years with the priests at Stanislas, almost obsequious. He would stoutly affirm his complete agreement with some passionate supporter of republican doctrines, "but at the same time, in the spontaneous remarks that escaped him . . . he seemed different, an admirer of wealth, authority, reaction; and all the trouble he took to appear to be in harmony with the entourage ended only by making his contradictions more obvious." [27] His friend Fernand Calmettes, who left this record of France's embarrassment, believed that mentally, at least, France really was a liberal, even though he could not resist the seductive charms of luxurious living. Calmettes probably was wrong. France, at twenty-four, was a republican because his father was a royalist, because he was poor, because he was unhappy, unloved and unknown.

Still, in 1868 he definitely considered himself a liberal. His public position was fairly moderate. He preferred the cool skeptic Voltaire to the passionate believer Rousseau, and when he wrote about the Revolution of 1789, he made it clear that he sat with the relatively moderate Girondists rather than with the followers of the incorruptible and intransigent Robespierre. He was not a revolutionary, but simply a quiet skeptic.

Toward the end of 1868, republican agitation against the imperial regime suddenly increased in volume and became more extreme than it had been in years. Opinions had not changed, but a new law, designed to appease liberal opponents of the Empire by easing restrictions on the press, had failed in its purpose: enemies of the emperor, instead of being grateful for the concession, took advantage of it to step up their attacks. When the campaign for the elections of May, 1869, began, republicans tried, as usual, to defeat the official candidates supported by the emperor's administration. They found themselves divided into two groups, moderate and extreme, the moderates asking only for a parliamentary regime, the extremists holding out for revolution.

Anatole France clearly belonged with the moderates. In an article published on April 16, 1869, he delievered a blast at democracy: "It lowers the level, it troubles the public taste, it abolishes traditions. . . . The deluge is mounting; let us take refuge on the summits." [28] He was still willing to write an article for a republican journal, but by January, 1870, after Napoleon III had made new concessions to liberals, he had rallied to the peaceful revolution that moderate, parliamentary republicans believed the emperor was gradually bringing about.[29] In *La Vogue parisienne*, a conservative family magazine for which he wrote regularly, he published an ode to Napoleon, signed only "France":

He goes, strong and tranquil like God who guides him,
His feet on solid rock and his face toward heaven,

> Pacific soldier, he has the gentle strength
> Of a providential force.[30]

The rest carries out the theme. Possibly some other "France," not Anatole, wrote this. More than likely, however, it came from the same author who had, three years before, compared the emperor to the tyrant of Syracuse. It expressed the opinion he held, and Jacques Lion, who knew France well many years later and spent a lifetime collecting "Franciana," found it worth preserving in one of his scores of scrapbooks.[31]

On July 15, 1870, the Franco-Prussian War began. Anatole France, who had just praised that pacific soldier Napoleon III and who had, three years before, joined a pacifist organization, may not have welcomed the war, but he supported it warmly. Patriotically he let the trees of liberty that were being cut down for defense purposes speak for themselves to the patriotic readers of *La Vogue parisienne:* "Our death will contribute to the defense of the capital, which is not, thank God! menaced by the Prussians, but which must be protected from every danger. The ditch where we once extended our green arms will be flooded. All our brothers of the Bois de Boulogne are ready to die as we are." [32]

The Bois survived; the Empire did not. Napoleon III, defeated by Bismarck's troops, lost his scepter to the provisional Government of National Defense. France, aged twenty-six, was called up to serve in the National Guard, but he languished in the reserve, doing guard duty while others fought. Sitting in a fort not far from Paris with his friend Calmettes, he watched French troops stave off a German attack while he himself had only to kill time,

reading Virgil, betting on the fall of German shells, or
gambling with his fellow soldiers.[33]

Nothing had happened before 1870 to make France
take politics seriously. His republicanism was a simple reflex; his pacifism was puerile. If he preferred Roland to
Robespierre, his choice was literary, not political, for he
had no basis on which to make a truly political choice.
The Girondists were moderates, and Robespierre was an
extremist: read classical for the former and romantic for
the latter. France had never been cold or hungry. The
only bonds that had restricted his movements were those
in which he was held by the priests of Stanislas and by
the father who had always represented authority. He had
rebelled against those quickly enough, but the Empire,
which he baited because to do so was fashionable, had
never touched him. At most, his politics was the politics
of tendency; he tended toward moderation.

In 1871, however, he got the scare of his life, and from
then on he had at least one political principle. At that
time his grasp on his career was precarious. His whole
mental outlook was in disarray as he cast about for an intellectual scaffolding that would look rational. Then, suddenly, the familiar world that he had always known became a sea of blood.

The Government of National Defense, formed to fight
the Germans after Napoleon had been taken prisoner,
finally signed an armistice in January, 1871. France was
discharged from his post as amateur soldier. But Paris was
not ready for peace. In March a group of revolutionaries
defied the provisional government's order to surrender
their weapons, seized control of the city, and ruled it for
three months. The leaders of the Paris Commune finally

became legendary heroes for revolutionaries everywhere, legendary monsters for others who preferred less dramatic change. To Anatole France they were "assassins," but for two months they left him "in tranquillity as sweet as it . . . [was] humiliating." [34] Early in May the Communards threatened to disturb him, probably by forcing him to join their army; he fled.[35] For a pleasant month he lived in the country with the Calmettes family, calmly awaiting the fall of the Commune. Troops loyal to the provisional government finally captured Paris on May 31, and less than a week later France returned to the city, where he was greatly satisfied to find "the government of Crime and Madness rotting on the field of execution." [36]

France's letters of the day contain several harsh comments, but they give no indication that this incident had any particular impact on him. The effect was there, however, even though it did not show up immediately.

On the surface France's life went on as before. He continued to write poetry, publishing his first and only collection in 1873; he continued to write reviews and essays for various journals, and he continued to do little chores for Lemerre. But he also wrote a novel, one so harsh that he could not, in view of his chosen aesthetic of moderation and genteel realism, bring himself to publish it. Even in the form it took when it was finally printed, much revised, ten years later, this work, *Les Désirs de Jean Servien*, was a bitter denunciation of the "government of Crime and Madness." In it France portrays the government of the Commune as both horrible and ridiculous; in its utter incompetence, its weird doctrine, its theatricality, the Commune France describes would be irresistibly funny were it not so thoroughly evil. One of France's characters, a charlatan who has, in the chaos, become a colonel, comments on the famous decree that ordered three prisoners shot whenever a partisan of the Commune was executed by order of the government: "It is an inimitable monument of popular wisdom." [37] Later Jean Servien tells the colonel about his rival in love, describing the man as "an enemy of the people." He cannot believe that he has actually "denounced a suspect." Instead, "he reassured himself; Colonel Tudesco was only a puppet and couldn't really arrest people." But indeed the colonel could, and Jean Servien dies at the hands of a mob because the colonel's power—and the mob's—is real indeed.

To Anatole France the Commune was a bloodbath, pure and simple. In *Jean Servien* he sneered at the idea of government by the people, and in other works of the 1870s and 1880s he always spoke reverently of order, which in those days very definitely meant government by an élite. Nevertheless, that particular attitude could still change when France learned more about the élite. What would remain was his horror of violence. From 1871 on he condemned violence not because of some lingering Aristotelian nicety but because it shocked him to the depths. In the past his intellect had found violence undesirable, moderation correct. The Commune took that attitude out of the realm of intellect and made it an emotional certainty. In later years France might find it possible to forgive violence after it had happened, even then grudgingly, but he could never bring himself to approve violence in advance, no matter what great end might, to others, seem to justify any necessary means.

II

France came back to Paris in June, 1871. For the next seventeen years, until he was forty-four, his political attitudes were thoroughly bourgeois and deeply conservative. Not until 1888 were new shocks to upset his composure, to teach him more about life, and to throw him back into political uncertainty.

Gradually he satisfied himself that his aesthetic philosophy was sound; gradually he came to accept life as an elegant skeptic. More important, he continued to build his literary reputation, and with it his self-confidence.

France's first important literary success came in 1876, when he published *Les Noces corinthiennes*, a long play in verse. His reputation as a poet was made. George Sand, herself a famous figure, and Hippolyte Taine, a great critic as well as a philosopher of history, both wrote him letters of congratulation.[38] In its indulgent anticlericalism and its gentle unbelief *Les Noces corinthiennes* was politically unexceptionable.

France's success was enough to prove false his father's dire predictions, but he was far from secure, and he was enough the son of his father to want some sort of income he could depend upon. In 1866, shortly after he left school, he had unsuccessfully sought a modest post at the Senate Library. Ten years later, his reputation established as a poet and critic, he tried again, with better luck. The library had expanded, for one thing, but even more important, France now had a friend on the inside—Leconte de Lisle was on the staff. On his recommendation, France was hired as a clerk with a starting salary of 2,200 francs a year. That was only a little more than Lemerre paid, but the work was supposed to take only a few hours a week.[39] With a steady salary in prospect, France could take a real chance: he got married.

The author of *Les Noces corinthiennes* was not the timid youth he had been a decade earlier. He had suffered other rebuffs since the days of his adolescent passion for the actress Elise Devoyod, but he was no longer a boy, no longer totally unknown, no longer poverty-stricken.[40] Somehow he met Valérie Guérin de Sauville, a girl of twenty who had "admirable skin," blonde hair, "marvelous" hands and feet, and an ancestry that was a good deal better than France's.[41] She came from an old family of painters and miniaturists, artists France admired. On April 28, 1877, two weeks after France's thirty-third birthday, they were married.

By 1877 Le Parnasse was beginning to break up; its members were getting older and getting on in the world. Thrilled to be accepted by a group of kindred souls, France had found in Lemerre's big studio an atmosphere in which poetry flowered. Married and working in the Senate Library, he gradually drifted away from the poetic environment. But environment was not all: he had things to say that were better said in prose than verse. Finally, married men have responsibilities, and in 1877 poetry paid only a bachelor's wage. Gradually France turned himself into a novelist, an essayist, and a philosopher.[42]

In the past France had occasionally published stories, and he had written and filed away his novel *Jean Servien*, but he made his real debut as a writer of fiction in October, 1878, when *Le Temps* published *Jocaste*, a novelette. Three months later, in January, 1879, *Jocaste* and another novelette, *Le Chat maigre*, were published together in book form. *Jocaste* was a melodrama; *Le Chat maigre* was a Dickensian farce. The volume sold poorly, but Flaubert, a generous man, told France that the first story was excellent and the second a masterpiece.[43] France continued to write reviews and articles while he worked on another novel.

That book, *Le Crime de Sylvestre Bonnard*, was a solid success. France published fragments of the book in various periodicals from December, 1879, through January, 1881, and the finished work in April, 1881. *Sylvestre Bonnard* was hardly a novel; it consisted of two episodes, related only in that they dealt with the adventures of the same hero. France had, however, developed a personal style that made anything he wrote delightful, and he had frankly designed the book to please his readers, particularly the ones who belonged to the French Academy. The Academicians, literary conservatives, were overjoyed to find in Anatole France a writer of genuine talent who carried the banner against naturalist "brutes" like Maupassant, Zola, and Flaubert. They called France's book a "delicate and distinguished work." [44]

After this success France began writing the series of fictionalized autobiographical anecdotes that he was to publish as his next book, *Le Livre de mon ami*, in 1885. Most of the stories collected there were first printed in February, 1883, in *La Nouvelle Revue*, then a prestigious literary journal.

France had been a poet and had become a novelist. In 1883 he became a popular journalist as well. *L'Univers illustré*, a highbrow news magazine, gave him a pseudonym, "Gérôme," and made him a man-about-town and commentator on virtually everything. Beginning on March 3, 1883, his column, the "Courrier de Paris," filled the first two or three pages of the magazine every other

week, alternating with Courriers written by another
Gérôme, an ex-captain who called himself Richard
O'Monroy. He continued to write those columns for ten
years, using them to tell charming stories, to advertise
his friends and ridicule his enemies, and to make remarks
either serious or frivolous on whatever events might pique
his interest.

In March, 1884, he produced a novel of the French
Revolution, *Les Autels de la peur*, which was published
serially in *Le Journal des Débats*, a conservative journal
of opinion. France never published this novel in book
form; later he broke it up into a number of short stories,
which he subsequently made into a volume. *Le Livre de
mon ami*, the memoir, appeared in March, 1885. In July
of that year France found another steady job, this one as
literary editor of a newly established review, *Les Lettres
et les arts*. His editorship lasted only nine months, because early in 1886 he got an opportunity that he could
not refuse.

In March, 1886, he began writing a regular weekly
column on "La Vie à Paris" for *Le Temps*. When he had
first managed, several years before, to get an occasional
article accepted by *Le Temps*, even his doubtful father
had recognized the value of his achievement; to become
a regular contributor was a far greater mark of honor.
Better yet, early the next year, having proved himself as
a columnist, France was allowed to turn over "La Vie
à Paris" to a successor in order to occupy the most coveted critical post in Paris: he became regular literary critic
for *Le Temps*.[45] He was, at forty-three, perfectly fitted
for his work. During his long apprenticeship as a teller
of tales and dilettante in literature, history, and philosophy he had developed a style exactly suited to his audi-

ence of refined, erudite readers. He was both more and less than critic; he was ironist in residence, intellectual companion to the élite of Paris. What his weekly columns lacked as criticism—sometimes he hardly bothered to discuss the book that had set him thinking—he made up by turning them into gemlike essays in worldly philosophy. In a very short time France was a personage, a man of influence. His conquest of the readers of *Le Temps* was an achievement even greater than that marked by the success of *Sylvestre Bonnard* five years earlier. By 1888, when he had been writing for *Le Temps* for two years, he had taken a long step toward the Academy.

In the early days of his marriage France wallowed in domesticity. Jules Breton, an eminent painter and poet, brought his wife and daughter to visit the new family in 1877, not long after it was established.[46] His host, wearing a loose dressing gown and hand-embroidered slippers, met them in the garden.

"Ah! dear friend," France bubbled, "how happy I am to show you my nest! You see, I have a garden! It's hardly bigger than my parlor, but it makes a delicious study. It's an extra room for our house. When the weather is nice we eat out here, my wife and I." And so he continued, until his bride appeared, tall and gracious, dressed in a long cotton peignoir. He introduced her.

"As I wrote to you," he said, "she is a descendant of the celebrated painter Guérin, and, as such, she loves the arts, painting in particular."

Breton replied that she would have made a perfect model for her great-grandfather, and even declared that she made him think of the Venus de Milo.

"True," said France, "but she has better arms!"

When she went inside the house to prepare refreshments, France confided to his guests that his bride was quite timid, but he was working to correct this fault. Certainly she had been pleased by Breton's flattering comparison, but she had not known how to reply. That would come. "I find it pleasant to complete the education of the woman I love," France said. "The husband should be an educator, so that he can in every way adapt his companion to himself." Then they fell to discussing Breton's latest work.

France was ecstatic when, on March 1, 1881, his wife presented him with a daughter. As soon as the little girl was old enough, father and daughter went together to the zoo and to the Guignol, the French equivalent of the Punch and Judy show. France, entranced, wrote down little Suzanne's every word, carefully preserving her conversations so he could report them to the world.[47]

Though France seemed to be happy at home, as soon as his literary achievement began to bring him opportunities to move about in the social world, he accepted them with pleasure. Sometime early in the 1880s he began to frequent the famous salon of Mme Aubernon, where he apparently cut a passable figure despite his obsequious air and his vestiges of timidity.[48] In 1885 he was named a chevalier of the Legion of Honor—not an important thing in itself, but a significant recognition of his growing importance. Wearing his new ribbon, he was introduced into other salons. He accepted invitations from the Princesse Mathilde, Mme de Loynes, Mme Juliette Adam, and the novelist Gyp (the Comtesse de Martel), all of whom were noted for the social and intellectual splendor of their soirées. In 1886 he began to frequent yet another salon, this one formed, like a medieval university, by a group that had seceded from an older company, and presided over by Mme Léontine Arman de Caillavet. When Mme de Caillavet first met France, in 1883, she found him unpleasant, mediocre, and gauche. By 1886 she was beginning to change her mind.

Mme de Caillavet was well fitted for her social role. She had been born rich and she had married rich. She had also been born Jewish, but she had married a Christian and had taken her husband's faith. Her father-in-law, a naval contractor and shipowner, had lost much of his money before he died, but she still had her own inheritance. Her husband was primarily interested in sports; he was a wastrel, worthless in business, and unsatisfactory as a husband, at least as a husband for a woman with her talents and her strength. She had one ambition: she wanted a salon of her own. For years she was a constant guest of Mme Aubernon, from whom she learned her profession (for the hostess who kept a great salon had to be an artist, and the techniques of success had to be learned). Her brother was married to the daughter of Alexandre Dumas *fils*, who was the "great man" at Mme Aubernon's table. When Dumas *fils* quarreled with his hostess, he took with him from her drawing room the nucleus of what was to become the salon of Mme de Caillavet.

When the dispute occurred, in 1886, Anatole France went with the clan Dumas, ceased to visit Mme Aubernon, and became a faithful guest at the house of Mme de Caillavet. Even this flattering move did not completely convince Mme de Caillavet that she should begin to like him. During the summer of 1886, while France was vacationing with his family at Saint-Valéry-sur-Somme, her husband wrote to ask him to visit them at Capian, their estate in the Gironde, but Mme de Caillavet wrote to her son that if France planned to come with his family she would find an excuse to put him off. "If he is coming alone," she added, "that would be another matter." [49] That year he did not go to Capian, but he had come a long way since the days when he was welcomed only in the modest parlors of his family's friends.

Marriage and a steady income brought France a new security, but not a new philosophy. Sylvestre Bonnard, created in 1879 and 1880, when France was living with a lovely wife and anticipating the joys of fatherhood, was just as much a skeptic as Jean Servien, offspring of France's days of desire and pain, child of 1872, when France had just begun to realize the implications of his skepticism. Nevertheless, France's viewpoint had changed a great deal, and his writings during this period of happiness reflected the new attitude as well as the old philosophy. *Sylvestre Bonnard* is so well known that it would be superfluous to describe it here; it was, quite simply, a charming story about a charming character. Optimism and tenderness dominate its pages, even though France gave the book an underlying sadness by making his hero an old man and an inveterate skeptic.

During the next few years, until the middle of 1888, France's writings continued to reflect the same mixture of philosophical pessimism and emotional tenderness that *Sylvestre Bonnard* had in 1880. Repeatedly some random notion sent him into a soliloquy on "the passing away of things," the eternal change that turned the lovely fingers of Mary Stuart into flowers in a field, or on the helpless condition of men, who live on an obscure ball of mud on the fringes of an unknown and unknowable universe. In 1885, when he published *Le Livre de mon ami*, a book as tender and full of charm as *Sylvestre Bonnard*, France still saw wisdom in a puppet who prefers to sleep rather than to look for treasure, for Guignol "knows the vanity of all things, and . . . aspires to repose as the unique good among the culpable or sterile agitations of life." [50]

Repose, however, is the opposite of life. France therefore did not try to justify action, he only declared that to act is human. For him, merely being human, acting and desiring, was somehow right. He was quite ready in one of his columns in *Le Temps* to admit that the skeptic Pyrrho was right to despise death, because life and death have equal value. Yet when he read of an old doctor, an atheist and materialist, who wept when he was condemned to die, France was touched. This man was not so wise as Pyrrho, but his tears, "though a little imbecilic, were more human than the virtuous insensibility of the sage of Elis." [51] To act is just as human as to fear death, France thought, and some actions might be worthwhile. Evil is everlasting, and sacrifice impotent, but "devotion and heroism are like great works of art: they have no object but themselves." [52] Men do good in the world, and even though their acts are futile, those acts are glorious.

In September, 1887, someone wrote an article on his philosophy that provoked him to reply: "He said that I have illusions. I have; the sad thing is that I know it. Nevertheless, I have them still, I have kept almost as many as I have lost. I have hundreds of them, and I could count them one by one. . . . They come in turn to play on my shoulder. . . . They never leave. . . . They are poet-birds! You have yours, my dear colleague, as I have mine; I divine that yours have plumage of shocking tones and warm colors. Don't you know that illusions would cover the world if they spread their wings together? I think they are the only realities of life." [53] Human beings, he believed, are governed by their illusions and hold strongly to them; humanity displays at all times the same quantity of folly and stupidity. Perhaps, in fact, old stupidities, consecrated by the ages, are the best. "Instead of rejoicing when I see some old error go, I think of the new error that will take its place, and I ask myself uneasily if this one will not be less convenient or more dangerous than the one it replaces." [54]

Illusions are dangerous, he believed, only when they lead to fanaticism. He profoundly revered the enlightened aristocrats, those "proud and charming" flowers of eighteenth-century culture, who brought into being "the spirit of tolerance, a profound belief in the rights of the individual person, the instinct of human liberty." He continued: "They wanted good for themselves and others and conceived the idea, new and strange at the time, that happiness was a desirable thing. Yes, those gentle heretics were the first to think that suffering is not good and that men must be spared it as much as possible. . . . These amiable ladies, these good seigneurs killed fanaticism. . . . They knew that life is a dream, and they wanted it to be a sweet dream." [55]

Fanaticism he saw as evil; superstition, good or bad, he saw as simply incurable. If religion was currently the most widespread superstition, there were other kinds as well: "If science reigns alone someday, credulous men will have only scientific credulities." [56] As long as those "credulities" stopped short of fanaticism, however, France could approve of science. (After all, it fascinated him.) In 1886 he remarked that the public had come to venerate scientists. That was not wrong. "Science can do a great deal for us; let us only take care not to ask of it more than

it can give. That was the error of the late eighteenth century. It wanted everything from science, even happiness.
. . . Without doubt, science explains a great many things; without doubt, it reveals many secrets; but there is one thing it does not reveal, and that is the secret of secrets. Science cannot teach us the reason of things, because that reason is outside of man, and science, which is human, cannot lead man to come out of himself." Scientific truths and vulgar truths are different only in their precision. This makes a big practical difference, but scientists still know only appearances and phenomena. They may see how things happen, but never why. Hence one cannot ask science for a moral. We may know now that the earth is just a speck, we may know what gases are burning in faraway stars, but that knowledge has not affected mother love or appreciation for female beauty. "It does not matter to men whether the earth is large or small. It is large enough that one may suffer upon it, and that one may love. Suffering and love—those are the twin sources of its inexhaustible beauty." [57]

France thought, however, that even though the deepest sentiments do not change, other attitudes might. He wrote in 1886 that some intelligent people still believed there had been absolutely no progress in morality across the ages; he thought they were wrong. "Amelioration is visible in our penal code, in the administration of hospitals and prisons, in the ordinary habits of citizens." [58] Still, he cautioned, men differ little from their grandfathers; human institutions should be modified slowly, since men themselves are so slow to change. [59] He was sure that progress is slow, and, moreover, that infinite progress is impossible. Regression would come, someday. The last human beings, he wrote, living on a cold earth beneath a dying sun, will be as primitive and stupid as were the first.[60]

All these ideas, culled out of France's writings of the mid-1880s, can be called a philosophy only in the broad sense of the term. France had no system, and he scorned any such thing. He remarked in the preface to the second of the four volumes he made of his columns from *Le Temps* that everyone ought to be allowed to possess two or three philosophies at one time—he was frightened by "souls exempt from all illogic." [61]

If he had no system, however, he had opinions on basic questions about human life. He also had opinions on religion, society, politics, and literature, and these tended to harmonize with his views on man's nature and destiny.

France's political position in the early 1880s was quite simply conservative. He was happy; he therefore preferred as a rule to ignore, or consider merely unfortunate, any unhappiness he might notice about him. At heart he belonged, he said, to Rabelais' Abbey of Thélème, where the rule was indulgent and obedience easy. "Indulgence, tolerance, respect of self and others, are the saints one honors there. If one is inclined toward doubt, it must be remembered that pyrrhonism [skepticism] cannot exist without a profound attachment to custom and to usage. But the custom of the greatest number is morality. There is no one like a skeptic to be always moral and a good citizen. A skeptic never revolts against the laws, because he has never hoped that good ones could be made. He knows that one must forgive the republic for a great many things." [62]

He was a patriot. He loved the army, and all it stood for. "An army is admirable! Think of it! So many hearts united in a single thought! Such a force, so well contained! Such beautiful order!" The military virtues, he believed, were the sources of civilization. Man is violent by nature, so war will never end. Even if a world of peace were possible, it would cost too much if it were bought at the price of the sentiments of courage, honor, and sacrifice that war has brought to men.[63] On the other hand, he was not a militarist. When he saw a general try to abuse the privileges of his rank by bullying a guard at a railroad gate, he regretted that he had to report such a thing, but report it he did, for the train guard had his duty to do just as the general did.[64] In his patriotism he kept his sense of justice. Justice, after all, is a form of moderation, a balance.

Occasionally, however, he betrayed the fact that his patriotism outweighed his devotion to liberty. In 1887 he bitterly denounced Abel Hermant's antimilitary novel *Le Cavalier Miserey*, which an army officer had forbidden his troops to read. France said he would rather have written the order of prohibition than the book itself. "A writer ought to be able to say everything, but he cannot be permitted to say everything, every way, in every circumstance, to every sort of person. He does not move in the absolute. He is in relation with other men. That implies duties; he is independent so that he may enlighten and embellish life, not so he may trouble and compromise it. He is bound to handle sacred things with respect." [65]

Religion, as well as patriotism, was a "sacred thing." France himself remained totally unreligious, and continued to make his position clear throughout this conservative period, but he insisted that toleration must work both ways. Most republicans agreed during the 1880s that clericalism was the great enemy; many of them failed to make the distinction France made between clericalism and religion. Religion was an illusion, but he considered one illusion as good as the next and thought that every man had a right to his own as long as he tolerated the illusions of others. France berated the notorious Léo Taxil, who had spent years as a propagandist for various freethinkers' leagues, even after Taxil had repented and joined the church. Unlike God, France was not willing to forgive the transgressor. Taxil had changed parties, France said, without changing souls; he would not be worth much more as a defender of the church than he had been as an attacker.[66]

France also argued that nuns had as much right as anyone else to teach children to read and to care for the sick: "They are suspect, I am told; if they teach, they will not fail to teach what they believe, and they do not know the truth. I doubt, in fact, that they do know it in its entirety. But I am not so sure that whoever might replace them would know it either. Error is not a privilege attached to the religious life, and laymen may also be mistaken." [67] He based his position, however, not only on the ideal of toleration but also on his belief that religion had a positive value. Speaking of St. Valery, who had preached to a group of pagan villagers after breaking their idols, France said "it was just that he should give them a God in exchange for those he had taken away, for anyone who destroys hope in men's souls is cruel." [68] Even as late as 1890, when all his ideas were changing, he could still say, "What does it matter what one believes, so long as that faith consoles!" [69]

The status quo that he supported so respectfully was embodied not only in religion but also in the conservative republic that was established in 1875 and firmly fixed in power around 1877. His memory of the Commune of

1871 reinforced his belief in gradual change and the deep opposition to revolution that stemmed from his conviction that social change was almost as slow as that of the earth itself. Whenever he had occasion to refer to the Commune in his newspaper or magazine articles, he attacked it as barbaric, "soiled with crimes." [70] When he spoke of the masses, he saw them as either innately cruel or naïvely good, sometimes changing suddenly from one to the other. In his novel about the Revolution, *Les Autels de la peur* (1884), he painted a glowing picture of the crowds gathered in July, 1790, on the Champs-de-Mars to prepare for the famous Fête de la Fédération, the day that contingents of the new National Guard from all over France came to Paris to swear allegiance to the king, the law, and the nation. In the holiday atmosphere no one feared thieves; men shared each other's wine, and fraternity was the order of the day. But one of France's characters was alarmed. "I wish there were a little less pressure," he said. "Is it proper to say, 'Be my brother or I'll kill you'?" [71] In a newspaper column France assailed Rousseau as the man responsible for the brutal (but not necessarily inexcusable) September massacres of 1792. Rousseau said that men are born good and happy but society has made them bad. "Then queens turned themselves into milkmaids, ministers became philosophers, legislators proclaimed the rights of man, and the people, naturally good, massacred the prisoners in the jails for three days." [72] Discussing an exposition of relics of the Revolution, France said he was most impressed by the utter naïveté the evidence shows: "The Revolution was made by fanatics." [73] And he did not like fanatics. Nevertheless, though he deplored the fanaticism of the revolutionaries, he did not condemn the Revolution in its en-

tirety. In the last scene of *Les Autels de la peur*, his hero
marches to the scaffold, still convinced that "France is
bringing justice to the world." [74] Clearly, the author saw
this creation of his as naïve, but he understood him, and
he was too wise to condemn an earthquake.

France had about the same attitude toward the Old
Regime that he had toward the Revolution that destroyed
it: it was as good as might be expected and as bad as one
might fear. Writing about the trial of the great financier
and minister, Foucquet, who was driven from office in
1661 by the young Louis XIV, he said that Foucquet had
served the state well until his reason became clouded.
When he fell, the public had a great deal of respect for
the court that was trying him. People hoped the court
would punish those who had oppressed them, and thereby
make their lives better. "Such illusions are very natural,"
France remarked, "and one may wonder whether any
government would be possible if unhappy people did
not, from day to day, expect something better on the
morrow." [75] By the time the trial ended three years later,
the public already hated Foucquet's successor, the great
Colbert, and was glad Foucquet escaped the death sentence.

Foucquet and his successors had finally been driven
from power, and the men who made the Revolution had
been tamed. In the 1880s neither king nor sans-culotte
governed; the nation was in the hands of the bourgeoisie.
Henry James wrote, long before Anatole France was famous, that Balzac and other French intellectuals hated
the bourgeoisie because they were almost all fugitives
from the bourgeoisie and because the bourgeoisie hated
them.[76] In the 1880s, however, France had not yet escaped his class; in fact, he had only recently begun to

belong to the real bourgeoisie, the small class of wealthy men and women who owned the factories and the banks and who actually controlled the country. As a child, he had been beneath that group, and the ambition that goaded him forward was at least partly a wish to join it. Until 1888 he had nothing to say against the Chamber of Deputies and the Senate that frankly ran the nation's government in the interest of the bourgeoisie. He may have been disgusted at some of the acts of the politicians, but he saw no hope for improvement. Moreover, he was still an employee of the Senate, and it would have been imprudent for him to attack the men who paid his salary. Paris, however, was run by a Municipal Council that was far to the left of the national government. It passed for "red," and it was fair game. When the Council decided to expel nuns from the corps of nurses that served in the city's hospitals, France called the action a "barbaric measure" that showed "the stupidity of our politicians," that is, the politicians of the Left.[77] His attitude exactly matched that of the vast majority of his readers, for most of the people who had voted for that left-wing city government did not subscribe to *L'Univers illustré*, in which he made these remarks. France's readers belonged instead to the group that ruled the nation, not the city, and, as a conservative, France attacked the Municipal Council but not the national government. In fact, neither France nor his readers had a high opinion of the politicians who worked in their behalf, but they were well aware that any government that might replace the one they had was likely to be far worse—for them, at least. That situation changed radically, however, late in the autumn of 1887. By then France himself was beginning to change his opinions, for

his years of solid success had subtly altered his view of
himself and of the world.

France's peculiar blend of mellow conservatism and
eighteenth-century skepticism, served up as it was in a
sumptuous style, pleased his editors and his public. During the years of patient labor that followed the success
of *Sylvestre Bonnard* he gradually became famous. He
who wrote about others began to be written about. In
February, 1883, a review especially aimed at French
youth carried a flattering essay on the author of *Sylvestre
Bonnard* written by an obscure young man named Maurice Barrès. In 1885 a colleague somewhat better known
than France, his friend Jules Lemaître, published the same
sort of essay in *La Revue bleue*, an important journal.[78]
France was hungry for this sort of praise. He had waited
long and worked hard for it. He basked in its warmth,
and year by year he grew more confident, more certain
of his worth, and more difficult to live with.

At the Senate Library he gradually came to feel that
he was too important to be treated as an ordinary clerk.
All he was supposed to do was keep the catalogue up to
date, but gradually he began to work less and less and to
expect more and more consideration. He had started at
a salary of 2,200 francs a year; his wage had been raised
first to 2,800 francs, then, in December, 1884, to 3,000.[79]
Nothing indicates that he ever worked hard at his job,
but presumably the salary raises would not have come
unless he had performed with at least a minimum of effi-
ciency for several years. In December, 1886, however,
just after the questeurs of the Senate had made up their
budget for the next fiscal year, France's superiors must

have intimated that they were less than satisfied with his work. In a column about Jules Sandeau, another writer who had been a librarian, France casually remarked that Sandeau never knew his library very well. "But who would hold it against him? His head was too full of beautiful books for him to be bothered with the people who filled his study room." [80] Sandeau got away with it; France did not. By the summer of 1888 his chief at the library was ready to report that France was doing no work at all.[81] He was, therefore, passed over, while a younger colleague was promoted. On August 4, 1888, he wrote to the questeurs to protest:

> This order . . . is an act without precedent in the French administration; it violates rights which until now have been constantly respected; it constitutes an unheard-of injustice, against which I must protest.
> My cause is that of equity. I would be culpable if I did not defend it with all my energy.
> And whom have you injured by this unspeakable, as well as unexampled, act? A man who has rendered services to the Library of the Senate, who has tried to merit your esteem and who was not totally unworthy of it, since his works have won him, still young, the cross of the Legion of Honor.[82]

Mme de Caillavet heard about his problem and was equally incensed: who were these people, to decide the fate of such a man as Anatole France? [83]

Several more letters passed back and forth before a temporary truce was made. The peace did not last, however, and France quarreled steadily with his superiors until he resigned on February 1, 1890.

France's squabble with the Senate was a farce. The destruction of his marriage was not so funny.

France had imagined that he would "educate" his young wife; he failed miserably.[84] Mme France was descended from a family of artists, but in fact, the domestic arts were the only ones that truly interested her. She was not interested, for example, in literature. She ran her home tyrannically, and in bad weather, when he could not work in the garden, France had to share his study with a wicker dress dummy. On occasion, too, Mme France, née Guérin, demonstrated execrable artistic taste; she failed, for instance, to agree with her husband's choice of a hanging for her parlor (the piece in question was a gift from Mme de Caillavet). She also let herself gain weight and allowed her teeth to deteriorate, thereby lessening her resemblance to the Venus de Milo. Clearly, she was resisting her husband's excellent instruction. Such things pained France in the extreme. If he thought he knew best how to educate his daughter, and his wife disagreed, then obviously he was right, for did he not discuss education quite often in the columns of *L'Univers illustré* and *Le Temps*? If she was proud of her ancestry, he shared her pride, as he had shown by writing an article about "les Guérin" in *La Revue alsacienne*.[85] But her ancestry, illustrious as it was, gave her no right to harp on the quality of her bloodlines, particularly when he himself had begun to produce personal achievements that compared quite favorably with those of her ancestors. She tended to imply, too, that their house was her property, since her dowry had paid for it, but, on the other hand, France supported her quite adequately. Worst of all, she began to tell all comers that her husband had no talent and did not know how to make money.

The disintegration of France's household was gradual, as gradual as his wife's loss of her beauty, as gradual as his own steady climb toward literary success. His home life became less pleasant, just as his life in the salons began to grow more enticing. How could Mme France compete with the brilliance of Mme Juliette Adam? the wealth of the Princesse Mathilde? the growing power of Mme de Caillavet? Particularly the last.

Mme de Caillavet had set up her salon in competition with that of her mentor, Mme Aubernon. Almost immediately, however, she found that a worse competitor still was Madame de Loynes, the former mistress of a Bonaparte prince, who sought to attract the same celebrities that Mme de Caillavet wanted to capture for herself. The custom of the salons decreed that any real hostess had to have her lion, a great man for her very own, but custom did not provide a simple method of determining who belonged to whom—that was left to a more primitive code. Temporarily, Mme de Caillavet made do with Victor Brochard, a distinguished professor who had written a classic study of Greek skepticism. Brochard, for some mysterious reason, was not wholly satisfactory. As for France, she liked "his style and his mind" but not "his character or his ways"—or his wife.[86] In the summer of 1887, however, he had made enough headway that he and his wife received the invitation to Capian that she had withheld the year before. Shortly before the visit was to begin she wrote to her son, already in the south, to tell him she had seen "the Anatoles Saturday night, he still trembling and stuttering before his imperious spouse." [87]

By then, however, even though no one knew it yet, the imperious spouse had lost her husband. Mme de Caillavet was ten years older than Mme France, and only three years younger than Anatole, but she was beautiful, intelligent, and strong. Obviously she was a far more suitable consort for a man of France's stature—or the stature he had come to believe he had—than the dowdy, carping descendant of "les Guérin." France fell in love. The only thing that might have deterred him from the course he set no longer was an obstacle; his pious and beloved mother, whom he never would have hurt, had died in 1886. Less than a year after that visit to Capian, Mme de Caillavet had captured her lion, and France had conquered a mistress. By August, 1888, he was writing delirious letters to her: "I have spent a day full of you and extremely painful. Be good and confident, my dear. Live in me, as I live in you, and all will be sweet, even sadness. I love you with all my heart, I love you with my tears. You tear me to pieces, bless you. I love you." [88] She answered: "Have confidence, my friend, have good courage, we have found the only reason to be alive: a love that can drown everything, submerge everything in its plenitude and its glory." [89]

France continued to live at home, but he rented a furnished room under an assumed name.[90] Word went round that Brochard, the old lion, had given way to a new. Mme de Loynes, who had had her eye on France, was a little upset, as was Jules Lemaître, France's good friend, who had entertained thoughts of displacing Brochard himself. Fortunately all went well. Brochard retired gracefully to visit elsewhere, as befitted a student of Pyrrho, and Lemaître became the great man of Mme de Loynes's salon.

France at last had a woman he considered worthy of him. Mme de Caillavet, however, was not really satisfied. She wanted a *great man*, and France was not quite that, not yet. But that could be remedied. Mme de Caillavet had her raw material, and it had certain virtues. She would mold it, smooth it out, polish it. She had a man; she would make him great.

2
The Anarchist
(1888–1898)

I

During the hot Parisian summer of 1888 Anatole France unconsciously closed a chapter in his life. His love for Mme de Caillavet came alive, he recognized that his marriage no longer counted, and he rebelled against his superiors at the Senate Library. He could still believe, as autumn began, that his skepticism necessarily implied "a profound attachment to custom and usage," to common morality.[1] Actually he had by then already broken that bond, but he had not yet made all the adjustments that his new position required.

Mme de Caillavet went to Capian in July. France, left behind, counting the days until he could join her there in September, poured out his woe in the letters he wrote to her.[2] Meanwhile he wrote his newspaper and magazine columns and planned a new novel. Once he dropped his guard, and a certain new bitterness, probably sharpened by the absence of his mistress, appeared in one of his articles. For the first time since he had begun writing for *Le Temps* he insulted his readers. Discussing the education of the daughters of the bourgeoisie, he remarked that bourgeois parents no longer even knew what they raised children for; how, therefore, could they know what those children should be taught? "Everything around them is uncertain and moving. They belong to a ruling class which no longer rules, and their incapacity and their egotism are marked with failure. They are part of an aristocracy that falls and rises according to its gain or loss of the money that is its sole reason for being. . . . They are themselves floating and abandoned." [3]

France went to Capian in September. When he returned, he struck up a friendship with General Georges Boulanger, who was methodically preparing to overthrow the government.

Boulanger had become prominent in 1886, when leaders of the Radical party made him minister of war in a coalition cabinet.[4] As a ranking officer, he carefully cultivated a reputation for loyalty to the republic that made him a distinctly unusual figure in a predominantly reactionary and royalist army. Once in office he irritated his more conservative colleagues by displaying, along with the most extreme patriotism, an appreciation for the hardships of common soldiers and striking coal miners. To the simple-minded citizens of Paris, Boulanger appeared to be the man who would avenge the defeat of 1871 and, at the same time, protect them from reactionaries, who had made an unexpectedly strong showing in the elections of 1885. With all this, he was also a consummate showman. At the Bastille Day review in 1886, astride his black horse, proudly displaying his great blond beard, he was the very personification of French pride and glory. The crowds went wild with admiration.

Anatole France was there that day, and he loved the show; that was the occasion that wrung from him his panegyric of "such a force, so well contained!" [5] This overdemocratic general, however, he did not like. In that same ecstatic column, though he pointedly omitted any reference to the general, he bitterly denounced the plan Boulanger and his Radical colleagues had offered for reducing the term of military conscription from five years to three. A few days later, in *L'Univers illustré*, he accused the general of showing off.[6]

Bismarck rattled his saber in the spring of 1887, and French *revanchards*, eager to recapture lost Alsace and Lorraine, demanded war. Cooler heads prevailed, however; both sides made concessions and the war scare subsided. The *revanchards* concluded that Boulanger had frightened the giant and immediately made him their hero. The Chamber of Deputies, alarmed at the general's sudden popularity, toppled the ministry in order to get rid of Boulanger, and overnight *le Boulangisme* was born. Paul Déroulède, a professional superpatriot, urged Boulanger to oust the politicians and set up an authoritarian regime based on universal suffrage, then lead the nation into war. Crowds in the streets shouted for Boulanger. France was still not impressed; in May, 1887, he called the chauvinists "ignorant." In July he labeled the theme song of the general's supporters, a music hall ditty called "En rev'nant de la revue," ignoble and inept; it was, he said, the "Marseillaise of bakers' boys and pastry cooks' apprentices." [7] Toward the end of the year he remarked that he liked Déroulède's collection of patriotic songs, the *Chants du soldat*, but not his "turbulent ideas." [8]

By this time real republicans were beginning to think they had created a monster. They had; in November, 1887, Boulanger sold out to the royalists. At the same time Daniel Wilson, son-in-law of the president of the republic, was indicted for selling decorations and peddling influence. President Jules Grévy resigned under fire. The scandal gave Boulanger, who was already playing heavily on the nerves of a population severely hurt by an economic depression, one more weapon.

Not many people knew that Boulanger, by then a national hero, had changed sides. In February, 1888, he got a total of 55,000 votes in several parliamentary by-elections, even though as an officer on active duty he was ineligible for public office. On March 26 the government, desperate, cashiered him from the army. On that same day Wilson, the seller of decorations, was acquitted. Corruption triumphed, people said, while virtue was unjustly condemned. Boulanger rode the crest. On April 15, having become a civilian and thus an eligible candidate, he was elected a deputy from the industrial department of the Nord. Immediately he had a party behind him. He had no program, but he was a patriot and he was defying the politicians; that was enough. To the crowds he was the embodiment of an illusion, the common illusion that all problems have a simple solution and will vanish if only the manipulators who make them seem complex can be replaced by a man of simple virtue and probity.

The literary critic of *Le Temps* had no business discussing the particulars of politics, but Gérôme, whose province was wider, could hardly ignore the existence of Boulangism in his "Courrier de Paris." Gérôme frowned on Déroulède's "turbulent ideas" in December, 1887, but by May, 1888, he was ready to be a little more friendly to the man on whom those ideas were centered. Soon after Boulanger's electoral triumph in the Nord, France discussed the great man in *L'Univers illustré*:

Him, always HIM!

I have . . . studied his psychology a great deal; it
is quite interesting, and one may affirm that it matters
to the republic. I have no need to explain that I am
speaking of General Boulanger.[9]

Then he went on to tell of the general's phenomenal
memory for names and his anxiety to please. This did not
explain the phenomenon of Boulangism, France said, but
he simply was adding his note to contemporary history.
Taken as a whole, his comments on the general in that
column were interested and respectful. He had not yet
joined the crowd, but he no longer ridiculed.

During the summer that followed it became evident
that Boulanger had shed his radicalism, and by that time
the idea of an authoritarian, not a Radical, coup d'état
had become quite acceptable to the new Anatole France.

Maurice Barrès, one of France's satellites in the early
1880s and by 1888 an avid Boulangist, claimed later, after
he had become France's enemy, that he remembered see-
ing France at the Restaurant Durand, where Boulanger
and his lieutenants liked to gather, sliding close to the
general to hand him his overcoat.[10] On a Tuesday in the
second half of October or, more likely, early in November, 1888, France had dinner with the general and only
one other person, presumably their hostess (the general's
mistress?).[11]

Mme de Caillavet twitted France about his infatuation
with Boulanger.[12] Obviously he was in a state of agitation.
She, however, had her own interests. She absolutely had
to have the general to dinner—his presence would be a
triumph for any hostess. She met her quarry early in
January and pursued him with determination until he was

in the bag. She filled her daily letters to her son Gaston, then doing his term of military service, with news of the chase: first the general was coming on January 30; then she was not sure he would come at all; then he accepted for the 20th; then it was the 30th again; finally, he came, on the 29th.[13]

By that time Boulanger had won his greatest victory. The death of a deputy late in December, 1888, made necessary the election of a new representative from the city of Paris. Boulanger became a candidate. Royalists were rallying to his banner, but since he lied so well and had so much (royalist) money to spend, he remained the hope of discontented republicans. The election was held on January 27. Boulanger defeated his Radical opponent by a huge majority. Jubilant crowds filled the boulevards of Paris, shouting "Vive Boulanger!" and "Down with the thieves!" Some of the general's backers urged him to make his move. The ranks of the police and the Garde Républicaine were riddled with his supporters; power was within his grasp, and if he had given the signal, the government could have done nothing to prevent a coup d'état. The general elected to wait: why storm the president's palace when he could take power legally within a few months? By the time he dined in the salon of Mme de Caillavet he was at the height of his power—or so it seemed.

The dinner was quite brilliant, Mme de Caillavet wrote to her son, but that was more than she could say for the guest of honor. "He makes me doubt the history books and ask myself if all those great figures who appear so imposing from afar were not made of a uniform, a plume, or popular infatuation." [14]

France disagreed. Rumor, probably unfounded, had it

that he was scheduled to become minister of public instruction in the coming Boulanger government.[15] In any case, in February he used his column in *L'Univers illustré* to tell how much more sociable and likable the general was than the politicians of the Radical party with their "mossy hats, greasy hair, and dirty beards." [16]

Sociable or not, in fact the general had missed his opportunity. On March 17, under pressure from his royalist backers, he made a speech that sounded suspiciously proclerical; it cost him more of his left-wing support. Worse yet, a new minister of the interior, Ernest Constans, no pillar of respectability himself, resolved to do what no one else had been able to: get rid of Boulanger. Constans carefully let it be known that the general would be arrested. Boulanger's mistress did not want her man in jail, and her man did not want to be there. On April 1 he fled to Brussels. A few days later his remaining support began to evaporate, for people who had built their hopes on a coward were not likely to forgive their fallen idol. His royalist financial backers dropped him. One good friend believed that Anatole France saw the end coming early in March.[17] At any rate, by May, when the great Paris Exposition of 1889 was opened, Boulangism was dead. Any lingering doubts were expelled by the elections of October, 1889, when Boulangist candidates won only forty-four of the more than five hundred seats in the Chamber of Deputies.

The France who dined with Boulanger was not the same one who wrote *Sylvestre Bonnard*. His flirtation with the general came hard on the heels of the beginning of his liaison with Mme de Caillavet and his quarrel at the Library. It is, however, more difficult to account for than either of those other two upheavals of 1888. France's books, along with the testimony of his friends, show why his marriage failed, but he never tried to explain why he joined Boulanger; again, letters and memoirs explain how trouble started at the Library, but only a few clues are left to indicate the reasons for his Boulangism. Charles Braibant, who has written the only careful study of France's political activities during this period, attributes France's turn to three sets of causes. First were his personal predilections: his chauvinism, his bedazzlement by the general's glory, and his taste for a strong regime that would not be dominated by the church. Second was his ambition. Third, and Braibant thinks it was the determining factor, was his quarrel at the Library, which led him to hate the politicians who made his position there untenable; Boulangism was an antiparliamentary movement, and Boulanger supposedly would have made short work of France's alleged persecutors.[18] Braibant conjectures also that Mme de Caillavet may have encouraged France's Boulangist tendencies on the chance that if the general succeeded, her protégé might benefit.[19] All these reasons probably played a part in France's decision to follow Boulanger. More than likely, however, France's ambition was a more important factor than his hatred of the senators who ran the Library. Just at this time France had found his coveted literary success, and his conquest of Mme de Caillavet put the seal on his triumph. He probably welcomed the opportunity Boulanger gave him to widen the scope of his activities, to become a public man as well as a literary figure. Another factor, which Braibant fails to mention, was a subtle resemblance France might have found between himself and Boulanger. Boulanger was a man of low birth who had fought his way to success and was on the threshold of even greater triumphs; so was France. When Boulanger's popularity grew too great, the "politicians" ousted him from the ministry of war and then cashiered him from the army; those same politicians ruined France's position in the Senate Library and, more important, hurt his pride. Boulanger was about to take revenge; so would France. Moreover, France's attitude toward the "ruling class" had always been ambivalent. He had envied his social superiors at Stanislas and in the salons, and he had also hated them. During his conservative period he had submerged the hatred in order to win a place for himself in the world of wealth and power; once there he could afford to unbridle the contempt he showed in his comment on the ruling class that failed to rule. Boulanger would rule, all right, and Anatole France would pay off some old scores. In any case, France's new pride, the product of his success, undoubtedly played a vital part in fertilizing the ground in which Boulangism grew.

France had been living in two worlds. While in one he followed the strange career of General Boulanger and radically altered his personal life, in the other he breathed the voluptuous air of ancient Alexandria. He began a new novel in the summer of 1888; a year later it was finished. Mme de Caillavet wrote to one of her friends that "*Paphnuce* is finished and sent to Brunetière, but we don't know whether the *Revue* will print it." [20] Ferdinand Brunetière was an editor of the *Revue des deux mondes*, which really was devoted not to two worlds (literature and public affairs) but to one, the world of orthodoxy, high society, and conservative politics. Brunetière had already rejected one of France's stories, having found it "quite irreligious." [21] The *Revue* finally accepted the new novel, but, wrote Mme de Caillavet a little later, "those imbeciles have demanded that it be cut so they can get it into two issues." [22] The cuts were made, but the novel, its name changed by then to *Thaïs*, had to run in three installments anyhow. The "imbeciles" had caused France trouble for nothing. They printed his book, though, and that was surprising.

Thaïs did not belong in the *Revue des deux mondes* because, in the words of a learned Jesuit, it "breathes hatred of the faith and of Christian virtue." [23] France re- told an old tale he found in his precious books of hagi- ography, but he added dimensions his pious predecessors had not recorded. The ancient tale is the simple record of the conversion of Thaïs, a courtesan of Alexandria, by a holy man. In France's version, Thaïs is converted, but Paphnuce, the desert father who brings her faith, ridden by desire, himself falls from grace. Even that story might not have been so shocking to the pious had not France artfully colored his narrative so that Thaïs' renunciation of the world is somehow pitiable, that world of passion a place of splendor and joy, and the religion of Paphnuce a hideous doctrine. *Thaïs* was an immediate success, for in the salons of literary Paris clever malice was always appreciated. The official guardians of the church could not, however, fail to recognize that this time France's apparently gentle treatment of "sacred things" barely masked a bitter attack. *Thaïs* was not like *Les Noces corinthiennes*. Both of them deal with the close of the pagan era and the triumph of Christianity, but in *Les Noces* France tried to treat religion with "sincere re- spect." [24] In *Thaïs* he condemned religion, and the veneer of respect was transparent. France's new confidence, his new harshness, was showing not only in his private life and his politics but also in his literary work.

The triumph of *Thaïs* lifted France from prominence to fame. He had been a power as a critic, but in 1890 he at last became a celebrity of the first magnitude. Soon he was being spoken of as a likely candidate for the Academy. Fortified in his new position, he rapidly finished liquidating his old way of life.

Mme de Caillavet used France to glorify her salon; in return, she made that salon a stage on which France could play to perfection the role that fame had thrust upon him.[25] For years the Wednesday dinners and the Sunday afternoon receptions in Mme de Caillavet's sumptuously furnished home played a large part in the social and literary life of Paris. The hostess, handsome, imperious, yet generous and loyal to her friends, presided in her eighteenth-century drawing room. France, forced to dress correctly, stood before the mantelpiece, ready to meet the guests he honored by his presence. In the best approved salon style, Mme de Caillavet gave him his cues, then he delivered monologues that had been carefully prepared under her critical eye. He rambled on, the center of attention, just as if he were an actor hired to perform; the guests listened just as if they had paid for the privilege. Because he never conquered his basic shyness, France sometimes would lose the thread of his talk, digress, and begin to correct himself. Then, as he once remarked, the audience could hear him "crossing words out." [26] Sometimes, particularly at the more intimate Wednesday gatherings, France read from his latest writings. Sometimes he was silent while one of his plays was acted or a well-known singer performed. Usually, however, France held the floor, talking of politics, art, literature, and history, and exhibiting his talent for paradox and irony.

The guests at these exhibitions were drawn from every walk of life; the only entrance requirements were talent or fame, promise or power. Writers, publishers, politicians, scholars, and, of course, beautiful women all came to meet each other and to hear "the master." Among the more or less regular attendants at one period or another were France's publisher, Calmann-Lévy; the editor of *Le Temps*, Adrien Hébrard; the actress Réjane; the dramatist Victorien Sardou; the writers Maurice Barrès, Charles Maurras, Sully Prudhomme, Pierre Loti, Marcel Proust, and France's old friend Jules Lemaître; the politicians Georges Clemenceau, Raymond Poincaré, and Jean Jaurès. And usually, too, the "master of the house," Arman de Caillavet, was there.[27] His method of introducing himself left one young lady astonished: "Permit me," he said, *"I am not Anatole France."* [28] But he confined his resentment at being relegated to a minor role in his own drawing room to minor displays of irritation.

Mme de Caillavet not only managed her salon, she also managed her lover. She sought out subjects for him to discuss in his articles, translated articles in foreign journals that she thought might interest him, and even took notes on his daily conversation so that no clever idea would be lost.[29] France grew to trust her taste and her ability so much that he often allowed her to write his semiweekly "Courrier de Paris." [30] She also wrote parts of various other articles and some of the prefaces he was called on to furnish as his reputation grew.[31] (The most memorable of those works of Mme de Caillavet was France's preface to Marcel Proust's *Les Plaisirs et les jours*.[32])

Her actual help was probably less important than her

encouragement: some intimate friends insisted that Mme de Caillavet virtually forced France to write when he would have preferred to loaf, and France himself said he worked at his best when she was near. Occasionally France was irritated by her officiousness, but for several years, at least, his love far outweighed the minor annoyances she caused him.[33]

Mme de Caillavet's lover and protégé continued to live with his wife for nearly four years after his new love had begun, but he clearly made no attempt to save his marriage. Finally, on June 6, 1892, after a particularly devastating quarrel, he walked out of his house in dressing gown and carpet slippers and left his wife permanently. From a nearby hotel he sent a messenger to pick up his clothes, and a month later he moved into a bachelor apartment. His wife sued for divorce on grounds of desertion, and won her case. The divorce became final on August 3, 1893.[34] Suzanne, eleven years old when the break came, remained with her mother. France saw his daughter every Sunday at the home of the Comtesse de Martel, who served as hostess for the weekly rendezvous permitted by Mme France. After he had left his wife France worked in his apartment and took most of his meals at the table of Mme de Caillavet.

With his divorce and his establishment as a fixture in the Caillavet household, France, at the age of forty-eight, put an end to a style of life he had lived for the fifteen years of his marriage and began to develop a new domestic routine that endured for nearly two tumultuous decades. The old life had been that of a promising writer and critic, the conventional existence of a man who was making his way in the world. The new life was the glittering career of a major public figure, the progress of a

man of wealth and connections who had only to keep
fresh the laurels he had already won.

II

To back Boulanger was to attack the status quo; to write
Thaïs was to declare war on orthodoxy; to take a mistress
and cast off a wife was to break with conventional morality. All these things France had done between the summer
of 1888 and the summer of 1892. By the summer of 1893
he had, almost unconsciously and without abandoning his
basic philosophy of extreme skepticism, brought his intellectual and political positions into harmony with the
radical line of action he had already begun to follow.

During those years France continued to make occasional excursions into metaphysical and epistemological
conjecture, just as he had done in the past. He maintained
his old position, arguing repeatedly that science is neither
moral nor immoral, that justice is a human idea not found
in any natural law, that men are moved by their emotions
as much as by their reason, that true knowledge is impossible, that the wisest course of conduct is to forget the
insoluble enigmas of life and live among the humdrum
cares of "daily duty and of sympathy." [35] He was still the
skeptic he had been for years.

France's underlying skeptical philosophy remained the
same, but the attitudes that philosophy supported changed
radically. On June 23, 1889, France published in *Le
Temps* a book review that showed the change.[36]

The book in question was *Le Disciple*, by Paul Bourget.
It had been written to start controversy. Bourget's main
character is a great philosopher, Adrien Sixte, whose

powerful presentation of the philosophy of determinism
has made him world famous. The present is, Sixte argues,
nothing more than the product of the past; there is no
such thing as "free will." If one knew every fact of the
past and the relations between these facts, one could predict every event of the future; thus good and evil are
nothing in themselves, they are simply the terms in which
society states its approval or disapproval of individual
acts. Sixte himself, however, lives a blameless life; he is,
France said in his review, a lay saint. Unfortunately, he
has a disciple who accepts his philosophy and all its consequences. The disciple sees nothing wrong in seducing a
virtuous girl, even though he has to join her in a suicide
pact to attain his end. Once satisfied, he refuses to honor
his contract. She kills herself, but he not only refuses to
die but feels no remorse at having done so much evil, for
what is evil to him? In the end he is shot by the girl's
angry brother, but that is beside the point.

Bourget's question, as France saw it, was this: "Are
certain philosophical doctrines, determinism, for example,
or scientific fatalism, in themselves dangerous and deadly?
Is the master who denies good and evil responsible for the
misdeeds of his disciple?" He goes on to say that philosophies that negate all morals cannot enter "the order of
facts" except in the form of crime; when they become
acts, they fall under the jurisdiction of the law. "I persist
in believing, all the same, that thought has, in its own
realm, indefeasible rights and that any philosophical system may be legitimately exposed." Everyone who has an
idea of the world should express that idea, he continues.
Besides, determinism, which so frightens people today,
existed in ancient Greece. "The moral liberty of man has
always been and always will be disputed. The rights of

thought are superior to all else. It is man's glory that he dares to hold any idea. As for the conduct of life, it should not depend on the transcendental doctrines of philosophy." What led the disciple to crime was not determinism but pride. France concluded by quoting Spinoza's statement that what one believes is unimportant, as long as one leads a peaceable and tranquil life.

Ferdinand Brunetière, one of those "imbecile" editors of the *Revue des deux mondes* who had taken the shears to *Thaïs*, caught the change immediately and rushed to the attack. A week later, in the same issue of the *Revue* that carried the first installment of France's novel, he bluntly asked what France might mean by his talk about the "indefeasible rights of 'truth.'" His view was different: "Morality is the judge of metaphysics. . . . Any time a doctrine leads logically to the questioning of the principles on which society is based, it is false, no doubt about it; and the enormity of the error may be measured simply by the seriousness of the evil that it can cause for society." [37]

Brunetière's doctrine was very close to the view France had expressed two years earlier in his attack on Hermant's *Cavalier Miserey*. Then France had said that writers are responsible to society, that they cannot be allowed to say everything to everybody at all times. Bourget's novel had caused him to state his new position; Brunetière's attack forced him to defend it. On July 7 he discussed Brunetière's article in *Le Temps*.[38] If philosophies are to be judged by morality, he asked, who will guarantee that the morality is itself good? Besides, the principles of society that Brunetière set up as norms are always changing. "It is thought that leads the world. The ideas of yesterday form the mores of tomorrow. . . . To subordinate philosophy to morality is to wish the death of thought, the ruin of all intellectual speculation, the eternal silence of the mind. And it is to stop with the same stroke the progress of morals and the rise of civilization."

The quarrel continued: Brunetière replied in the *Revue* on September 1 and France answered in *Le Temps* on September 8. The arguments flew back and forth, but essentially they remained the same. Brunetière insisted that ideas that might lead to immoral action should be suppressed, while France demanded freedom on three grounds: first, that no one could ever predict the consequences of any act anyhow; second, that only through freedom of thought could progress be made; third, that tolerance was in itself a good thing. France still remained a skeptic, doubting everything (including his own arguments), but whereas his skepticism had formerly led him to favor restricting liberty because he doubted that liberty was worthwhile, that same skepticism now led him to support liberty because he doubted the value of current morality. His basic skepticism had not changed, but he had chosen another of the varying lines of thought that might come from that basic position. He had left his conservative skepticism behind and embraced the iconoclastic skepticism of Voltaire.

Not much later France publicly changed his position on two questions that were then burning issues among the literati.

First, he concluded that perhaps, despite his earlier condemnations of the movement, the poetry produced by the new school of symbolism did have a certain merit.[39] This was apostasy for a Parnassian, and it led France, in devious ways, to a violent quarrel with his old mentor, Leconte de Lisle, who was so incensed by some of France's remarks that he demanded a duel. France graciously replied that such a great man was "untouchable." But he carefully edited a newspaper column about Leconte de Lisle when he republished it in book form so that the "great poet" became just "the poet." [40] On the other hand, he wrote a highly laudatory column about Stéphane Mallarmé, whose contribution to *Le Parnasse contemporain* for 1873 he had caused to be rejected.[41]

Second, he revised his opinion of the works and character of Emile Zola, both of which he had savagely attacked during the eighties.[42] Writing about Zola's novel of peasant life, *La Terre*, in 1887, France had condemned the book and said of Zola that "his work is bad and he is one of those unfortunates of whom one can say that it would be better if they had never been born." [43] Several more attacks followed, but by 1890 France was able to praise Zola's *Germinal* and to remark that he objected not so much to naturalism in itself as to the attempts of Zola's school to make themselves dictators of letters.[44] Then, in *Le Temps* on March 22, 1891, he admitted that he regretted "a little" his violent outburst against *La Terre*. In 1892, he praised almost without qualification *La Débâcle*, Zola's famous novel of the defeat of 1871.[45] Though he still could not be classed as an admirer of naturalism, he no longer condemned the movement in toto, and some naturalist works he frankly admired.

Neither of these changes in opinion represented a major change in France's principles of aesthetics. He had opposed both symbolism and naturalism on the ground that they "kill thought": symbolist poetry he called unintelligible, naturalist novels brutalizing.[46] In his later period France understood symbolist poetry better and saw virtues he had not noticed before in naturalist novels. Having ceased to make convention the arbiter of his philosophy or his personal morals, he no longer allowed convention to influence his critical views. This new attitude of tolerance was to make it easier for him to win friends among the younger writers; his reassessment of Zola was to be of incalculable importance in his political life only a few years later.

To break with his past cost France a great deal. Despite the new life that opened for him, despite the new love he had found, despite the warmth of his new fame, he was disturbed. Dismay at "the passing away of things" had been a recurring theme in his work since he was an adolescent. His own life was passing away as he approached middle age, and he was not, after all, one of those followers of Horace who could grasp at evanescent pleasures and laugh at life's impermanence. As the changes in his existence and his attitudes multiplied, France was uneasy. He thought, moreover, that he could detect all around him the same mood he felt in himself.

On March 31, 1889, he headed his column in *Le Temps* with a question: "Why are we sad?" He wrote that he had just read two novels, both of which left him with a feeling of melancholy.[47] Melancholy is nothing new, he said, but modern man, more refined and more delicate than his ancestors, is also more ingenious at tormenting himself. "We have eaten the fruit of the tree of science, and in our mouths remains the taste of cinders." We have seen how short life is in contrast with geological ages; as we lost our ignorance we lost our faith. Worse still, the new society we have constructed sharpens the struggle for existence. "With faith and hope we have lost charity.

. . . Who will bring us a new faith, a new hope, a new charity?"

In 1890 he pointed out that at the same time that naturalism came into fashion in literature spiritualism, with its poltergeists and ouija boards, had come into vogue in society. "The insensibility of nature desolates us. The deadly majesty of laws of nature confounds us. We look for mystery. We call on all the sages of the Orient; we throw ourselves head first into this psychic research, the last refuge of the marvels that astronomy, chemistry, and physiology have chased out of their domains. We are in the mud or in the clouds. No middle ground." [48]

A few weeks later he published a long discussion of the spirit of the younger generation. Many observers think, he said, that youth is turning away from eighteenth-century rationalism and becoming mystical.[49] Of course it is, he wrote, because one must believe in something, and modern young people know that one can believe in nothing. Moreover, he added, the intellectuals are incapable of providing any new faith. But perhaps there is one hope, although it may be slim: "Young men, if the need to believe bothers you, go, throw yourselves into the obscure masses of the people, run, search. The people think very little, practically not at all. But that nothing is everything. The masses elaborate the faith of the future and murmur confusedly the ritual of the new religion; but they can hardly be understood and they do not themselves understand." France did not pretend that he himself could understand that murmur.

France chose to draw a peculiar moral from the humiliating case of General Boulanger. Shortly after the general fled the field, France mournfully agreed when someone said the country still needed a new broom. "We need a broom," he wrote, "but which one?" [50] Not long after that, however, he apparently concluded that not even a new broom would help.

In 1886, as a good conservative, France had urged that institutions be changed very slowly because men themselves change slowly. To support Boulanger was not to reverse that stand, for by the time he won France's favor, Boulanger stood for a vague program of reaction: he would "restore" to the nation not only its lost territory but also its vigor and glory. France did not, however, expect the general to put a stop to social evolution. In a column he wrote in November, 1888, soon after he had become closely associated with Boulanger, he indicated what he expected the future to bring. Discussing Shakespeare's play *The Tempest* and, more particularly, Ernest Renan's social interpretation of that play, he wrote as follows: "The future is Caliban's. Ariel, just between us, is finished. In the opposition, [Caliban] is priceless. He has an astounding aptitude for destruction. He understands nothing; but he feels, because he suffers. . . . What makes him redoubtable is that he has instincts and little intelligence. Intelligence is subject to error; instinct is never deceived." [51] He went on to say that the triumph of the masses would destroy a great many beautiful things and beautiful ideas; it would ravage civilization. Nevertheless, civilization would survive, because Caliban would someday have children who would be less ugly than he is. At best, then, France hoped Boulanger would be able to salvage something during the time of troubles he expected to come.

Boulanger failed. Soon afterward France began stating simply that whatever men might try to do social change was quite beyond their control. He compared social change to geological change, arguing that the two were very similar. "The conservative spirit and the revolutionary spirit might find in this a ground for conciliation. Persuaded that they remain unnoticeable when they operate continually, the conservative would not oppose necessary changes for fear of accumulating a destructive force at the very point he would place his obstruction. And the revolutionary, on his side, would stop imprudently soliciting energies that he would know to be constantly acting." [52]

But if change was slow, it was sure, and he still believed that even though prophets of doom always had a great deal to say, progress could still be made. "For my part, I do not see in humanity any sign of decline. I have heard a great deal about decadence. I do not believe it. I do not even believe that we have arrived at the peak of civilization. I believe that the evolution of humanity is extremely slow, and that the differences in customs that show up from one century to another are, if carefully measured, smaller than people think." [53] Thus the foreseeable future would, he thought, be neither much better nor much worse than the past.[54]

France thought rapid change was impossible, but he had supported Boulanger because he distrusted the parliamentarians who ruled France, and the fact that Boulanger failed did not change his opinion. He remained a Boulangist without a Boulanger. He still preached aristocratic doctrines, he was still patriotic, he still castigated the politicians of the republic. "Democracy is supposed to suppress the barriers that separate classes, not to suppress classes themselves. There is in society a necessary hierarchy." [55] A grocery boy is below a student in this hierarchy, he continued, because his function is inferior to that of a student. All functions are useful and necessary, but some are "noble" and some are not, even if the least noble functions are the most necessary. In another article, commenting on the fact that a painting offered to the Louvre had not been popular, he said: "The opinion of the mass is unimportant in artistic matters (and it could be wished that it was a little less important in political matters)." [56] When a left-wing municipal councilor, defending the interests of the nation as he saw them, protested against a plan to make the birthday of Joan of Arc a school holiday because Joan was proclerical and royalist, France replied that he agreed she was prejudiced: "Her prejudice was love of her country." [57] That prejudice, he went on, had saved the nation; he hoped the councilors' prejudices would do as much. At about the same time he remarked that what he liked the least about Mme de Staël, Napoleon's famous antagonist, was her "anti-French" political stand.[58] When he spoke of republican politicians, he spoke harshly. A certain deputy would make a good minister of public instruction, he wrote, if he were not a deputy. But custom required that ministers be chosen from among the deputies, "who are generally the refuse of the nation." [59]

French socialists celebrated May Day for the first time on May 1, 1890. France duly noted the event in his column in *Le Temps*: "Last Thursday's commotion happily was kept in hand, but its size revealed the existence of a significant new power. As the dust of the capital stirred in the spring sunshine, I was led by chance into the peaceful rooms of the Musée Guimet. Alone there amid the Gods of Asia, in the shadows and silence of study, I was still thinking of contemporary matters, which no one is permitted to ignore. I thought of the hard necessities of life: the law of labor, the sufferings of existence. Stopping in front of the image of an antique sage whose voice is still heard by more than four hundred million men, I tried, I admit, to pray to him as a god. I asked for that secret of the good life for which governments and peoples search in vain." [60] Buddha answered that men should have pity on each other and resign themselves to fate. France approved, but he knew that the sage's voice would go unheard. Men demand action, not contemplation. France wished it were otherwise.

During 1890 France was still a conservative, but even then his opinions were subtly changing. In the summer of that year Paris was deserted (as it still is every summer) by all those who could afford to leave. France spent a good deal of time wandering around the town, and he saw things he apparently never had seen before. His life was changing rapidly; his angle of view changed with it. Suddenly he began to take an unusual interest in the condition of the poor.

He had visited charity hospitals and written of poverty in the past, and had even attacked unmercifully a physician who demanded his fee in advance when a life was at stake, but that summer he seemed to develop a kind of sympathy for the unfortunates of Paris that he had never shown before. [61] He devoted large parts of three of the seven "Courrier" columns of the summer to discussions of the poor, deserving and otherwise. On July 12 he described at length the plight of Henriette Poulaillon and Joseph Didier, both old, blind, and crippled, one a pencil seller and the other a purveyor of *bonne aventure* (little colored slips of paper with fortunetellers' predictions on them), who were jailed for begging. [62] A zealous policeman had noticed that passers-by were dropping money into the cups displayed without taking the merchandise they had bought. Neither Henriette nor Joseph minded being in jail, where at least they were fed ("and that is an important point," France remarked), but neither had any idea what they would do when they were released except to return to their old stand. France was equally puzzled. He respected the law, he said, but the one that had incriminated "this good woman and that good man" was "a little pit pharisaic." Two weeks later, in his next "Courrier," France remarked on the emptiness of Paris, deserted by the rich, left to be "the city of the poor." [63] He wondered what passed through the minds of the beggars he saw, and called them "these unknowns, tired and resigned."

On September 26 he discussed poverty again, and that time he advanced from simple description, mixed with pity, to philosophical comment:

> Some English economist has violently attacked people who give coins to street beggars:
> "Thus they easily satisfy," he says, "the needs of their vulgar sensibility, without thinking of the difficulties they raise at the same time for the state as well as for private persons."
> There is a grain of truth in what this English economist says. Private charity, which is disbursed in the streets, feeds mendacity there and perpetuates it, with its train of vices. It is an evil. And it is an evil without remedy.[64]

Four years earlier he had taken a simpler view: he had cited his economist and replied that, whatever such people say, one can give to the poor without any danger.[65] In his new mood he no longer denied the existence of an evil, but he was not yet ready to accept any suggestions for its cure.

That summer's concern for the poor of Paris may have been nothing more than the concern of a columnist hunting grist for his mill; probably, however, it was more.

Socialism and anarchism were making progress. On May Day in 1890 the socialist parties (there were several) had made their existence known. On May Day in 1891 they had so frightened the authorities in the northern industrial town of Fourmies that troops fired on a group of demonstrators and killed ten people, seven of whom were women or children.[66] In the Paris suburb of Clichy police and a tiny anarchist band exchanged shots. Such clashes were horrible for the victims, and socialists hated anarchists as badly as the police did, but for the labor movement in general and the socialist parties in particular they were invaluable because they brought publicity that was otherwise unobtainable. As a result of that publicity, the various socialist parties won members among the workers and sympathizers among the intellectuals. Anatole France, literary critic for *Le Temps*, took notice of the new developments in his "Vie littéraire" of January 31, 1892.[67]

Socialism is not new, he wrote, but it is news. "It is talked about and written about; our entire society is occupied with it. . . . Elegant women interest themselves in it, and soon it will be a fashion among them, like the Economists and parrots were under Louis XVI." He added that in the Chat-Noir, a cabaret featuring a comedian who specialized in political lampoons, socialism was already the order of the day. Opening a discussion of socialist literature, France said that he found the poetry of Jean Allemane and Jules Guesde, two socialist leaders, mediocre. The verses of Louise Michel, the "Red Virgin," were better—"they are inspired." Inspired, but too full of hatred to quote at length. Turning to prose, he discussed a "socialist novel," Georges Renard's *La Conversion d'André Savenay*, that he thought smelled too much of the lamp. The author's hero, he said, seems barely alive when compared with the real socialist leaders sketched in a new monograph on the socialist movement in Europe. The descriptions of meetings were far from realistic, not nearly so stirring as the artist Jean Béraud's old painting of the Salle Graffard. In that painting, he commented, there was a figure that told him more about the socialist worker than would twenty volumes of history and doctrine. "[It is] that of a little bald man who is all head, without shoulders, who sits at a desk in his muffler, a skilled worker without doubt, and a man of ideas, sickly and without instincts, the ascetic of the proletariat, the saint of the workshop, chaste and fanatic like saints of the church in the early days. Surely, that man is an apostle and one feels when one sees him that a new religion is born in the people."

France was fascinated by fanatics—his books are full of people like the doomed hero of *Les Autels de la peur* and old Paphnuce—but even though he could be moved by a painting he was far from ready to admit either that socialism really was the new faith or, more unlikely still, that this new faith could gain his loyalty. In the novel, he said, the author showed his ignorance of the real relation between the bourgeoisie and the workers. Talk of class hatred was ignorant, France argued, when all that existed was a conflict of interest. Such an error, he thought, was particularly lamentable because Renard wanted a peaceful transformation of society. Then France went into his familiar refrain: peaceful or not, any transformation of society would be made slowly, as slowly as the operations of nature. On the other hand, if he attacked the novel and disputed the author's doctrines, he could certainly agree with the end in view: who could not say with Renard, he asked, "For the little, the disinherited, the weak, always more justice, always more pity, always more fraternal goodness, that is what we must will without cease"?

France had chosen just the wrong moment to deny the existence of a class struggle. Exactly two weeks after that column appeared several thefts of dynamite were reported. A month later, on March 11, 1892, a bomb destroyed the house occupied by one of the magistrates who had helped send to jail the anarchists involved in the Clichy incident of May Day, 1891. On March 15, four days later, a barracks was bombed. On the 27th the home of another of the officials involved in the Clichy trial went up in smoke. Among the more timid elements of the Parisian bourgeoisie there was a mild panic: what would happen next? On March 30 a fanatical anarchist named Ravachol was arrested in a Paris café. Confronted with evidence obtained from informers, Ravachol confessed that he had planted the two bombs in the magistrates' houses. His trial was scheduled for April 26; on the night of the 25th, the restaurant in which he had been arrested was bombed; a customer was killed and the owner, who had called in the police when Ravachol was recognized, was injured so badly that he died several days later. At his trial Ravachol, who, it developed, had worn gloves and a top hat while he worked, not only confessed to his bombings but proudly admitted that he had robbed a grave in an attempt to get money to finance anarchist propaganda.

The case fascinated the public, and although a great many people considered Ravachol a monster, a surprising number, including some romantically inclined members of the upper classes, thought he was, however misguided, a martyr to his faith. Speaking to the jury, Ravachol explained why he destroyed: "Society is rotten; in the workshops, the mines, and the fields, there are human beings who work and suffer without being able to hope to acquire the thousandth part of the fruits of their labor; there are women who are dying of hunger and children that they have no bread to feed. Beside that terrible misery, we see fat bourgeois lead lives of pleasure and respond with disdainful laughter to the tears of the starving." [68] As Ravachol spoke, the government was bringing troops to Paris to prepare for another May Day.

In the midst of the alarm set off by those three months of violence, Anatole France wrote a "Courrier de Paris" for publication on April 30. He, at least, was calm. "On the eve of the first of May, if I had any pretention to elegance, I would call myself a socialist. The socialists are in fashion today. They have on their side the marquises, the Jesuits, and the Chat-Noir. They also have the future. They lack only the peasants, which they will never have; but the peasants are not an army, and, when they don't vote, they don't count. The workers are, on the contrary, an army that obeys socialism." [69] France's swipe at the Jesuits referred to the new liberal social doctrines growing out of Pope Leo XIII's encyclical *Rerum Novarum*, published the year before. But if he joked about the church and about people who took up socialism as a fad, he was quite serious in his remarks about the workers. He continued, saying that the instinct of the masses, the strongest force of all, was with the socialists. Nevertheless, socialism seemed to be coming like a breeze instead of like a tempest. "One should not fear the first of May, primarily because one should fear nothing—fear makes man stupid and mischievous. One must not fear it also because it brings more warnings than dangers. Let us not be troubled. Of all evils, fear is the only one that is real." He went on to say that Peter Kropotkin, the Russian "anarchist prince," had predicted that parliamentarianism would die during the nineteenth century. "I don't know. I had a close view of parliamentary politicians for several years. They are, except for a small élite of superior minds, the most mediocre type of men that I have ever had the opportunity to observe. Their insufficiency is equaled only by their power, which is sovereign. Since they subsist without talents and without knowledge of any sort, obviously they are indestructible." Evidently France was more amused by the discomfort of his enemies in the Senate (not to mention his friends among the rich guests of Mme de Caillavet) than he was frightened by the rising tide of socialist power.

Without knowing it France had written the last of his gentle laments. As he worked on through the summer, writing a new novel, the alarms begun by Ravachol continued to grow. In July, 1892, the anarchist "martyr" was executed. In November an attempt to blow up the Paris headquarters of a great mining concern failed, but the bomb intended for the capitalists killed five policemen. At the end of the year the Chamber of Deputies passed a series of laws designed to prevent further anarchist violence. France kept his own counsel as these events passed by, discussing less striking matters in his columns. In

June, 1892, however, he suddenly about-faced on a significant issue.

Zola had just published his new novel, *La Débâcle*. In his review, after commenting that Zola had improved through the years and that his new book was excellent, France went on to say, coolly, as if he had never said anything different, that though their military sentiments had not weakened, Frenchmen no longer loved war for itself.[70] "They are quite right." He went on to praise Zola for making his soldiers ignorant and hungry. That matched his experience in 1870: as a soldier, he was always hungry and he never knew what was happening. A week later, in reply to a letter, he added a note to his column: "When M. Zola paints in his book the ferocity of the man who fights, when he shows war changing inoffensive and tranquil beings into furious beasts, he is quite right." [71] So perished the lover of the military virtues. Perhaps he had learned more about those virtues from Boulanger.

Toward the end of 1892 France published a collection of short stories and a new novel.

L'Etui de nacre, the volume of short stories, was made up of miscellaneous tales France had written for various periodicals during the past nine years. Several of them were episodes taken from the novel *Les Autels de la peur*, which had appeared in serial form in 1884 but was never published as a book. Among the others two stood out; they are probably the most popular stories France wrote. One was "Le Procurateur de Judée," in which Pontius Pilate is shown as a forthright, conservative, patriotic old man, retired from government service, who, when asked about the case of Jesus the Nazarene, replies: "Jesus?

Jesus the Nazarene? I don't remember him." The other was "Le Jongleur de Notre Dame," France's reworking of an old legend that contrasts the virtue of sincere simplicity with the sin of pride. The whole volume was France in his usual vein, and it won him new critical acclaim.

France's real triumph of 1892 was, however, the novel he published in weekly installments in *L'Echo de Paris*, a popular daily newspaper, from October to December. This novel, *La Rôtisserie de la Reine Pédauque*, won even greater applause than *Thaïs*. It also created greater alarm among the supporters of contemporary morality.

La Rôtisserie is an eighteenth-century tale in both style and subject matter. In it the Abbé Jérôme Coignard, who was to become one of France's most famous characters, lives his rollicking life, teaches his Epicurean philosophy, and dies an exemplary death; all of this is reported by the abbé's young protégé and pupil, Jacques Tourne-broche. Unlike most of France's books, *La Rôtisserie* has a complex and well-constructed plot, but the meat of the book is its wit, its irony, and—for the first time—its sensuality. France's abbé is no atheist; like any number of eighteenth-century philosophes, he solves the conflict between reason and religion by insisting on the inherent irrationality of religion, thus deriving for himself a license to turn reason loose on everything not explicitly reserved to faith. He has contempt for human affairs, and, like his creator, he thinks human beings can be judged only with irony and with pity. He cheats at cards, brags of his amours, drinks himself into a stupor. No matter, he will repent, and God's mercy is assured. Several critics admired France's style and his verve, but deplored the fact that *La Rôtisserie*, for all its gaiety, undermined all the everyday virtues of civilization.[72] The reading public read it anyhow.

Politically, *La Rôtisserie* had little to say, unless the abbé's ingrained disrespect for human laws, social classes, and "everyday virtues" could be called political. As it stood, the book made ever more clear France's growing contempt for convention, but it also showed his continuing doubt that any positive effort to improve society would have any appreciable effect.

France still believed that the speed of progress had to be measured in generations. Nevertheless, in a book review he wrote early in 1893 he began to show signs of impatience.[73] Maurice Barrès had just written, in a novel called *L'Ennemi des lois*, a plea for a society based not on reason but on instinct. France doubted that such a thing was possible, and he was sure it was undesirable. "Savages bow to instinct more than we do," he wrote, "and they are, if possible, still more cruel and more unhappy than we are." Clearly, to repeal all laws overnight would be an error. But "can one argue . . . that our codes are excellent in every way, and that we did well the other day to condemn to six months in prison a poor man who had stolen a loaf of bread?" The law, he continued, should correspond with social mores, which had recently grown less harsh. Contemporary laws, which were products of the revolutionary era, were less harsh than those they had replaced, but they were still too strict in certain areas. Finally, he said, "the enemy of the laws" was right in one thing: "Dream for dream, I like better that of a world in which we will be very free than that of a 'store-state' that we would all be bound to serve." Barrès' hero was not an authoritarian socialist, and that stood to his credit. In that review France conceded a great deal: he admitted that a revolution had produced a change, and a change for the better at that; and he implied that one could conceive that further changes might be made, even if all that were changed were obsolete laws rather than obsolete customs.

By the beginning of 1893 France had come a long way from the days when he complacently used his critic's chair to point out the virtues of the conservative republic. He had also left far behind the chauvinistic doctrines of Boulangism. Nevertheless, he had so far only toyed with left-wing politics; he was restless, not revolutionary, troubled, not enraged.

In February, 1893, France's amusement changed into disgust, his ironic contempt for the "mediocre" politicians who governed his country turned into hot anger. For he and most of his compatriots discovered then that occasional hangers-on like ex-President Grévy's son-in-law were not the only public figures who were infected with a desire to enrich themselves at the expense of the nation. The disease had spread, and the seat of the new epidemic was the Chamber of Deputies.

The great scandal that reached its climax in February, 1893, grew out of Ferdinand de Lesseps' failure to duplicate in Panama the triumph he had engineered in Suez.[74] The Panama Canal Company, formed in 1879, went bankrupt in 1888. De Lesseps underestimated the amount of money the Panama project would require; at the same time, he insisted on raising his capital by selling shares in the company to small investors rather than to large banks, because bankers might attempt to hamper his freedom of action. The first shares sold well, but fever-carrying mosquitoes and stubborn mountains slowed construction and forced de Lesseps to look for more money. Aware that bad news would hurt the sale of new shares, he (or his partners in the project) began paying newspapers for good publicity. As the years dragged on and the failures mounted, the company began to pay journalists simply for silence. Even so, new capital became increasingly hard to find. To lure investors, the company planned a lottery scheme, but for this government permission was needed. To get it, the company bought a majority in the Chamber of Deputies. The lottery failed, however, and the company collapsed. Complaints poured in, but the government was reluctant to prosecute, because officials preferred to leave unscathed the reputation of the great de Lesseps, because they knew what a scandal an investigation would produce, or because bribes were still changing hands. Not until four years after the failure, and then only because newspaper campaigns forced the deputies' hands, did the affairs of the company reach the floor of the Chamber. Then the din was terrific. Overnight, reputations were ruined and careers wrecked. The Chamber first discussed the subject in mid-November, 1892; by the end of the year, most important members of the ruling party, the conservative Opportunists, and a number of opposition deputies had been implicated, and some of them had been indicted on charges of accepting bribes. New pieces of evidence, even more damaging than those already uncovered, came to light in January and February, 1893. When the accused deputies were tried, all but one, who made the mistake of confessing, were acquitted. De Lesseps, the eighty-eight-year-old hero of Suez, and his son, who had helped him set up the company, were each sentenced to five years in prison, but six months later their sentences were set aside by a higher court. Most of the individuals concerned escaped punishment, but during the furor two ministries fell, and dedicated republicans generally feared that the regime was in danger. After all, Boulanger had barely failed only a few years before; a government weakened by such a widespread scandal might not be able to resist if a new attack came. In the end, however, only a few politicians were seriously hurt. At the next election, in September, 1893, republicans won a solid victory, even though Clemenceau and a number of other leading figures who had been tarred by the scandal were defeated.

At the height of the scandal, the Abbé Coignard, who had died in the faith at the end of *La Rôtisserie de la Reine Pédauque,* suddenly came back to life. France, incensed, published in *L'Echo de Paris* a series of episodes he called "Opinions de M. l'abbé Jérôme Coignard sur les affaires du temps." From March 15 through July 18 the abbé commented weekly on political affairs—ostensibly, on affairs of the eighteenth century; actually, on affairs of 1893. When he wanted to talk about the Panama scandal, the abbé discussed the Mississippi Bubble; for the parliamentary cabinet he substituted the ministers of the king. The disguise was transparent, and besides, France often discarded it and let his abbé make "conjectures" about "the future." For the first time in more than twenty years, France said what he really thought. He not only discussed politics, he discussed the entire social system, in general and in detail. His days of caution were over. His freedom was all the greater because he was about to resign his post on *Le Temps,* probably because the pressure of writing a weekly column, no longer to be borne out of necessity, was too great to bear for the sake of pride or power. The last "Vie littéraire" by Anatole France appeared on April 30, 1893.

By then the Abbé Coignard had begun his weekly subversion. In the first article, published on March 15, the learned abbé set the tone for all the rest. Said he: "A government that scandalizes the people by overstepping the bounds of mediocre and common honesty ought to be deposed. . . . The newcomers couldn't be worse than the old, and who knows? They might even be a little better." [75] A week later, however, he said, "It is almost immaterial whether we are governed in one way or another." [76] Why? Because "power is divided between fools and knaves." [77] He took little interest in what was done in "the king's cabinet," because such acts do not change the course of life. "Men are not changed by legal reforms; they remain egotistical, avaricious, cowardly, and cruel; they are in turn stupid and insane. . . . The numbers of newborn babes, bridegrooms, cuckolds, and gallows-birds never change—which demonstrates the beautiful stability of our society. Nothing can trouble this stability, sir, because it is founded on human misery and imbecility, and those foundations will last forever. They give the whole edifice a solidity that defies the efforts of the worst princes and their ignorant officials." [78]

As for democracy, which the abbé thought would come to France in a century or so, its major effect would be to reduce still further the little power possessed by secretaries of state, whose names, "chalked on the walls by little scribbling schoolboys, will make the bourgeois laugh." [79] Certainly "Demos" will not know what he wants, and if he did he would not know how to carry out his wishes. He will order badly and will be badly obeyed, so he will always think he is being betrayed. His deputies will have to train themselves to speak without saying anything. Nevertheless, the people should not be any more unhappy than before, because their own incompetence and turbulence will prevent their ministers from being able to plan "useless and disastrous wars"; there will be no more foreign policy, "and that will be a great piece of luck for unhappy humanity." [80]

For the abbé did not like war. "I have worked," he said, "at all trades except that of the soldier, which has always filled me with disgust and terror because it is characterized by servitude, false glory, and cruelty, all quite contrary to my pacific nature, to my savage love of liberty, and to my mind, which judges glory clearly and values that of musketry at its true worth." [81]

Though he could hardly outdo his contempt for governments and armies, the abbé saved some of his most penetrating comments for human justice. "Justice has for its object not the just, but the useful, and . . . it is inspired only by the interests and prejudices of peoples. . . . Crimes are punished not in proportion to the evil in them, but in view of the damage they cause or it is believed they cause to society." [82] Counterfeiters are boiled to death, he continued, not because they are evil but because they damage the public, and particularly the financiers. Thieves are hanged not because it is perverse to steal a loaf of bread but because people are attached to their property. "It is worthwhile to reduce human justice to its true principle, which is the material interest of citizens, and to disengage it from all the high philosophy in which, with pompous and vain hypocrisy, it envelopes itself."

In the last article of the series, France condemned violence once again and pointed out that although the abbé had the utmost contempt for governments "he never would have been a revolutionary." [83] He believed too strongly in original sin. "Robespierre believed in virtue:

he made the Terror. Marat believed in justice: he demanded two hundred thousand heads. The Abbé Coignard is, perhaps, of all the spirits of the eighteenth century, the one whose principles are most opposed to the
principles of the Revolution. He would not have signed a
line of the Declaration of the Rights of Man because of
the excessive and iniquitous separation established there
between man and the gorilla." [84]

A few months later, in September, 1893, France reworked his articles in order to publish them in book form
as *Les Opinions de Jérôme Coignard*. He used his concluding article, part of which is quoted just above, as the
preface to his book. To this he added several strong paragraphs. They are worth quoting at length, for in them
Anatole France first spoke the language of socialism.
These significant paragraphs followed a remark with
which the abbé closed a dialogue:

> "After the destruction of all false principles, society
> will remain, because it is founded on necessity, whose
> laws are older than Saturn and will still reign when
> Prometheus has dethroned Jupiter."
>
> Since the time when the abbé made this comment,
> Prometheus has dethroned Jupiter several times, and
> the prophecies of the sage have been verified so liter-
> ally that today, because the new order so resembles the
> old, some people believe that the old Jupiter still rules.
> Some even deny that the Titan has come to power. One
> no longer sees on his chest, they say, the wound from
> which the eagle of injustice tore out his heart, the
> wound that should bleed eternally. He knows nothing
> of the pains of exile. That is not the worker god that we
> were promised and that we await, it is the fat Jupiter
> of the old and laughable Olympus. When, then, will he

appear, the robust friend of man, the bringer of fire, the Titan still chained to his rock? A frightful noise from the mountain tells us that he has raised his torn shoulders above the evil rock, and we feel upon us the flames of his faraway breath.[85]

France went on to suggest to his readers that a study of the opinions of the Abbé Coignard might well help them examine their consciences:

With a little good faith and impartiality, we would quickly recognize that our codes are still a nest of injustices, that we still have in our mores the hereditary harshness of avarice and pride, and that we esteem only wealth and do not honor labor. Our order of things would appear to us what it is in fact, a precarious and miserable order, condemned by abstract justice if not by that of man, an order that has begun to fall into ruins. Our wealthy would seem to us as stupid as those May bugs which continue to eat the leaves of trees while little beetles, inside their bodies, devour their entrails. We would no longer let ourselves be lulled to sleep by the false and flat declamations of our statesmen. We would have pity for our economists, who dispute among themselves the price of the furniture while the house is burning. The words of the Abbé Coignard show us a prophetic disdain of those great principles of the Revolution and those rights of democracy on which we have established during a hundred years, with all kinds of violence and usurpation, an incoherent succession of insurrectional governments that have, without irony, condemned insurrections. If we begin to smile a little at these pieces of foolishness, which appear august and were sometimes bloody; if we perceive that modern prejudices have like ancient ones

ridiculous or odious effects; if we judge each other with
charitable skepticism, the quarrels will be less lively in
the most beautiful country in the world, and M. the
Abbé Coignard will have done his bit for the universal
good.

France was still cautious. If he heard a "noise from the
mountain," he nevertheless seems to have been able to
hope only for the quarrels of his day to become "a little
less lively." Braibant, in his study of France's turn toward the Left, correctly pointed out that the "noise from
the mountain" was France's symbol for the anarchist
bombings.[86] France's comments on the belief that
"Prometheus" was yet to come, that "fat old Jupiter" still
ruled, alluded to the constant refrain, shouted by the
French Left ever since 1789, that the Revolution was not
yet complete, that the political conquests of the nineteenth century should be followed by social conquests of
even greater magnitude. In the preface just quoted France
simply says "some people" believe this, but the opinions
of the abbé make it quite clear that France was one of
those people. In *Le Lys rouge*, a novel he published the
following year, France spelled this out in detail, making
a character he used to expound socialist ideas say this:
"Since the Revolution was carried out by crazy men and
imbeciles to the profit of men who acquired national
property [confiscated from the church and the émigré
nobility], and since it ended only in the enrichment of
peasants and bourgeois usurers, it built, in the name of
equality, the empire of wealth. It delivered France to the
men of money who have devoured her for a hundred
years. They are lords and masters. The apparent government, composed of poor devils who are pitiable, shabby,

miserable, and prone to disaster, is in the pay of the financiers." [87]

Les Opinions de Jérôme Coignard thus marks the moment of France's turn from ironic amusement at the antics of politicians he considered contemptible to active hatred of the government in power. But the abbé "would never have been a revolutionary," and Coignard spoke for France. For the next few years France openly scorned the bourgeoisie and its deputies and cabinet ministers, but he only criticized. As for the socialists, he sympathized with them and predicted their eventual triumph, but he did not join them in battle. He still thought that progress must come slowly, like geological change.

III

From 1893 to 1897 France gradually increased his wealth and fame. Under the benevolent eye of Mme de Caillavet he wrote new books: from October through November, 1893, he published in *L'Echo de Paris* most of the stories that made up *Le Puits de Sainte Claire,* a collection of stories set in Renaissance Italy that was offered as a volume in February, 1895; in November, 1894, he published *Le Jardin d'Epicure,* a collection of epigrams and parables culled from newspaper articles printed between 1886 and 1893; from April through June, 1894, *Le Lys rouge* appeared in the *Revue de Paris;* in 1895 he started a new series, "Histoire contemporaine," in *L'Echo de Paris.* He also wrote dozens of articles about Joan of Arc, in whom he had been interested for several years, for the *Echo* and other periodicals, and published occasional articles and stories in other journals.

France no longer hesitated to fill his works with political and social commentary. Several of the stories in *Le
Puits de Sainte Claire* play on themes mentioned earlier
by Jérôme Coignard; one, "L'Humaine tragédie," serves
as a vehicle for a sympathetic presentation of anarchist
principles, although, of course, the "tragedy" is that such
principles belong to a simplicity that is beyond the capacity of human beings. France was still pessimistic. That
story also served to illustrate once more France's attitude
toward religion. The main character, Fra Giovanni, tries
to model himself on the patron of his order, St. Francis of
Assisi. Doing so, he is bound to advocate at least one principle France held to strongly: he had to believe in gentle-
ness, he must oppose cruelty in any form. His conduct,
France implied, was directly the converse of that of the
organized church, which had construed poverty to mean
wealth and had organized the meek to build a powerful
army. France was not, however, urging the church to reform; Fra Giovanni's ultimate fall from grace was meant
to prove that his whole theory of conduct, the Christian
theory, not only was unworkable in an evil world but was
in the end less desirable than the Epicurean system based
on the savoring of pleasures, the very pleasures of sense
and intellect that Satan used to cause Fra Giovanni's fall.
Like the juggler of Our Lady, Fra Giovanni is a sympathetic character, whose simple goodness stands out
sharply against the background of an evil society. In "Le
Jongleur," however, France had shown simplicity triumphant; in "L'Humaine tragédie" simplicity is defeated.
France would have liked an anarchist world in which all
men were simple and good, but he would have liked even
better an anarchist world in which all men were sophisticated and good. He was convinced that neither was pos-

sible. He thought true Christianity was true anarchism, and that both were utopian. The Christianity of the organized church he hated. He loved the beauty of Christian mythology, and he could sympathize with men who really believed that mythology was true. He was convinced, however, that such men were doomed to destruction or disillusion, and that the church neither believed the mythology nor tried to follow the impossible ethic Christ had preached.

Le Jardin d'Epicure has often been called the ideal exemplar of France's philosophy in this period.[88] In it he put together a random collection of statements that together convey the whole of his complex attitude. Contempt for the works of humanity stands beside guarded hopes for some measure of progress; a completely skeptical distrust of reason and science is offset by an even greater distrust of human instincts; over all, France's two favorite judges, Irony and Pity, hold sway. The empire is divided, however. In matters of justice, government, wealth, and the church, irony is uppermost; whenever poor human beings are on trial, pity tips the scales.

Mme de Caillavet was responsible for *Le Lys rouge*.[89] As France's "manager," she was determined to make him show that he could write as well of the contemporary scene as he had written of ancient Egypt, Renaissance Italy, and eighteenth-century France. She seems also to have wanted him to write a book just for her. She was modern, romantic, and of the great world; hence *Le Lys rouge* was set in the present of the mid-1890s and dealt with romance in the world of the salons. France had a plot at hand; he simply disguised the story of his own love affair with a great lady of the salons and made it a novel. But France was still France, and *Le Lys rouge* was "Francian"—in its realism it stripped the great world of all its greatness, and of all the characters only the half-crazy poet Choulette, whom France made into a prophet of socialism, is treated with more pity than irony. *Le Lys rouge* was a literary triumph; it appealed not only to the highly sophisticated, erudite public that admired everything France wrote but also to the huge class of readers for whom were written what the Victorians referred to simply as "French novels." (*Le Lys rouge* is the only one of France's books that has been republished recently in the United States as a cheap paperback on its own supposed merits, that is, without the telltale warning that here is a "classic." [90]) *Le Lys* also signalized France's own triumph: he never could have written it without first becoming a full-fledged member of the society it portrayed, the world of wealth he had so much craved to enter when he stammered and blushed in the little salons of Parnassus twenty-five years before.

Once in the modern world, France remained there. On January 22, 1895, he began writing his new series of stories, the "Histoire contemporaine," in *L'Echo de Paris*. Only seven installments of the series had appeared, however, when it suddenly stopped; readers had a chance to discover only that France was beginning to examine the complicated maneuvers by which less than savory clerics climbed the ladder of preferment in small provincial towns. The examination promised to be enlightening to the public and highly irritating to both church and government. But after April 2, 1895, the "Histoire contemporaine" disappeared for a little more than a year; instead, the column set aside once a week for France's contribution contained childhood reminiscences or studies of various aspects of the great legend of Joan of Arc.

France did not explain why he dropped the "Histoire" and began writing sugar-coated stories of his childhood, but later events cleared up the mystery. He simply drew in his horns temporarily in order to avoid antagonizing the august, and generally quite conservative, Immortals of the French Academy. For at last France, self-appointed critic of the vanity of men, had a chance to achieve his childhood ambition. The door to the Academy was half open, and if he were careful he might be invited to enter.

The invitation did not come unsought. Like other aspirants to that particular honor, France had to announce his candidacy and then he had to campaign. He made formal visits to each of the thirty-odd Academicians who voted to fill the vacancies. France had been mentioned as a likely candidate in 1892. Zola was in the running that year, and some of the Immortals were afraid their colleagues would vote to accept him; France might have his flaws, but he was infinitely preferable to the vulgar creator of naturalism. But France had already begun to respect Zola's talent, so he refused to enter the race.[91] By 1895 France's renown was greater than it had been in 1892, but he was also a great deal more radical than he had been then. Still, the competition was weak. Mme de Caillavet, who used all her talents to push France ahead, said that she would not allow him to run unless she was certain of the outcome.[92] A deal was arranged: the Academy "Right" would vote for France if France's supporters would cast their ballots for Costa de Beauregard, a nobleman of ancient lineage who wrote mediocre histories, for a second seat that was vacant.

On the morning of January 23, 1896, the election was held. France and Mme de Caillavet, awaiting the decision, dined in splendor at the Tour d'Argent. Finally the news

came. Fernand Gregh, one of France's talented young
admirers, ran all the way from the Institut to tell France
that he had been elected. Gregh later reported that France
was greatly moved; Mme de Caillavet had to assure him
that the election was really over, that at last he, too, was
an "Immortal." [93] Congratulations poured in, and French
and foreign newspapers wrote laudatory articles about
the new Academician. In December, 1896, France was
officially received into the Academy, amid the usual pomp
and circumstance. His speech, glorifying the man to
whose chair he was succeeding, was tactful, scholarly, and
pleasant—even though his predecessor was Ferdinand de
Lesseps, creator of the Panama debacle France had so bitterly attacked. France dwelled on de Lesseps' earlier triumphs, and blamed not the entrepreneur but his associates
for the miserable failure of the Panama project.

So France entered the Academy, was "moved" to hear
of his election, and carefully avoided hurting feelings
when he spoke at his reception. Still, shortly after the
election and several months before the reception, he
began again to publish installments of the "Histoire contemporaine." [94] World famous at last, an immortal, he still
had contempt for the world that honored him.

During those years of growing fame, France gradually
grew accustomed to his life of wealth and ease. He wrote
a great deal, but he also played. He continued to grace
his lady's salon. In the summers, beginning in 1893, he
took long tours with Mme de Caillavet. They went to
Italy almost every year; in 1895 they also visited Holland
and Belgium, and in 1896 they traveled all the way to
Egypt. As his books brought in more and more money,
France gradually cut down his journalistic output. In
1896, after his election to the Academy, he severed his

connection with *L'Univers illustré*, the last obligation
that held him to a regular schedule.[95] He began occasionally to make speeches to various groups: to the historical
society of Auteuil and Passy (1894), to a girls' school
(1894), to a society for the preservation of the Provençal
tongue (1894), to a banquet of students (1895), at a
celebration in honor of the romantic poetess Marceline
Desbordes-Valmore (1896).[96] On March 9, 1897, he even
made a political speech. Introducing an Armenian refugee
writer who was to tell the Société de Géographie about
Turkish oppression in his homeland, France compli-
mented the speaker for having raised the "horror and
indignation of a public kept almost in ignorance by its
government and by most of its newspapers." After the
speech he offered a comment: "The blood of martyrs will
not cry in vain. A force is with us, dispersed but powerful—it is the sympathy of generous hearts and noble
minds." [97]

Readers of the opinions of the Abbé Coignard, or of
the more recent early chapters of the "Histoire contemporaine," might well have asked France just how powerful he really thought the force of sympathy was. When he
spoke at a meeting organized to help right a wrong, he
was, of course, almost forced to sound optimistic. In
fact, no matter how much he deplored the cruelty of
men, his skepticism prevented him from giving himself
wholeheartedly to any cause. M. Bergeret, who was
emerging as the major character in the "Histoire contemporaine," was the Abbé Coignard stripped of his vest-
ments and his faith in God's infinite mercy. His attitudes
toward war, government, and justice were those the abbé
had expressed earlier. And he, too, had little hope for
the future: "It is true," said M. Bergeret, "that men hold

it the prime social duty to learn to kill other men regularly, and that, among civilized people, the glory of carnage surpasses all others. After all, that man should be incurably malicious and incorrigibly given to doing evil does very little harm in the universe, because the earth is nothing but a ball of mud in space, and the sun a ball of gas that soon will be consumed. . . . It is difficult to conceive that reasoning, sensible men nourish the hope of rendering life on this little ball supportable." [98]

France was nearly fifty-three when he wrote those lines. He had attained his greatest ambition: he was famous, he was rich, he was a member of the Academy. He had a charming home of his own—the Villa Saïd, near the Bois de Boulogne, bought in 1895—and he had a mistress who not only loved him but made herself extremely useful in his career. Still, he was melancholy. He had won the glory he had always wanted, but he had lost something in its pursuit.

3
The Crusader
(1898–1906)

I

France was not alone in his melancholy. The intellectuals of his day all seemed to sense that they lacked something, something indefinable but exceedingly precious, that alone could bring them joy. What they lacked, of course, was a faith.

The philosophers of the eighteenth century jettisoned religion, but they found a substitute in progress. That faith survived the disasters of the Revolution and lived on in the romanticism and utopianism of the 1830s and 1840s, but 1848 dealt it a severe blow. It lingered awhile: Renan, skeptic that he was, could still muster a belief in progress, even though he clearly expected very little of the immediate future. Le Parnasse, despite its militant republicanism, was hardly a bastion of faith: without an emperor to revile, what would that republicanism have been? Then, 1871: for Frenchmen, an unparalleled disaster that pride could barely support. Another, more subtle disaster came, however, after the war: the republic arrived, and virtue was still nowhere to be seen. Through the 1880s Renan's gentle skepticism held sway—dilettantism was its label. Symbolism, in poetry, reflected the

times; it was an affirmation of total individual independ-
ence, a kind of social nihilism. The generation of the
1890s was impatient for something better. Nurtured on
Taine's hard-boiled determinism and Renan's irony, feeling themselves as irresponsible as the "disciple" portrayed
by Paul Bourget, discontented young men looked for a
new absolute that would tie them to society and give their
lives a meaning they could swear by. The period that
began, roughly, in 1890, ushered in what has been called
by a brilliant scholar "the crisis of humanism." [1]

Micheline Tison-Braun, writing of that period, speaks
of a "polarization of minds" between the two extremes
of anarchy and social absolutism.[2] Political anarchism
took the forms described in the preceding chapter; in
literature, the anarchistic tendency showed not only in
symbolism but in the enormous popularity of *Ubu-Roi*,
Alfred Jarry's brutal social farce, and in the welcome
given the works of Nietzsche, which began to be known
in France during the 1890s.[3] The cult of energy, made so
popular in France by Maurice Barrès, was another symptom of the same trend. Mme Tison-Braun argues that it
was inevitable that spirits in the grip of such nihilistic
doctrines should attempt to make their escape by leaping
into faith. Some of them embraced the racism of Gobineau, rationalized by social Darwinism; some heard the
voice of Leo XIII—or, perhaps, that of their own class interest—and returned to religion. Some followed Tolstoy,
whose mystical Christianity had become immensely popular in France after the publication of the Vicomte de
Vogüé's *Le Roman russe* in 1886. Others fought frankly
in the name of tradition: Charles Maurras, for example,
helped to lead a group of young poets in an attempt at a
new classical renaissance.[4] All of these new movements

had two things in common: they tended away from the easy skepticism of dilettantism and toward some kind of absolutist ethic, and they led toward social conservatism.

The effects of the crisis showed in the chaotic condition of poetry in the late 1890s and the decade following. The young poets scorned symbolism; schools proliferated, but none came along to sweep the field.[5] Among the established intellectuals the effect was even more marked. René Doumic, writing in the *Revue des deux mondes* in January, 1900, said that successively Bourget, Brunetière, Émile Faguet, Lemaître, and Barrès, all products of the tradition of Taine and Renan, had abandoned agnosticism and turned to militant conservatism. "All that generation of deliquescence," he concluded, "would be in the future a generation disappeared, forgotten, abolished, if, in order to remind us of it and keep it under our eyes, M. Anatole France did not remain its exquisite and delightful representative."[6]

France was not untouched by the winds of change. He, too, was unsatisfied, seeking. He, too, found dilettantism too little. He, too, wanted "a new faith." He never found it; instead, in the powerful emotional storm that was the Dreyfus Affair, he discovered that his old skeptical humanism meant far more than he had ever realized.

Everyone knows at least the basic story of the Affair. Captain Alfred Dreyfus, the only Jewish officer on the French General Staff, was convicted of espionage in January, 1895, and sent to Devil's Island. He was not guilty, but before his conviction was reversed the case had split the upper echelons of French society into two enemy camps, both of which finally saw justice for Drey-

fus as far less important than the crushing political victory someone was going to win. The Dreyfusards were
so well treated by the historians for so long that the
inevitable reaction has set in, and now the standard pro-
cedure is to blame both sides equally, or, more often, to
imply that the whole struggle was simply the outcome of
a series of errors by well-meaning men.[7] In fact, as Professor Paul Gagnon recently wrote, neither view is right:
errors there were, but there were also heroes, fools, and
villains.[8]

The fools, as usual most numerous, can be ignored. The
outstanding villains were a Major Walsin-Esterhazy, who
was finally unmasked as the real traitor; Colonel Henry,
who took it on himself to help the case against Dreyfus
by forging documents to take the place of nonexistent
evidence; and, more than likely, some still unknown army
officers who were criminally involved with Esterhazy and
Henry. The outstanding heroes were Colonel Picquart,
the Catholic anti-Semite whose notions of honor and duty
led him to destroy the case against Dreyfus despite his
own prejudices and the pressure of his superiors; Matthieu Dreyfus, the victim's brother, whose tenaciousness
kept the case from being forgotten immediately; Senator
Auguste Scheurer-Kestner, who dared the wrath of his
colleagues to force the case back into the headlines, and
Emile Zola, whose famous letter to President Félix Faure,
"J'accuse," will probably be remembered longer than
even the best of his great novels. Among the lesser heroes
was Anatole France.

France was writing weekly installments of what was to
become the third volume of his "Histoire contemporaine"
when the drama opened. Scheurer-Kestner, after having
tried fruitlessly to win the support of the premier or the

president of the republic for a new investigation in the case, publicly demanded a new trial for Dreyfus on October 30, 1897. On November 23 the new Affair found its way into one of France's regular chapters, printed routinely in the conservative *Echo de Paris*. In that column, entitled "Les Juifs devant l'Eglise," France ignored the question of Dreyfus' guilt or innocence.[9] Instead, he examined the impact of the Affair on the upper-class provincial society he was writing about. He created a scene in which an aristocrat, a Catholic lawyer, a retired general, and a priest discuss the news from Paris. They agree that the "agitation" that has begun "is nothing and could be nothing but an execrable maneuver" of the enemies of their country—"and of religion," adds the priest. They cannot believe that a military court could err. The whole business is the work of a conspiracy of freethinkers, Freemasons, Protestants, and Jews. The lawyer, the general, and the aristocrat dislike Jews, who, they say, "take our money and destroy our national energies." The cleric agrees that Jews are criminal, but when it is suggested that they be expelled from France, he demurs. The Jews are not heretics, he explains, but infidels; moreover, some of them have been quite benevolent toward the church, and some of them have been converted. The three laymen view these arguments as frivolous; converted or not, Jews are Jews, and "they do not bring good luck to France."

This analysis of the reception of the pleas for Dreyfus in aristocratic society was shrewd. France was right to place the aristocrat and the devout lawyer squarely on the side of the soldier, and he was not far wrong in his estimate of the ambiguous position of the priest. The army was a stronghold of the aristocracy, which controlled the officer corps. Aristocrats and wealthy members of the bourgeoisie, potential victims of any social change, put their faith in the army as a bastion of reaction. Many of them had supported Boulanger, and they still hoped the army would save them from what they called "the social peril." Most of them were royalists. Most of them also were strong supporters of the church. The aristocracy clung loyally to the old alliance of throne and altar, while the wealthy bourgeoisie, once revolutionary and anticlerical, had been so frightened by the class strife of 1848 that it had long since turned to the church for protection. Pope Leo XIII, convinced that the monarchy was a lost cause, had tried in the 1890s to build in France a strong conservative and Catholic republican party but had failed. Catholicism and monarchism were almost inseparable, because a great many monarchists and a great many sincere Catholics were convinced that neither monarchy nor church could return to the glories of old without the aid of the other. Hence France was right to suggest that clerics sympathized with their reactionary friends, but he tended to overlook the fact that whatever they felt they had to act with considerable discretion: the pope was still a republican.

As France indicated, however, most reactionaries refused even to consider the possibility that Dreyfus had been wrongly condemned. They clothed themslves in the mantle of patriotism and called any criticism of the army, no matter how mild, treason. They held that the fate of the nation was at stake: the campaign for revision of the Dreyfus verdict impugned the honor of the army and damaged its morale, and weakened the faith of Frenchmen in the force that existed to defend them. The other side, the Dreyfusards, contended that justice must be done though the heavens fall. Because all sorts of partisans of authoritarianism, from royalists, Bonapartists, and former Boulangists to conservative republicans, displayed the same attitude, the Dreyfusards lumped their opponents together and called them all "nationalists." The question of Dreyfus' guilt or innocence ceased to be the real problem almost as soon as it was raised. The struggle quickly became part of the perennial conflict between the political Right and the political Left.

France and others like him, anticlericals as strong in their opinions as any religious fanatic, helped put the church in the nationalist camp. The reactionaries France portrayed in the "Histoire contemporaine" assumed that Dreyfus was being defended by a conspiracy of heretics and traitors—a Jewish syndicate; France and many other Dreyfusards assumed that the church must be the soul of the nationalist opposition. In fact, the pope ordered his clergy to maintain a strictly neutral stance. The anticlericals made Dreyfus' cause their own, however, and the clergy, already unsympathetic, soon began to react to anticlerical accusations by joining the nationalists. Members of the militant order of Assumptionists were to become especially notorious for their venomous attacks on the Dreyfusards, which they circulated widely in their highly popular newspaper, *La Croix*.

The masses of ordinary Frenchmen ignored the battle. In politically conscious Paris, however, the nationalists found a great deal of support in the lower economic classes. The glories of the armies of the Revolution and Empire still brought a thrill of pride to nearly every Frenchman. Despite the internationalist propaganda of the socialists, the masses were stubbornly chauvinistic, as they had amply demonstrated on the eve of the War of

1870 and in the Boulanger crisis, and were to demon-
strate time and time again. Anti-Semitism, ever present,
had become stronger since 1870, at least partly because
the Jewish population of Paris had greatly increased when
the loss of Alsace drove many French Jews to the capital.
The dream of upper class nationalists was a powerful
state with a docile population in which they would be
the dominant class; at least one of the dreams of lower-
class nationalists was a glorious state that would protect
them from the machinations of clever and unscrupulous
Jews. The dreams overlapped, and neither of them
seemed likely to be fulfilled under a republican regime.
Certainly they would not be if that regime were to allow
a mere Jewish captain to overturn the verdict of a duly
constituted military court.

On November 23, 1897, the same day that France's
first comments on the Affair appeared in *L'Echo de Paris*,
a rival journal published a long interview in which he
explained in detail his attitude toward the case.[10] He refused to take sides. He had seen no evidence but a
brochure written for the Dreyfus family by Bernard Lazare, a brilliant Jewish publicist, so he had no basis on
which to judge. But whatever the facts, he said, the case
could lead to trouble. Certain institutions, like certain
organs of the human body, outlive their usefulness and
then begin to cause disorders. Military justice, he thought,
was such a survival. "Its forms contradict the democratic
instincts of the masses. . . . Every time democratic instincts clash with survivals of the past—of the Middle
Ages—there will be disorder, unrest." He was not blam-
ing anyone, he hastened to add. He was a philosophe, a
man who simply demonstrated the facts and then paid no
attention to the effects of his demonstrations.

France heard the case discussed everywhere during the next few weeks, but he remained neutral.[11] So did most other people, for both the army and the government were stifling every attempt to reopen the case. Colonel Picquart, whose inconvenient honesty had led him to furnish the evidence that caused the furor, was under arrest. Quiet prevailed, at least on the surface. Then Zola sent his famous letter to Clemenceau's paper, *L'Aurore*. It was published on January 13, 1898, and from then on the Affair was a crusade.

Zola's facts were garbled, but what mattered was the call to arms, because he was right on his main point: Dreyfus was innocent. All kinds of rebels flocked to join Zola's assault on the "establishment." All kinds of conservatives joined to defend it.

Within weeks the lines were clearly drawn; as the months passed, they hardened. Socialists split over the case. While Jean Jaurès, then one of the leading independent socialists, carried one faction into the battle on the grounds that socialists had to fight injustice whenever it arose, Jules Guesde, the leading intransigeant Marxist, treated the Affair as a bourgeois quarrel of no interest to the proletariat. Most politicians of the non-socialist Left and Center stayed neutral as long as they could, then chose a side. In the end the Affair split the Progressists and the Radicals just as it had the socialists. As a result, the Progressists became more conservative, but so did the Radicals, whose ranks were swollen by social conservatives whose loyalty to individualism put them in the Dreyfusard camp. More and more the Affair became political; at the same time it remained a struggle for justice. Clemenceau, for example, became one of the leaders of the Dreyfusards. Certainly he was fighting for justice.

but just as certainly he used the Affair to rebuild the political career he had lost as a result of the Panama scandal. Though Jaurès was assuredly an idealist, he obviously milked from the Affair every ounce of political advantage he could. In the opposite camp the same process was visible. Anti-Semites like Edouard Drumont cared little for justice and a great deal for their own cause, but the honesty of others among the anti-Dreyfusards is more difficult to impugn. Maurras, for example, laid the foundation for a lifelong role as the leading exponent of monarchism in France by writing his article glorifying the "patriotic forger," Colonel Henry. His argument was that Henry's act hurt only enemies of France, so it was not a crime but an act of heroism. Maurras was not the only man of letters among the anti-Dreyfusards; the Right had its Academicians and professors just as did the Left. One of Anatole France's oldest friends, Jules Lemaître, was president of the nationalist Ligue de la Patrie Française.

Like everyone else, France gradually mixed his idealism with a heavy dose of politics. He believed in the search for truth, at least in so far as truth might be said to exist. He had said time and time again that "justice" was simply a convenient term for the decisions of the powerful, but he obviously dreamed of something better even as he doubted that it was possible. He hated the army, and he hated the church: here was a chance to strike a blow against both of them. Perhaps most important of all, Dreyfusism could become a faith, at least for a while.

France joined the crusade the day Zola's letter appeared. As soon as that famous edition of *L'Aurore* was on the streets, someone began circulating a petition demanding a public investigation of the Dreyfus case. It was published the next morning. Zola's name led the list of signers; Anatole France's signature came next. Hundreds of professors, lawyers, and scholars also signed the "Protest," and the "intellectuals"—so named by people who disliked their petition—came to be a class apart. Until that day the term had been practically unknown in France; since then it has been used constantly to describe the disgruntled men who not only live by their pens but use them for weapons.

Marcel Proust and Fernand Gregh, in 1898 young men just beginning their literary careers, both claimed in later years to have enrolled France for the cause. Proust casually remarked in a letter that he thought he was the first Dreyfusard, because he had got France to sign the petition.[12] Gregh, in his memoirs, described the scene in great detail and took the credit himself.[13] He found France at Mme de Caillavet's home, he wrote, and asked France to sign the document. France read it. "Given my opinion," he said, "I could not refuse to sign."

"But, Monsieur," cried Mme de Caillavet, "you'll get us in trouble with the Félix Faures!"

"Ah, Madame, I can't be responsible for that," France replied. "What do the Faures matter? Anyhow, listen, my friend, it would be useless to get ourselves put in jail."

"Now, dear sir," answered Gregh, "it's I who can't be responsible."

"Who is with me?" France asked.

"All youth," said Gregh.

"Of course," said France, "but I need some people my own age. Without them, I'd look a little ridiculous. Whom do you have?"

"Zola," answered Gregh.

"Oh! him, he doesn't count, that goes without saying," said France. "It's his career."

"Ludovic Trarieux," said Gregh. (Trarieux was a former minister of justice.)

"Ah, good, perfect," France answered. "You can use my name."

Whether Proust or Gregh got the signature is unimportant. Perhaps both of them went, and each neglected to mention his friend.

In any case, from that day France was an ornament of the Dreyfusard band. When Zola was arrested on a charge of criminal libel for having written "J'accuse," France testified at his trial. He turned many of the chapters of his "Histoire contemporaine" into Dreyfusard tracts, and he began to speak at public meetings. With many others of the "intellectuals" who signed the January 14 protest, he became a charter member of the Ligue pour les Droits de l'Homme et du Citoyen, a new organization designed to carry on the fight for Zola and Dreyfus and for every other human being the Ligue deemed to have been denied his civil liberties. France also became a close friend of Jean Jaurès. Though his progress was slow, he drifted gradually and quietly into the Socialist party.

France had revised his estimate of Zola long before the Affair began; after "J'accuse," he was ready to brave the mob that howled for Zola's head outside the court building to testify to Zola's "admirable good faith and absolute integrity." [14]

On February 15, 1898, just a few days after the Zola trial, the first of France's openly pro-Dreyfus columns was published. It purported to be a letter from an Italian scholar, Aspertini, to M. Bergeret. Aspertini, after discussing at length another subject, ends with a postscript telling M. Bergeret that he can't understand why the French persist in upholding a judicial decision that all the rest of the world knows is wrong.[15] Intermittently, during the next few weeks, France discussed forgers and forgeries, obviously alluding to developments in the case. Two episodes dealt with a fabulous forger named Vrain-Lucas, who was supposed to have made a fortune selling autographed letters of great men and women from every age and nation—all of them in excellent modern French.[16] Vrain-Lucas succeeded so well because the public was gullible; what is more, he might have gone on swindling people forever if the circumstances had been favorable: "Do you think that the papers of Vrain-Lucas would have been publicly recognized as false if popular passions and interests of state had created in the whole nation a generous desire to find them authentic?" [17] Intelligence, M. Bergeret continues, is often overbalanced by emotions, which are the determining factor in human survival. "Men can subsist only on condition that they understand badly the little that they understand. Ignorance and error are as necessary to life as bread and water. Intelligence must be, in societies, excessively rare and feeble in order to remain inoffensive." [18] The ironist, the skeptic, the pessimist, in France still ruled. There was, however, another passage. M. Bergeret's listener replies to the long discourse he has just heard on the dangers of intellect: "I see, M. Bergeret, that you have a lover's quarrel with intelligence. You cover her with reproaches because she is not queen of the world. Her empire is not absolute. But she is a good lady who is not without credit in several respectable houses. Her powerful sweetness acts even in this city." [19]

Even after France had committed his literary alter ego,

M. Bergeret, to the cause of revision, Bergeret was still prey to doubts. The truth is by no means sure to triumph, he argued. The truth is inferior to the lie, he said: it is single, while the lie is multiple; it is rigid, while the lie is plastic. The lie is the natural product of the senses, source and reservoir of illusions; the lie is moral, for it conforms to the ideas of good and evil that men have formed on the basis of ancient errors. As for the masses, the truth is not in them: "Popular enthusiasm is not constructive. It is essentially subversive." [20] In another episode of the "Histoire contemporaine," written a little later, Bergeret remarks that bad laws, not applied, are better than good ones that are enforced.[21] Such a doctrine is, of course, anarchical. Despite his desire to save Dreyfus and to uphold the cause of justice, despite the faint hope that truth could somehow win the day that is barely discernible in the columns of this period, France was far from ready to base his picture of the future on the beneficent action of the people or on political reform. He was still a skeptic, but he had gone into action. He was no longer the philosophe, merely demonstrating, that he had claimed to be six months before.

When Colonel Picquart, already cashiered, was to be tried, late in 1898, for being too honest, Dreyfus' innocence was already obvious. The generals, however, had not yet decided to give in. The Dreyfusards were infuriated at their impudence. Several newspapers combined with the Ligue des Droits de l'Homme to campaign for Picquart, issuing a petition protesting this new persecution of the "heroic artisan of revision." France was the first signer.[22] The protest was followed on November 28, 1898, by a meeting of students and professors. France spoke from the platform: "No vain words! Acts! We are

not going to separate without having taken a solemn en-
gagement to save Colonel Picquart from the interested
hate of Mercier and Boisdeffre, the disastrous stupidity
of Zurlinden, the tortuous egoism of Félix Faure, the
ruses and violence that all the criminals of the General
Staff have used to get rid of the heroic denouncer of their
names." [23] Mercier, Boisdeffre, and Zurlinden were generals, two of them former ministers of war; Faure was, of
course, president of the republic. In an episode of the
"Histoire contemporaine" that was published just a few
days before the Picquart meeting, France had poured
scorn on Esterhazy and all his accomplices.[24] A week later
he attacked again, this time recounting a story of Greek
gods on trial, the guilty freed and the innocent condemned.[25]

Still nothing happened. Picquart testified before the
investigators of the Cour de Cassation, but he was still to
be tried on December 12, 1898. Another meeting was
organized for the night of December 3. France spoke
again. How could justice be done?

> With what force do we oppose our adversaries? What
> means do we employ to gain satisfaction? The force
> of thought, the power of reason.
>
> Thought, a breath, but a breath that conquers all; the
> reason that, opposed and mistrusted, always prevails in
> the end because one cannot live without it.
>
> We will win, because we are right, and because
> reason is on our side.[26]

France had completely reversed his earlier stand. Despite
its many superiorities, the lie would not win. M. Bergeret
had allowed himself to be convinced in December by the

same argument, or the same wish, that he had ridiculed in April. Truth would prevail, after all.

The Cour de Cassation saved Picquart by ordering his trial delayed indefinitely, but the nationalists still persevered. Among the still unconvinced was Paul Déroulède, the nation's most famous incorrigible revolutionary conspirator. Undaunted by his defeat in the Boulanger adventure, Déroulède brought his Ligue des Patriotes into the fight against revision. As the nationalists lost ground in the courts, he and his followers began to plan a coup d'état.

Anatole France did not need to be told that plans for a coup were in the making. Like Jaurès, he had concluded long before that the republic he so often condemned but occasionally appreciated was in danger. Mobs still roamed the streets, and they could be led. On December 27, 1898, France let his apprehensions show in his newspaper column. "Life is hard and one must be indulgent toward Pécus [the mob], who lacks discernment. He is not bad when he is not unhappy. He is not violent when he is not oppressed. He may still expect the most freedom and the most happiness from the republic." [27] Less than a month later, in January, 1899, France lost his platform. *L'Echo de Paris* chose the other side in the battle, and M. Bergeret had to rest for six tumultuous months.

While France was silent, the Affair moved toward its climax. Déroulède's coup turned out to be a comic opera farce: when he tried to lead the troops of the Paris garrison off to the Elysée Palace as they marched away from the funeral of President Faure in February, 1899, the commanding general whisked him off to jail. But the trouble was still not over. On June 4, 1899, the day after Dreyfus was finally granted a new trial by the Cour de

Cassation, an irate nobleman attacked the new president, Emile Loubet, at a crowded race track. The uproar that followed finally led to the downfall of the government, whose critics insisted that the president had not been well enough protected, although he was unharmed. René Waldeck-Rousseau, a thoroughly republican, thoroughly conservative senator, took office as premier. Waldeck-Rousseau was determined to put an end to the Affair, and he did. Suppressing riots regardless of consequences, he forced through the retrial of Dreyfus and confidently awaited the return of peace and quiet.

Anatole France apparently regarded victory as certain after Dreyfus had been brought back from his island prison. M. Bergeret returned to the public print on July 5, 1899, this time speaking in the pages of *Le Figaro*, a Dreyfusard newspaper. France wrote of the triumph of the Dreyfusards as achieved, even though many of the innocent still had not been cleared, even though Dreyfus still faced another ordeal in the toils of military justice. From his new tribune France could speak far more openly than he had before; he no longer had to resort to allegory. He devoted one column, the first in *Le Figaro*, to a condemnation of the decision of the Marxist socialists to remain neutral in the Affair.[28] In another he ridiculed the anti-Dreyfusards who believed their own propaganda: their gullibility amused him.[29] He attacked republicans who, accepting the nationalist argument that the Dreyfusards were weakening the national defense by attacking the army, refused to help the cause of justice.[30] He praised freedom of the press, saying that uncensored newspapers were the key weapon in the struggle for victory.[31] As the Dreyfus retrial got under way at Rennes, he talked of the new proceedings.[32] On August 16 he devoted an entire column to a panegyric of Picquart, a hero he knew personally.[33] (A year later, when this sketch appeared as part of the final volume of the "Histoire contemporaine," an eminent historian who was also a leading Dreyfusard called it "an incomparably beautiful page of history." [34]) When Dreyfus' attorney, Labori, was wounded by a would-be assassin during the opening days of the trial, he, too, received a column of tribute.[35] As the trial neared its end, France printed a "Letter Written from Holland to M. Bergeret" that expressed the desire of the Dutch people, and of foreigners everywhere, that justice be done.[36]

The Dreyfusards were doomed to disappointment. After hearing evidence for more than a month, the military judges issued their notorious verdict: Dreyfus was guilty of treason—with extenuating circumstances. Like all his friends, France was appalled: "When are our politicians going to understand that the whole republican party, to which they belong, was condemned with Dreyfus by the judges of Rennes and that the republic will not be rehabilitated until Dreyfus is rehabilitated?" [37] Waldeck-Rousseau, however, was ready to put an end to the Affair as quickly and as simply as possible. He did it by forgiving Dreyfus the crime he had not committed: Dreyfus was pardoned on September 19, 1899.

Loose ends had to be tied up. Déroulède was tried and exiled, and various nationalist rioters were punished. So was a group of young Dreyfusards who had sacked a church. In a letter read at a meeting held to protest the convictions France warmly approved plans to demand an amnesty—for the Dreyfusards, not the nationalists.[38]

Amnesty was in the air. Waldeck-Rousseau, still hoping to finish once and for all with the Affair and the disorder it had brought, introduced in the Chamber a bill to amnesty everyone charged with illegal acts connected with the prosecution or the defense of Dreyfus. Dreyfus, his health broken, had been glad enough to accept his pardon, though he had announced that he would continue to attempt to clear his name. France, however, along with most of the members of the Ligue des Droits de l'Homme, was bitterly opposed to this amnesty, for it would, he argued, free the guilty along with the innocent and it would not remove the shadow from the name of the republic. At the urging of France and many others, the Ligue backed a petition against the passage of the amnesty bill and demanded punishment for men who had used high office to commit criminal acts.[39]

France also attacked the amnesty in *Le Figaro*, but by mid-November he was ready to recognize that if the victory of the Dreyfusards was not complete, it was nevertheless a victory. Reaction had finally failed, he said; it was dead. The republic would endure. Only the decimated troops of the rich and the idle would attack again, and they could not conquer: "Nothing more. The bourgeois looks on with kindness, but he will not fight, and he will serve reaction only by applauding nationalist doggerel at the café-concerts. But the enormous mass of workers, grave and somber, will no longer be amused by politics and riots. The people who one day will be able to demand everything, since they produce everything, are organizing, learning to think and getting ready to want." [40] The amnesty was voted, but France was not ready to quit fighting.

One injustice had been corrected; France was ready to vanquish them all. At the end of 1897 he had been his old self, a philosophe, skeptical, examining life, exposing folly, but remaining above the battle. During the spring of 1898 he had plunged into the crusade for Dreyfus, but he still had little hope that justice would be done. Then, during the second half of 1898 he had gradually reversed his stand: the truth would be heard; "the power of reason" would prevail. Earlier he had seen the masses as children who could never grow up; now he saw them "organizing, learning to think." His skepticism was not dead, as later events were to show, but it was in abeyance. With this statement of November, 1899, this prediction of a worker's awakening, he began to fight, as a socialist, for the triumph of socialism. He had found his crusade, his chance for comradeship, and it had led him to an even greater crusade, one that promised a future without injustice.

II

Through the 1890s Anatole France had broadcast his disgust with bourgeois society and his doubt that anything much better could be found to replace it. Even after he joined the Dreyfusards, he allowed M. Bergeret to talk his way through a full year of the Affair as a republican of the Left, vague about his politics despite his strong opinions on the vices of reactionaries, priests, judges, soldiers, students, prefects, capitalists, and women. As late as December 27, 1898, M. Bergeret was still quite pessimistic about possible improvements in human society: "I think that changes in institutions can have little effect if mores are not changed. Laws can be reformed without too much difficulty. They are changed from the outside; the legislator works on them in the same way a sculptor works on a figure. But mores, like the living bodies from which they come, cannot be modified except from the inside, and that treatment is more difficult. It is also more necessary. A society with bad laws, but good mores, is supportable. One cannot live in a country in which the laws are equitable and the mores cruel, because mores are active and laws inert. And what forms mores is neither the white horse of the Trublions [France's coinage, meaning the royalists], nor the president's coach, but the air, the earth, the water, the plains and the coasts, the forests, the mountains, the vine and the harvest, labor and days." [41]

Within seven months, however, M. Bergeret became more optimistic. Having moved to Paris, he ordered some bookshelves built in his new apartment. While they were under construction, the professor struck up a conversation with one of those worker-paragons so familiar to readers of books by left-wing intellectuals: a carpenter, uneducated, but shrewd, logical, perspicacious—and, one cannot help but feel, trustworthy, loyal, brave, clean, and reverent.[42] (France was very seldom fatuous, but by this time he was well into the process of conversion, a phenomenon that seems often to have an unfortunate effect on prose styles.)

A few weeks later M. Bergeret adopted the socialist militia plan for army reform.[43] Then, on November 15, 1899, came the column in which France turned the corner to see the masses, who produce everything and one day will demand everything, "learning to think."

For a mandarin like France, the urge to help speed the awakening was overwhelming. On November 21 he stood on a platform to preside at the opening of a "popular university," a night school staffed by volunteer teachers that was designed to educate the workers. They would study, he said, the origins of the present state of society. "By discovering how capitalist force was formed and brought to its present strength, you will judge better the means that must be employed to make yourselves its masters." [44] They would better understand their own position, and assure themselves a share in the building of a new and better order. "It is time, citizens, that your force is felt and that your will . . . is imposed to establish a little reason and equity in a world that has come to obey only the suggestions of egoism and fear. We have seen in recent times [that] bourgeois society and its chiefs [are] incapable of assuring us justice, not the ideal justice of the future, but the old lame justice that survives from ages of barbarism." [45]

By July, 1900, France was saying that the victory of the proletariat was certain: "Our own divisions and the indecision of our method are more likely to retard it than the disordered efforts of our adversaries. It is certain because the very nature of the things and the conditions of life ordain it and prepare it. It will be methodical, reasoned, harmonious. It is already imposing itself on the world with the inflexible rigor of a geometric construction." [46] "Our" divisions; "we," the proletariat.

France's change of position was basically one of temperament, not of rational conviction. He had seen men as pathetic, deserving to be treated with a nice balance of irony and pity. Irony and pity were still his watchwords, but his actions showed that he could also regard men with sympathy. He could even face the fact that he himself was one of these pathetic creatures; that, as to eschew politics was in itself a form of politics, to eschew the struggle of life was merely to deceive oneself as to the nature of that struggle.

France's evolution, despite its different outcome, was not really so very different from that of the other intellectuals of his day. As René Doumic pointed out, France came of the same intellectual origins as Lemaître, Barrès, and other disciples of Taine and Renan whose philosophical meanderings ultimately led them into the ranks of the political, and philosophical, Right. All of them, including France, had found dilettantism uncomfortable and naked determinism intolerable. Even Zola, self-appointed scientist of humanity, eventually found himself writing semimystical novels far different from the lockstep chronicles of the Rougon-Macquart family upon which he had built his fame. Accidents of upbringing and fate led these men, however, to take different paths. Lemaître, like France a lion of the salons, apparently succumbed to the luxury of society; Brunetière, the uncompromising polemicist, found his comfort in the ranks of the mighty army of Roman Catholicism; Barrès, the Lorrainer, his eyes always turned toward the east, chose as his gods the power and energy that would someday undo the German victory. France could not move to the Right without acute discomfort. In the old days he had rebelled against his father's politics and his teachers' religion; he could remember the taunts of richer schoolfellows and the titters of ladies who found him too awkward for polite society. Events of his later years—his undignified squabble with the Senate, his divorce, and his liaison with a Jewish mistress—made him less likely to support an authority that would stand for institutions and attitudes that he had rejected. Others changed; he did not. He remained the disciple of Renan, the quiet humanist, while

other famous members of his literary generation abandoned the field and turned to follow gaudier banners.
Then, just in time, during the Affair, he found a way out.
Socialists fought the same battles that he fought. They,
too, had contempt for the rules laid down by the rich,
but they also had what France lacked—a positive goal, if
not a faith. With Jaurès he found friendship, and on
socialist platforms he found a respect and a warmth that
the approving audiences of Madame's drawing room were
unable to provide. Every student of the Dreyfus Affair
has remarked on the deep emotional fellowship that
joined the Dreyfusards; socialism promised to make that
fellowship last forever.[47]

None of his biographers has discovered just when
France actually became a full-fledged member of a socialist party. From 1899 on he was closely associated with the
Independent Socialists led by Jaurès. In April, 1901, a
writer discussing his work in *La Revue socialiste*, obviously in a position to know France's status, still referred
to him as moving closer and closer to socialism,[48] but a
month later France addressed his listeners at a meeting
of a "communist" organization as "comrades," using the
term publicly for the first time.[49] Quite possibly, therefore, he joined a socialist group, either the Independents
or Jaurès' new Parti socialiste français, which was then
being formed, in March or April, 1901. In any case, by
the beginning of 1900 he was a socialist, formally or not,
and he soon made his adhesion official.

To say that France was a socialist in 1900 is to say that
he accepted the general aim of socialism: the abolition
of private property and the construction of a classless
society. That is, however, merely the beginning of a defi-

nition. As a socialist, France presided at party meetings, exhorted the proletariat, fought for various liberal causes, signed petitions, and wrote propaganda articles. But he was, above all, a crusader. During these years he wrote as a socialist, but his socialism was really little more than his old humanism in a militant dress.

In the last volume of the "Histoire contemporaine," the one he was writing in 1899, France began offering, along with the attacks on bourgeois society for which he was well known, occasional rather tentative prescriptions for socialist reconstruction. In 1901 he wrote "Crainquebille," the story of a Parisian vegetable peddler who was the victim of social forces he could not even dimly understand, much less resist. That short work, a superb piece of anticapitalist, antibourgeois propaganda, cemented France's position as a champion of the proletariat. It was remembered, and praised, whenever France's name was mentioned in socialist circles. A few months after it was first published, "Crainquebille" was combined with several episodes of the "Histoire contemporaine" and published in the Bibliothèque socialiste as France's *Opinions sociales*.[50] This put France on the same shelf, if not in the same class, with Marx and Engels, William Morris, Fourier, Babeuf, and other socialist thinkers whose works were included in the collection. But France still had written only social criticism; most of the other authors on the list had created grand constructions of one kind or another and had indicated what the new society should be like or, if they were vague about that, had at least given some directions on how to bring the new society into being. Before he set himself to remedy that deficiency, France reworked and published a novel he had begun nearly ten years before, the *Histoire comique*. It was

good, it was ironic, it criticized; but, aside from a general
left-wing tendency, it was not really political. Then, in
1904, France allowed Jaurès to publish, in the first few
issues of his new socialist journal, *l'Humanité*, a new
utopian novel called *Sur la Pierre blanche*.[51]

Sur la Pierre blanche is a philosophical conversation
that stresses, among other things, man's inability to fore-
tell the future. But, argues Nicole Langlier, a character
France used as his spokesman, prophecy does not always
have to be wrong. One may look at history and at the
current scene, he insists, and forecast the general trends
of years to come, even though particular details may be
impossible to foresee. First he shows how one might go
about deciding whether socialism will triumph; then,
using similar methods, he commits himself to the proposition that there will someday be an end to wars. As for
socialism, one can decide by observing trends whether it
will come, "not because it is just, for there is no reason
to believe in the triumph of justice, but because it is the
necessary outcome of the present state and the inevitable
consequence of capitalist evolution." [52] Having shown the
mechanics of prediction in his discussion of socialism, he
does not venture to predict on that particular subject.
On war, however, he is not so cautious:

> Without doubt there will be more wars. Ferocious
> instincts, united to the natural greeds—pride and hun-
> ger—which have troubled the world for so many cen-
> turies, will continue to make trouble. . . . But these
> better times that we will not know we foresee. By pro-
> longing into the future the curve already begun we
> can determine in advance the establishment of more fre-
> quent and more perfect communications between all
> races and all peoples, a stronger and more general

sentiment of human solidarity, the rational organization of labor and the establishment of the United States of the World.

Universal peace will be realized someday, not because men will become better (one cannot hope for that) but because a new order of things—a new science, new economic necessities—will impose on them a state of peace, just as in other times the very conditions of their existence placed them and kept them in a state of war.[53]

The last paragraph was a refrain that France repeated often during the years to come, a cardinal principle that he never repudiated. Having put it into the mouth of one of his spokesmen, he had set the stage for the presentation of his utopia.

Hippolyte Dufresne, another participant in this philosophical conversation, reads a fictional report on the state of mankind in A.D. 2270. Here socialism has triumphed; the new world is very different from the world of 1904. The citizens of the "European Federation" own in common all means of production. Everyone works, six hours a day, and has, if not all he wants, at least all he needs. Production, rationally organized, has increased four- or fivefold, and no one need be poor. Lawyers and judges are no more, for the suppression of poverty has resulted in the disappearance of crime. Violence still occurs, but only in the case of crimes of passion: these are dealt with by ordinary citizens, who are called upon to judge their comrades only when the occasion arises. Money no longer circulates, for prices are reckoned and wages are paid in units based upon hours of work. The pope, his church vastly diminished in size, is a dry-cleaner in the Via dell'Orso, Rome. Liberty, equality, and fraternity no longer serve as ideals: liberty cannot exist in any society, for it does not exist in nature; equality is a false ideal, for each person must give what he can and receive what he needs; fraternity has given way to peace and "harmony." People still complain about taxes and suffer from the ravages of difficult love affairs. "We have with us, as in the past," says a man of the Federation, "misers and spendthrifts, the industrious and the lazy, rich and poor, happy and unhappy, satisfied and discontented. But everyone lives, and that, after all, is something." [54] He continues: "Perfect happiness is impossible for human beings. One cannot be happy without effort, and all effort brings with it fatigue and suffering. We have made life supportable for everyone. . . . Our descendants will do better." [55] Stripped of all its verbiage, France's proposition was that men can be happier in a better world—and socialism, a better economic and political system, will produce a better world. This was offered not as a certainty but as a logical probability. He was optimistic, but only to a degree.

That optimism was confined within a system of philosophy that was, if taken as a logical whole, a stark and radical skepticism. In several passages of the general conversation that serves as the main thread in *Sur la Pierre blanche* both before and after the talk on the socialist future, France reasserted his steadfast conviction that man can never know a purpose, a beginning or an end of life. He speculated on the possibility of multiple, identical universes, and on the likelihood that man is only a step, not the final product, in the chain of evolution. He had not yet changed his belief that all men are like prisoners in a darkened cell; he only had given men the right to construct a tiny island of light in the midst of the void.[56] In earlier days he had emphasized the futility of the drama, but now he was willing to allow it a certain grandeur as well.

The promised land lay in a shadowy universe, but France protested that it could be reached. Two roads seemed to lead that way, however, and every pilgrim had to choose one or the other. In *Sur la Pierre blanche* France not only described the destination but showed how he thought it best to travel there. Dufresne hears a thumbnail history of the period from 1900 to 2270. Wars ceased, his informant says, because the masses, not as bellicose as their rulers, gradually built up their power in all the nations of Europe. Representatives of the people in the various parliaments, meeting informally with the representatives of other nations, developed a spirit of international cooperation that led to a sort of embryo United States of Europe. Without wars, armies ceased to have a reason to exist and were gradually disbanded, much to the displeasure of the capitalists. Finally, with little fighting, in most countries at least, socialists gained control of governments. Despite a resurgence of primitive nationalism and serious difficulties encountered in the establishment of functioning socialist governmental systems, the spirit of peace and cooperation, assisted by certain strong leaders of the proletariat, gradually triumphed, and the "European Federation" was formed. France thus accepted revolution, but revolution of the "when-the-time-is-right" variety. He apparently contented himself with the hope that a few weeks of fighting against die-hard reactionaries would be enough to seal the triumph of socialism; his old hatred of violence was still a major aspect of his mental attitude.

In 1904 France was a reformist, a reluctant revolution-

ary. He was a representative figure in his party, for not
until 1905 was reformism "outlawed" by the unified
French Socialist party.[57] This new party, formed by the
merger of several smaller groups, was to be above all a
party of the class struggle. Socialist deputies were to continue to serve in the Chamber, but they were to be fully
under the control of the party. They were to propa-
gandize and to serve the interests of the working class in
every possible way except one: no Socialist was to become a minister in the government. Their real aim was to
be, however, revolution. The new program seemed to
have little effect; actually, it was politically impossible.
France himself, for instance, did not publicly urge the
working class to prepare for revolt. Had the Socialists become a truly revolutionary party, as the Communists did
later, they would have lost much of their power to help
the working class through peaceful means. In fact, most
Socialists in the French party did about what Anatole
France did: they talked revolution but did their best to
ignore the practical aspects of revolution. By remaining
flexible they kept their allies, without whom they would
have been powerless. Without those allies, humanitarian
Socialists like France would have been left to organize
their own demonstrations for the many causes they supported; and they would have been forced to do without
the votes of many sympathizers who supported those
causes but would have been appalled at revolution. As it
was, France, Jaurès, Francis de Pressensé, and dozens of
other prominent Socialists could be found supporting all
sorts of public movements initiated by liberals of every
stripe, and, in turn, could expect those liberals to support
many of the projects they began.

III

When the Affair came to an end, it left scores that had to be settled. France's first great political campaign as a Socialist was one for which he had been enlisted most of his life. The church had remained above the battle, but its noisiest supporters had not. The Dreyfusards, firmly carrying on a century-old tradition of anticlericalism, believed that the time had come to win a final victory by forcing the separation of church and state.

Among Frenchmen, demands for separation of church and state were not usually based on a belief that separation would, as it had in various other countries, assure religious freedom.[58] They were, and had been for more than a century, the cries of unbelievers who were confident that without state support the church would die. Religious freedom, of course imperfect, existed. Not only Catholic priests but also rabbis and Protestant ministers received stipends from the government. Careers were open to men of any faith or none. Supporters of the system in force could claim with a great deal of justice that the French system was much fairer than, for instance, that of England, under which only one church was subsidized. Subsidies, however, were not the major issue; in reality, Catholics and unbelievers or deists were fighting for control of the nation's educational system. For a century the battle had gone on, and, though one side often gained a lead, neither side had been able to demolish the other. Generally speaking, the opposing sides were constituted along traditional political and economic lines: the "party of order" (to use terms long out of date but still useful), traditionalist, conservative, supported the church;

while the "party of movement," demanding change, attacked. The Radical party, the left-wing republican group, had gradually come to rival in strength the more conservative republicans once led by Gambetta. It was vehemently anti-clerical, and it was a Radical premier, supported by the Socialists, who was to carry through the fight for separation. Anatole France at last had an opportunity to do lasting damage to the church that he had hated so long.

France began attacking the church in public speeches during the election campaign of 1902. The fate of the church had once more become a burning issue in French politics. Waldeck-Rousseau had opened the new chapter in the struggle between church and state in France by offering the Chamber of Deputies a bill that would regulate the activities of the regular clergy. The bill was designed not to stamp out the orders but to clarify their status, give them legal recognition, and, by regulating them, to prevent them from overstepping the bounds of republican propriety. The majority in the Chamber went about this task more enthusiastically than the premier had intended, and the law finally passed in July, 1901, was a good deal more strict than the draft that Waldeck-Rousseau had introduced.[59] Thenceforward no regular religious order could be formed without prior authorization by the passage of a law, but any order could be dissolved by a simple decree. Moreover, no member of an unauthorized order would be permitted either to direct or to teach in any school whatsoever. The general election that came in 1902 was the first since 1898. The electorate was asked, therefore, not only to approve or disapprove the government's handling of the Dreyfus case but also to make clear its attitude on the new church legislation. Both sides, "nationalist" and Dreyfusard, girded for battle. The groups that had fought for Dreyfus organized a political alliance they called the Bloc des gauches: Radicals and Socialists banded together to consolidate their gains. Anatole France was an indifferent speaker, but during the campaign he served loyally as an agent of the Bloc des gauches.

France made his first election speech on December 21, 1901, when he presided at a joint meeting of the Sixteenth Arrondissement sections of the Ligue des Droits de l'Homme. (He had been president of the Porte Dauphine section since it was formed earlier that same year.[60]) Introducing the main speaker, a vice-president of the Ligue, France remarked that the "reactionaries and clericals," half-beaten, had not given up the battle: "They talk of nothing but liberty and the rights of men." [61] He added that the Left must combine to defeat these enemies who spoke such fair words, and pointed out that even though he was no admirer of French parliaments, he did not want to see them replaced by "patrols of cavalry." In another speech, on March 2, 1902, this one made at a Victor Hugo centenary celebration, he again condemned the clerical demands for "liberty" and praised Hugo for his stand against the clerical "loi Falloux" in 1850.[62] The situation in that year had been much like that of 1902, France said; clericals were clamoring for a liberty that would give them control of education and would stifle the liberty of their enemies. He urged his listeners to work for the establishment of the ideal republic, for social justice and true liberty, "that which recognizes no liberty against itself." In April, 1902, the month of the election, France became chairman of a campaign committee in his arrondissement and led the effort to unseat the incumbent nationalist deputy. He spoke one week before the election to a general assembly of the Ligue, urging voters not to cast their ballots for so-called liberals "who respect every oppression and every iniquity," but to vote for Radicals, Radical-Socialists, or Socialists.[63] He spoke again, in similar terms, between the two rounds in the election.[64]

The Bloc des gauches won its victory. Jaurès, who had lost his seat in the Assembly in 1898, won a new place on the first round of the 1902 election, and when the second round was over, the Bloc held a 53-vote majority in the Chamber of Deputies. Waldeck-Rousseau, having won the nation's approval, resigned the premiership and left the government in the hands of a Radical stalwart named Emile Combes.[65]

Combes hated Catholicism with a zeal easily as powerful as that displayed, in other directions, by the Jesuits who had educated him. He had one aim: to demolish the enemies of the republic. The chief enemy, as he saw it, was the church. Armed with the law of 1901 and backed by his parliament, he closed more than 2,500 clerically operated schools. Riots erupted in Catholic Brittany; stormy debates shook the Chamber. Waldeck-Rousseau protested that even though Combes was within the letter of the law he was violating its spirit. Combes, with the assent of his supporters, held firm.

To Anatole France, Jaurès, and thousands of other veterans of the crusade for Dreyfus, the battle for separation of church and state was just another phase, though an important one, in their struggle for justice and equality. To others, men who had been just as sincerely and actively dedicated to the vindication of Dreyfus, the case was not so clear. When Dreyfusism became separatism, they deserted in large numbers. Combes's campaign against the clerical schools was the signal for their revolt. By this time the poet Charles Péguy, a leading Drey-fusard, had begun publishing his *Cahiers de la Quinzaine*, each number of which was devoted primarily to a single work of fiction or to a discussion of current controversy. To the issue of August, 1902, which appeared about two months after Combes took office, Péguy added a supple-ment given to an examination of the new premier's anti-clerical policies. Péguy called the actions of the govern-ment "idiocies." [66] Among the documents he printed was a letter from the Comité Catholique Pour la Défense du Droit, a pro-Dreyfus Catholic group, and another from Gabriel Monod, a Protestant who was a lecturer at the Ecole normale supérieure and a supporter of separation; both letters attacked Combes's school decrees as intoler-ant. These letters had attracted the attention of "impeni-tent Dreyfusards," Péguy said, so he had asked Bernard Lazare, one of the first to come to Dreyfus' aid, to write a "consultation" on the subject of the laws concerning religious orders. In this article Lazare asserted that he had, in formulating his opinion, applied to the study of con-temporary affairs exactly the same principles that had guided him during the Affair. He pointed out that "all the reactionaries" had protested against the new laws in the name of liberty. Republicans had approved those laws, arguing from the necessities and rights of civil society. "This is a grave situation," Lazare wrote, "for it means nothing less than the reversal of positions taken in recent years." [67]

The legal questions involved were complicated, but few of the partisans of either side bothered to examine the problem from the legal angle; and the moral question was only too simple. Lazare's summation of the stands taken was factual, and his accusation was obviously just. Whatever the value of the stake, the issue was clear: the explosive question of the rights of the individual in the face of the state was the kernel of the argument, just as it had been in the case of Captain Dreyfus. Lazare was right: the cause of individual liberty had fled one camp to turn up in the other. The clerical forces, had they won, certainly would have suppressed the rights of their enemies as quickly as possible; the Catholics in France had cried liberty more than once in their attempts to quash the liberties of others. That, however, was a political consideration that could not affect the moral question. Jaurès and by far the larger number of the Dreyfusards had dropped the mystique to make room for the politique. Monod, Lazare, and the Catholic Dreyfusards left the coalition.[68] Jaurès, annoyed by these defections, railed at his former supporters, describing them as "lawyers gone mad, ridiculous knights-errant." [69] A few idealists might raise an alarm, but the machine must roll on: the fate of the republic was at stake.

Anatole France, despite the fact that he was on good enough terms with Péguy to allow the *Cahiers* to publish a collection of his speeches and one of his novelettes,[70] ignored the delicate question raised by Péguy and his friends. He was in Paris to mourn the death of Zola in October, 1902,[71] then he went south to Mme de Caillavet's country estate. There he took time to write a letter regretting that he could not attend a great Socialist "solidarity" rally to be held in Paris on December 21.[72] He aimed a barb at conservative republicans who sympathized with the incessant clerical demands for liberty.[73] He sent his "best wishes" to a banquet honoring the staff of *Jean-Pierre*, a children's magazine that published articles by important liberals twice a month, and, just as often, infuriated good Catholics.[74] (One later critic called the magazine a "diabolical enterprise" that taught children to regard all priests as "nauseating hypocrites." [75] The editor was Jeanne Maritain, and the contributors included her brother Jacques, who later became prominent in other circles.) In short, Péguy's moral fervor had no effect at all on Anatole France.

Combes was not ruffled either. In March, 1903, he announced that all unauthorized orders would be dissolved. The Council of State, the highest body of governmental advisers, ruled that if an order applied for authorization and was refused by either of the two houses of parliament, such a refusal amounted to an order dissolving that order.[76] Of the 535 orders that applied, only five were granted authorization. Throughout 1903 the process of dissolution proceeded.

Anatole France applauded. He made his position thoroughly clear in May, 1903, in a letter to Domenico Oliva, a reporter for a Rome newspaper: "It would not be easy for any government to reduce these rebellious monks to obedience. Monks of every order have for some years fought furiously against the republic. The republicans are defending it. The battle will be, on both sides, without mercy. If the clericals win, liberty will be finished for a long time; we will no longer be able to hope to prepare for the coming of social justice. The intellectual development of the country will be interrupted. But the clericals will not win." [77]

In September Combes braved hostile Breton crowds in Tréguier, the birthplace of Renan, to dedicate a monument to the great apostate. France was at his side, not afraid to point approvingly to Renan's view of the origins of piety: unlike the philosophes of the eighteenth century, Renan felt that the religious man was the victim not of a fraud but of his own sick mind.[78] In December, 1903, France returned to print once again, this time for a major undertaking. Combes, defending his position, published a collection of his speeches entitled *Une Campagne laïque*. The preface was by Anatole France. This preface was long; in it France gave an impassioned résumé of the activities of the clerical orders during the Affair, told the story of the church legislation passed under Waldeck-Rousseau and his successor, praised Combes for carrying on despite the abuse of his enemies, and ended by accusing the papacy of still pursuing an age-old objective: conquest of the world.[79] He also devoted a few paragraphs to a critique of Christian morality, which he found wanting. It was horrible, he thought, to teach children to obey by giving them little books full of pictures of busy demons torturing the souls of the damned.[80] The preface was an excellent piece of propaganda. France did not have to lie to make his point, for the monks had given him plenty of evidence to work with. As for his history, his interpretation is now generally accepted; Adrien Dansette, the Catholic historian whose history of religion in France is now widely followed, tells much the same tale. France's description of the objectives of the papacy was, of course, subject to dispute, but one can safely say that it had a wide appeal in the non-Catholic world. The preface, having appeared once in *L'Aurore* and again in Combes's book, was reprinted as a pamphlet under the title *Le Parti noir* in March, 1904. An expanded version, about twice as long, was issued in January, 1905, as *L'Eglise et la République*.[81] Mme de Caillavet was glad that France had written these pages—she thought that

"that nice Combes" was worth encouraging, and, besides, France's work would please some old friends.[82] No doubt it also irked some old enemies, and that was a consideration that would not have escaped its author.

France did not have to wait long to see his enemies discomfited once more. Combes, seizing on a diplomatic blunder made by the Vatican, started the proceedings that would finally sever all connection between church and state.[83] The text of a confidential papal diplomatic dispatch, leaked to the press, seemed to indicate that the Vatican was interfering in French politics. The public outcry that followed helped to produce the right mood for a decisive act. Combes recalled the French envoy at the Vatican, and, on May 27, the Chamber approved his action. Two months later diplomatic relations between Paris and the Vatican were broken. Combes followed through immediately. On July 7 he forbade any monk, regardless of order, authorized or unauthorized, to teach in any educational institution. When the Chamber opened its new session in October, Combes introduced the separation bill.

Then the anticlerical machine ground to a halt. A new scandal had come to light, and it was manna for the clericals. Once more there was an affair; this one came to be known as the *Affaire des Fiches*.[84]

In October, 1904, several newspapers reported that there existed a secret file of political dossiers on army officers. The implication was, of course, that the officers whose opinions pleased the government were the ones whose careers would prosper; good Catholics were not likely to be promoted. General André, Combes's minister of war, had to admit that the charge, and all it implied, was true. Sordid details followed. Combes himself apparently had approved the system (though he denied the charge), and the Grand Orient, the unorthodox French Masonic lodge, had furnished the agents who turned in the reports that caused all the trouble. Jaurès attempted to minimize the scandal. It was, he said, a political intrigue stirred up by reactionaries to divide republicans. He was certainly right that the reactionaries were pressing the charges, but the fact remained that the charges were not just mud thrown but secrets uncovered; the system existed.

The Dreyfusards were shaken. Another group of purist republicans deserted their old comrades on the ground that what was illegal and immoral if done by reactionaries was equally illegal and immoral if done by republicans. Among the men who espoused this refreshing view was Joseph Reinach, a charter member of the Dreyfusards and, in 1904, a member of the central committee of the Ligue des Droits de l'Homme. Francis de Pressensé, Dreyfusard, Socialist deputy, and president of the Ligue, wrote in the *Bulletin* of the Ligue that the organization condemned the system, but opposed the condemnation of individuals who were responsible for its application. He pointed out that the evidence had been stolen (which it had), and that the attack on the government was led by men so reactionary as to be automatically suspect.[85] Reinach was not satisfied. He had for some time doubted the justice of the stands taken by the Ligue, and, faced with this new equivocation, he felt that he must resign.[86] Paul Guieysse, a deputy, and Emile Bourgeois, one of the chief theorists and political leaders of the Radical party, resigned for the same reasons.[87]

The Chamber held Combes responsible for the system, but, thanks to the efforts of Jaurès, he managed to survive the parliamentary assault that followed its discovery. He won a vote of confidence by six votes. Recognizing the extreme weakness of his position, he resigned his premiership a few weeks later, at the end of the legislative session. His successor, Maurice Rouvier, had to worry through the final steps in the process of separation. The separation bill was passed in the Chamber in July, 1905, and became the law of the land in December of that year.

The Affaire des Fiches had not, after all, defeated the partisans of separation. It had, however, demolished the Dreyfusard party. This time not only Catholics and "lawyers gone mad" had rebelled; this time raison d'état as used by the so virtuous Dreyfusards had alienated men not widely believed to be tinged with mysticism. The mystique was gone.

Anatole France had gone into the Dreyfus Affair very much infected with the mystique, but by the time of this new and not so tragic affair, he was all politician. Having tasted the pleasures of political writing in preparing his preface for Combes, France welcomed an opportunity to become a regular political analyst for a Vienna newspaper, the *Neue Freie Presse*, early in 1904. He changed neither his opinions nor his style when he took up the burden of enlightening the citizens of Vienna on the state of French affairs. His first column, published on January 31, 1904, was a blow aimed at the church, and many of the others followed the same pattern; several of them were added to the Combes preface to make up the final manuscript of *L'Eglise et la République*.[88] He confidently discussed the coming of separation, and did his best to help it along.

When the scandal of the fiches broke upon the scene, France was immediately involved, though indirectly. His daughter Suzanne, never really close to him since he had left his wife, had married an army captain named Henri Mollin. She was unhappy in her marriage, and France was on bad terms with his son-in-law.[89] Not that there was anything wrong with Captain Mollin's politics—indeed, quite the reverse: he was not only a zealous Mason but the personal aid of General André, the very republican minister of war. When the revelations began, it developed that Mollin had served as André's liaison with the Masonic order; he was, in fact, the man who administered the network of informers. His disgrace, which followed immediately upon his exposure, gave France's daughter an excuse for a divorce, and she grasped the opportunity. France had been involved in an embarrassing scandal, but he had profited by the loss of an undesired relative.

He was, however, involved in the scandal on yet another plane. How would Combes's collaborator, who had so often impugned the morals of the nationalists, react when he found that "that nice Combes" was not exactly simon-pure himself? He could follow Reinach's example or he could listen to the soothing words of Pressensé. The same issue of the *Bulletin* of the Ligue that reported Reinach's resignation from the central committee announced proudly that the place vacated would be filled by M. Anatole France.

France could not have made his position more clear, but he reinforced the choice he had made when he presided, two weeks after the scandal had begun, at a meeting of six thousand Socialists. He spoke of the Affair, the rabid monks, the bands of anti-Semites, and the brave men who had opposed them, conspicuous among whom was one of the speakers of the evening: Francis de Pressensé.[90] He recalled those perilous days, France said, because it was clear that another attack by these enemies of the modern spirit had begun, and republicans must preserve their unity in the face of that growing threat. The implication was obvious: when reactionaries forged evidence against an innocent Jewish captain, they were moral lepers; when republicans secretly probed the religious opinions of other officers equally innocent of any crime, they were patriots defending the modern spirit.

France's propaganda writings showed no change after the scandal. Writing while the Affaire des Fiches was at its height, he set down in logical form his reasons for demanding separation and offered his answer to the demands for liberty posed by partisans of the church. The separation bill must be passed, he wrote, because the church does not recognize the modern state (here he cited the *Syllabus* of 1864); the church interferes in the affairs of the state (the Loubet visit and its consequences); the Concordat violates freedom of conscience by forcing people to pay for the support of churches they abhor; and, above all, even if one accepts the Concordat as a legitimate agreement, the church has, in actuality, denounced that agreement by violating its provisions (a list of violations followed).[91] On the subject of liberty, France said: "In France, where [Catholicism] is the religion of the majority, it does not want to be free, it wants to be sovereign."[92] He said also: "The state must give the church what it owes, and only what it owes: that is, liberty—certainly not that metaphysical liberty that does not exist and, in fact, designates privilege, but a real liberty, limited by other liberties and defined by the conditions of the political and social environment."[93] France had chosen his side, and he had abdicated his position as a disinterested critic. He had once been inflexible, but now he was willing to compromise, if compromise was the price of success.

IV

Socialists and Radicals, closely allied in the struggle for separation, found it worthwhile to work together in other matters as well. One of the foremost of these causes, in the early years of the century a major project for European liberals, was agitation for colonial reform and equitable treatment of ethnic minorities.

France joined the crusade for minority rights even before he became a socialist. One of his first political acts was to sign, in the spring of 1899, a protest against the order of Tsar Nicholas II that abolished the semiautonomous status Finland had enjoyed since 1809. In August of that same year he wrote a preface for a book attacking the tsar's policy in which he said that the Russians might be able to destroy Finland but would never make it a Slavic nation.[94]

Anatole France was even more active on behalf of the Armenians, a people suffering worse tribulations than the Finns. Turkey, Russia, and Persia shared control of Armenia under an agreement made at the Conference of Berlin in 1878, and each was supposed to guarantee the safety of the Armenians, particularly against the violent Kurdish tribes installed in the area.[95] Meanwhile, Armenian nationalism, encouraged by students returning from Europe, began to flourish in the early nineties. The sultan of Turkey, already hard put to keep his empire from collapsing, allowed the Kurds free rein, then sent in his Moslem troops to help them massacre the Christian Armenians. The project of extermination took two years (1896–1898), and even then was not finished; the massacres continued for several years. The Armenians made their complaints heard all over Europe, but the European governments had important diplomatic and economic reasons for staying out of the sultan's affairs. Not until after World War I was any serious effort made to protect the Armenians. Meanwhile, Armenian propagandists, aided by European sympathizers, kept up a steady barrage of protest. Anatole France was in the forefront of the sympathizers; he spoke at a banquet organized for the benefit of Armenian orphans in June, 1900; he served for several years on the editorial board of *Pro Armenia*, a propaganda journal, beginning at the time of its foundation in November, 1900; he wrote an announcement in June, 1902, to promote an international congress that was to be held to protest the massacres; he spoke twice in March, 1903, once in Rome, at protest meetings; and, in general, he lent his name or his presence to the Armenian cause whenever it was needed.[96]

France also worked steadily for another minority, closer to home—the Jews. He had always opposed anti-Semitism.[97] In his books he could be hard on Jews, but not simply for their Jewishness: in his "Histoire contemporaine," for instance, he ridiculed Jews who, out of ambition or greed, kowtowed to reactionary noblemen. There are also indications that he could not forgive the Jews for having given birth to Christianity and for having given the Christians a stern and jealous God.[98] But he did not consider that reason enough to hate all Jews. In one of the selections in his *Opinions sociales*, a "Dialogue sur l'anti-sémitisme," France argued that anti-Semitism was largely caused by economic factors, and that it was not widespread among the workers, who not only knew that poor Jews existed but were well aware that they would gain nothing if the rich Jews were despoiled.[99] He cited the anti-Semitism of the nationalists as one of the many reasons for voting against them when he made campaign speeches before the election of 1902, basing his argument on the empirical philosophy that was ingrained in his nature: "A people cannot be hateful as a whole, for it includes within it all kinds of opposites—women, men, the old, the young, rich and poor, idle and industrious, evildoers and doers of good. A race? But a race is made of very diverse and unlike individuals. To hate a race is to hate indiscriminately men very different from each other. It's a stupid idea." [100] He made much the same point in one of the articles he wrote for the *Neue Freie Presse*, and repeated it in *Sur la Pierre blanche*. Later he protested against pogroms in Russia.[101]

In Africa not a single race but an entire continent suffered persecution. Colonial administrators were often as brutal as the most primitive of their charges, and some incidents in this routine of horror in Africa aroused waves of indignation in France. On July 14, 1903, the day in every year when Frenchmen celebrated the end of the Old Regime and the cruelties they associated with it, an official in the French Congo chose to make an example of a native guide who had led his party into an ambush: he fastened a lighted stick of dynamite to the man's neck and set him free. The sound of the resulting explosion took more than a year to reach the banks of the Seine, but when it did the cry that went up produced a reform movement that actually got results.[102] Pierre Savorgnan de Brazza, a veteran explorer renowned as much for his friendliness to the natives as for the fact that he was the man who had won the Congo for France, was named chairman of a government commission formed to make an investigation of the colonial administration of the Congo. Brazza made his tour, but he died on the way back to Paris. Although the government refused to publish the report filed by Brazza's companions, Félicien Challaye, a young author Brazza had taken along, refused to be silent. His report was devastating.

Socialists had always deplored colonial conquest. As early as 1902 Anatole France had called it folly, and in 1904 he said that Russia was paying for the imperialism of all Europe with her defeat in the Russo-Japanese War.[103] He considered the colonies a pure liability: they were valuable not to the nation, but only to a few rich merchants; and, since other nations coveted them, they kept the country constantly in danger of war.[104] When Challaye began telling what he had seen on the Brazza expedition, Gustave Rouanet, one of the editors of *l'Humanité*, began a newspaper campaign to force publication of the full report and the accomplishment of reforms in the colonial administration.[105] On January 30, 1906, France presided over a meeting on colonial reform sponsored by the Ligue des Droits de l'Homme, one of many meetings at which Challaye spoke. Introducing the speaker, France asserted that colonial policy was simply capitalist policy, and demanded that the natives be accorded civil rights and treated justly.[106] France continued to denounce imperialism, and Rouanet kept hammering at the ministry of colonies in his newspaper columns. In February, 1906, the Brazza report was finally published.[107] France helped to organize, and sent his greetings to, a banquet held on March 20, 1906, to honor Rouanet for his work.[108] The commercial concessions in French Africa were gradually liquidated, and, in a few years, the worst of the brutality had been stopped, though real reforms did not come for decades. Rouanet, Challaye, and their supporters could, therefore, claim credit for at least a modest achievement.

France and his friends accomplished far less in their attempts to influence other aspects of the government's foreign policy. In several speeches and articles of this period France discussed the danger of war. He called Théophile Delcassé, minister of foreign affairs in cabinet after cabinet, "the crazy man of the ministry" and referred to "the black dwarf of the Quai d'Orsay" who was preparing "to make Europe explode." When the conference of Algeciras was held to settle a grave dispute between France and Germany over their respective rights in Morocco, Anatole France presided at a meeting held to demand an end to secret diplomacy. Introducing Jaurès, the chief orator of the evening, France said that French nationalists, bellicose as they seemed, did not really want war; they only wanted the menace of war, a menace they could use to maintain their control over the people. Secret diplomacy, he said, was a weapon in their hands. Needless to say, neither his speech nor the resolution passed by the crowd at the meeting had the slightest effect. Despite the ineffectiveness of his efforts, however, France was to pay increasing attention to the problems of peace as the years went by.[109]

In their preoccupation with mass oppression and national policies, France, the Socialists, and French liberals in general did not forget their concern for the stricken individual. For instance, France signed a writers' petition deploring the prosecution of Georges Eekhoud, a Belgian novelist whose works were said to be "contrary to good morals." [110] Later, in 1903, he sent a letter joining in a demand for freedom for a number of Andalusian working-class agitators who had been in a Spanish prison for years on a charge that had finally been proved false.[111] He also wrote a letter to be read at the trial of the poet Laurent Tailhade, charged in 1901 with writing an article in an anarchist journal that urged the murder of a visiting potentate, Tsar Nicholas II. He had not read the article, France admitted, but that did not matter: "I cannot well conceive of a crime of words among a free people. Making thought pay fines and putting doctrines in prison is, in France, a great undertaking." [112] No one accepted Tailhade's suggestion, if that was what it was; the tsar was probably safer in Paris than in St. Petersburg. He was, nevertheless, none too popular in France, and in 1905, when his people rose in revolt, French liberals loosed a mighty roar of encouragement.

For years Russia had been a sore point for a great many democratically oriented Frenchmen.[113] After her defeat in 1871 France had faced the newly founded German Empire alone. After Bismarck's departure, however, the German emperor neglected to renew his alliance with the tsar. French diplomats took advantage of their opportunity; together France and Russia were more than a match for Germany. By the turn of the century Russia was France's ally, and the tsar, most absolute of autocrats, had been heard to sing the revolutionary verses of the "Marseillaise." For left-wing Frenchmen the situation was acutely uncomfortable. Most of them really were glad to see Russia help to keep Germany tied down, but they hated to see French money, invested in Russian bonds, used to bolster the sagging tyranny of the tsar. Every time the inept Russian government did anything at all highhanded, and that was often, French Socialists and liberals, Anatole France included, condemned the tsar loudly and publicly.

The first act of Russia's twentieth-century revolution was played in March, 1901, when the Russian government began to enforce a law providing that university students who engaged in political activity should be drafted into the army. The students rioted in protest; police fired on them. On April 29 Anatole France signed a protest against "the massacres of St. Petersburg, Moscow, and Kharkov, and against the mass arrests that followed the massacres." [114] A week later he wrote a letter that was printed in *L'Aurore:* "Since Russia has been born to the life of the mind, her intellectual and social emancipation can no longer be prevented. The hour of her liberty will come. . . . Historical law, this time, too, will be obeyed: Russian democracy will pay with its blood for its liberty." [115] That time the tsar's police had had their way; the riots were suppressed, the arrests made, order restored.

The next act opened on January 22, 1905 (New Style). The hardships and humiliations of the war with Japan then in progress had made themselves felt. A priest, Gapon, led a mass of demonstrators to the Winter Palace to present to the tsar a petition for social and political reforms. Troops fired on the marchers; a thousand people were killed, a thousand wounded. Strikes broke out, sailors revolted. Members of the Russian Bolshevik party began organizing soviets in St. Petersburg and Moscow. Maxim Gorki, the famous novelist, wrote an "Appeal to All Russian Citizens and to the Public Opinion of the European States," and was immediately jailed. [116]

In Paris a frenzy of pro-rebel activity began. Anatole France was first on a list of contributors to a fund for

"the families of the victims of the Russian massacres." [117]
On January 27, five days after the massacre, he spoke at
a protest meeting organized by the trade-union associa-
tions of the Paris area and attended by five thousand of
their members. On January 31 he joined a group of
French intellectuals in protesting the arrest of Gorki.
During the month of February he spoke or wrote on five
different occasions specifically for the Russian rebels,
and on February 26 it was announced that he had become
president of a new organization, Les Amis du Peuple
russe et des Peuples annexés (Armenian, Finns, and
Poles).[118]

In his speeches France called the massacre of January
22 unprovoked, and predicted that it would have dire
consequences: "The tsar has had men massacred who,
dying of misery and hunger, were only guilty of having,
in their distress, prayed to him as to a father. To their
fervent prayers, their filial invocations, their tears, he responded with the charge of Cossacks and the bullets of
grenadiers. Those bullets struck his own image, carried
in the hands of the priest Gapon. Just in spite of himself,
the tsar has killed the tsar . . . and has raised the revolution that will devour tsarism. Nicholas Alexandrovitch
already may be said to exist no longer, and the universe
will execrate his memory." [119]

But the victims of the tsar were, France continued, not
alone in their plight. The Russians, who deserved better,
might have the worst government in the world, but the
governments of Western Europe were not very good
either. The bourgeois republicans who governed France,
for instance, were devoted to imperialism, nationalism,
and social injustice. Their alliance with the tsar, a disgrace, was only to be expected, for reaction was every-

where and all oppressors were allies. "For its safety and its freedom . . . the proletariat must rely on itself alone. Against all oppression, against tsarism, against imperialism, against nationalism, proletarians of the entire world must unite. They must all unite against the universal triumvirate of the priest, the soldier, and the financier." These men, truly internationalist by virtue of their religion, their capital, and their fraternity of arms, made up the international of servitude and violence. "To that international . . . let us oppose the international of the proletariat, the international of liberty, of harmonious work, and of peace."

France's speeches all followed the same pattern: the massacres in Russia were crimes against humanity, but the tsar was not the only criminal: he was only the worst of the reactionaries who ruled everywhere. The Franco-Russian alliance was worthless to France; it benefited only the bankers who traded in Russian bonds. The only alliance Frenchmen recognized was that of "a people with a people," not that of "a people with a man," and the only real safety lay in the union of all the workers of the world.[120] The revolution in Russia was a forerunner of the triumph of oppressed over oppressors everywhere.

In Russia triumph seemed near, but it was not. The rebellion dragged on for nearly a year; its failure was not certain until the tsar had crushed a general strike in January, 1906. While there was still hope, Anatole France cheered the rebels on. On March 18, 1905, presiding at a meeting of the Société des Amis du Peuple russe, he protested vigorously against plans to float a new Russian loan in France. The money would not be paid back, he argued; the tsar, defeated by Japan and in the midst of a revolution, would not last long enough to settle his debts; moreover, to send money to the tsar was to finance his crimes. He attacked this loan again, even after the revolution had definitely failed and the French government had consented to the transaction.[121]

France still hoped for the triumph of the rebels as late as December, 1905, only a month before they were finally crushed. On December 16 he presided at a meeting organized to protest the pogroms that were taking place in Russia in the aftermath of the revolt. He made his speech twelve years too soon:

> The Russian revolution is a universal revolution. It has revealed to the proletariat of the entire world its means and its ends, its forces and its destiny. It menaces all despotisms, all oppression, all exploitation of man by man. . . .
> The fate of the new Europe and of future humanity is being decided at this moment on the banks of the Neva, the Vistula and the Volga.
> Strange exchange of notions and ideas!
> Our fathers of 'eighty-nine taught Europe the bourgeois revolution, and there, in return, Russian proletarians are giving us lessons in social revolution.[122]

It was as near as he had come to advocating real revolution in France. He soon realized, however, that his hopes for Russia had come to nothing. Early in August, 1906, he joined in sending a plaintive message to the president of the Duma, a representative body the tsar had first authorized and then dissolved. French intellectuals proclaimed their faith in the coming of liberty to Russia: "The Duma is dead! Long live the Duma!" [123]

Purists like Jules Guesde, Marxists who believed that only the triumph of socialism could put an end to the

injustice that was inherent in capitalist society, thought
that effort exerted on behalf of isolated reforms was effort
wasted. Anatole France showed by tilting against injustice on so many different fields that he was too impatient to share such a cold-blooded attitude. True, he
seemed to believe, only socialism could end all oppression
in one fell swoop, but in the meantime single men and
even entire nationalities could be saved from destruction
by timely protests and tireless propagandizing. He acted
in the old liberal tradition, fighting oppression as a whole
by working for a better society, but still trying to right
immediate wrongs even though the new dawn was still to
come. All his many activities—his speeches on behalf of
persecuted Jews, his articles on the plight of the Armenians, his literary diatribes against warlike nationalists—
he made a coherent whole by basing his arguments on a
socialist political philosophy. All his public actions served
a double function; each one supported a limited end, such
as the reform of colonial administration, and at the same
time was a piece of socialist propaganda. His disagree-
ment with the purists was a matter of method, not of
final aims.

In two areas France worked directly for the triumph of
socialism, with no intermediate end in view. He strongly
supported a movement for the education of workers, because he thought that, once educated, they would fight
for socialism; and he fought hard to promote the election
of Socialist political candidates.

Free, universal education had long been a favorite ideal
in France. Most of the philosophes of the later eighteenth
century had considered free education a necessity; if a
people was to govern itself it must be "enlightened."
Their schemes were far from realized. The French school

system was so organized in Anatole France's day that thorough and extended education was available to only a few. Competitive examinations weeded out the stupid and the overly creative, but economic disability was a far more effective barrier to uncounted thousands of prospective students. The glaring deficiencies of the system were apparent not only to Socialists but to thoughtful men of all classes. Most voters—and taxpayers—naturally were hostile to every major reform proposed in the Assembly, but surprisingly large numbers of private citizens were willing to support any good private remedy.

"Popular universities," the first of which was founded in 1897, seemed for a while to be a major step in the right direction. If the state would not educate the workers, the workers, with a little help, could educate themselves. Some of the founders of the popular university movement intended simply to give intelligent workers a chance to improve their minds—according to one early enthusiast, "to elevate their souls." [124] The early curricula included heavy doses of cultural courses, such as literature and philosophy; but even then the political aims of others among the founders were clear, for along with traditional subjects the workers were offered courses in the history of the labor movement. Vocational training was not included; that could be left to the technical schools. At first the opposing political philosophies that underlay the movement caused little trouble. Young idealists like Edouard Herriot, who was to lead the economically conservative Radicals in stormy days, gave up their evenings to teach workers whose formal education was rudimentary.[125] Guesde, adamant as usual, was reported to consider the universités as just another attempt of the bourgeoisie to corrupt the proletariat, and one of his chief lieutenants, Paul Lafargue, fought them from the start.[126] Other Socialists, prominent among them Anatole France, saw the universités as a training ground for future comrades, and supported them warmly.

In 1900 France told an audience of worker-students what he expected them to gain from their study of science. That study, he explained, must be objective; it must be approached without a social bias. But, on the other hand: "It is to betray science not to introduce its teachings, wherever one can, into social life. Science teaches us to fight fanaticism in all its forms; it teaches us to construct for ourselves our ideal of justice without borrowing the materials from erroneous systems or barbarous traditions." [127]

France preached this curious blend of scientism and socialism during the early days of the movement; two years later he was more explicit: "What retards . . . our emancipation? The people have numbers and power; they could disperse the heavy obstacles amassed before them with a breath, as if they were made of straw. They could, but in fact they do not. Why? They do not lack the courage. They do not act because they do not yet know sharply and precisely the social, industrial, and economic conditions of their emancipation; they cannot because they do not yet know how to proceed with scientific rigor to their methodical and certain liberation. . . . The conquest of political liberties was made in the eighteenth century by means of reason and thought; the emancipation of the worker will be accomplished, in the twentieth century, by means of science and thought. May the proletariat, with the power of reflection, finally become conscious of itself and of the world; may it unite completely in unanimous consent to demonstrated truths and in the application of a rational method; and, as it is the only force, it will become the only authority." [128] France appeared before such audiences several times during the years from 1900 through 1905, and also helped to inaugurate a cooperative press and supported the creation of a "popular theater" along lines similar to those of the popular universities.[129] All the while he took it for granted that these workers planned to use the education they got, not for personal advancement or to "elevate their souls," but to make themselves masters of the world.

Such attitudes, displayed regularly by the Socialists in the movement, could not have failed to alienate the bourgeois idealists who also supported the popular universities. The bitter polemics that resulted from the conflict between Socialists and more conservative sponsors simply destroyed the entire movement. It broke up around 1905, its initial idealism spent; most of the groups disappeared, and the few that survived were controlled by one side or the other, Socialists or liberals.[130] Such an idealistic program faced almost insurmountable obstacles from the first: money was scarce, and the number of workers willing to give the little leisure time they had for so little tangible reward was not likely to be as large as the generous intellectuals who conceived the idea had hoped. La Coopération des Idées, the one popular university of which a history has survived, was still operating in 1910, and the author of the history, at least, was optimistic about its future; but the group was racked by squabbles between socialist and bourgeois sponsors and between workers and intellectuals, and also was suffering from financial scandals, a chronic lack of funds, personality problems in its administration, and natural catastrophe (the Paris flood of 1910 left its rooms a wreck).[131] Despite the obvious problems, the movement had been astonishingly successful until the political strife began to come to the surface. Anatole France undoubtedly helped, by lending them his prestige, to build the popular universities; but the strong socialist stand he took in his speeches probably helped to destroy them.

The failure of the popular universities was just another example of the death of the unifying mystique that had made something more than a mere political machine of the Dreyfusard party. The universités benefited from the idealism generated by the Affair and collapsed when that idealism deteriorated.

By 1906 Anatole France seemed to have been touched by that deterioration. In 1902 he had spoken at election rallies and predicted glorious victories. When 1906 brought another election, France followed the campaign closely, analyzing the pre-election situation at length in an interview that was published in the *Neue Freie Presse*, but he did not mount a single platform.[132] Instead, he traveled leisurely through Italy with Mme de Caillavet.[133] He still was watching new developments with interest, and he contemplated the future "with serenity." [134] After all, Dreyfus had been saved, even though the Dreyfusards had fallen out when their job was done; the monks had been punished, even though the men who chastised them no longer worked together. These were triumphs. But the crusade was no longer going so well. Perhaps the next few years might bring not more victories but defeat.

4
The Socialist
(1906–1917)

In 1904, at the height of the battle over separation of church and state, Anatole France had confidently predicted that socialism was the wave of the future, "the inevitable consequence of capitalist evolution." The socialist utopia of *Sur la Pierre blanche* exuded confidence. During these first years of his association with socialism, however, France could call himself a socialist without convincing anyone that he meant it. The brand of socialism Jaurès preached was not the uncompromising revolutionary doctrine of Jules Guesde; the battles Jaurès was fighting until 1905 were not really skirmishes in the class war but simply continuations of old conflicts that had existed before socialism was anything more than a curiosity. France's actions during this period differentiated him hardly at all from any warmhearted reformer.

After 1905, however, the political situation changed rapidly, and to be a socialist came to mean much more than it had in the heady years of the "Dreyfus Revolution." Only after 1905 was it clear that France was anything more than an enthusiast, ready to sink into dejection at the first sign of difficulty. After 1905 socialism was no longer fashionable. France proved then that his conversion was more than a gesture meant to attract attention.

I

Radicals and socialists, fresh from their joint victory in the struggle for separation of church and state and their mutual disgrace in the Affaire des Fiches, found in the general election held in the spring of 1906 that most French voters wholeheartedly approved of their actions. They won handily and returned to the Chamber of Deputies with their numbers increased. Clemenceau, the destroyer of cabinets, finally agreed to become premier himself in October, 1906.[1] Anatole France was jubilant: he was sure that Clemenceau would enforce the separation law to the letter, and he was confident that Clemenceau's government would handle other matters just as agreeably. The Bloc des gauches had been strained since the palmy days of the Combes administration, but France, like Jaurès, believed that Clemenceau would have to make new and more important concessions to the Socialists. Otherwise, France wrote, "caught between the extreme Left and the Right, he is lost." [2] France was wrong. Clemenceau, leading the powerful Radicals, kept his own party under control, added the votes of a few moderates, and proceeded to ignore the Socialists.[3] Passage of the separation law actually produced a rapprochement of Radicals and moderates: on other spiritual matters they differed profoundly, but they could not have agreed more fully on the sanctity of private property. To make matters worse, from the Socialist point of view, Clemenceau's government tried to solve the labor problem by killing strikers. Twenty workers were killed and nearly seven hundred wounded by government troops "keeping order" during 1907 and 1908.[4] The number and violence of the strikes of those years, combined with the extreme harshness of the government's reactions, produced a chronic state of apprehension throughout the nation. As early as 1906, before the situation had reached its most critical point, the Confédération générale du travail (CGT) reported as follows: "There was an amusing flight of capital, emigrating to foreign countries in the name of the purest patriotism. Provisions were stocked in cellars. . . . The government was afraid." [5] The Dreyfusard party no longer existed. The men who had been its leaders, Clemenceau and Jaurès, exchanged insults in the Chamber. The Radicals were in control, and the extreme Left was near revolt.

Like other Socialists, Anatole France surveyed the wreckage of his hopes and went into opposition. Less than four months after Clemenceau took office as premier, France was saying that Briand wanted to give the nation back to the priests and that Clemenceau, dazzled by his friendship with the king of England, wanted to start a war with Germany.[6] Furious, feeling betrayed, France spent most of 1907 constructing a book that surpassed in violence any he had written before.

Fragments that were to make up the first part of that new book, *L'Île des pingouins*, had been published in a newspaper in 1905 and 1906. Obviously France had already planned the book to be what it was, a parody on French history, but the later chapters, written after the reign of Clemenceau had begun, reflected a bitterness absent from those early fragments. In fact, France overshot his mark, for instead of discomfiting his reactionary enemies he convinced them that he had turned against socialism. Many of his Socialist allies, equally shocked, thought he had plunged into nihilism.

The book, finally published in 1908, is divided into three major sections: the first carries the history of the "Penguins" from ancient times to the recent past; the second, almost half the book, covers the period Frenchmen knew as that of the Third Republic, with a strong emphasis on the famous Affaire Pyrot (Dreyfus); the third carries the history into "Les Temps futurs."

Socialists should not have been seriously disturbed by Parts I and II. France followed Rousseau in attributing the origin of private property to violence; [7] he ridiculed religion on every second page. He continued to attack capitalism: its buildings were ugly, its cities "Americanized," its justice still for sale (and quite expensive), and its statesmen still even more ignorant than their constituents.[8] Its financiers still got the blame for everything: "The Penguin state was democratic; three or four financial companies exercised in it a power that was more extensive, and, above all, more effective and more stable, than that of the ministers of the republic. Those ministers were little lords, secretly governed by the companies and obliged by intimidation or corruption to favor the companies at the expense of the state. When ministers remained honest, the companies destroyed them by turning against them the calumnies of the press." [9]

Socialists who refused to help save Pyrot came in for a gentle reproof,[10] but Socialists who deserted to the bourgeoisie were impaled on shafts of irony: "It was then one of the most solemn, most rigorous, most severe—and, I should say, most cruel and most terrible—customs of politics to place in each ministry destined to fight socialism a member of the Socialist party, in order that the enemies of fortune and property should feel the shame and the bitterness of being struck by one of their own, and so that they could not meet among themselves without looking at the man who would attack them on the morrow. Only a profound ignorance of the human heart would permit a belief that it was difficult to find a Socialist to perform this function." [11] Another passage appeared to be a general indictment of human intelligence: "One believes what one desires. . . . The faculty of doubt is rare among men; a very small number of minds carry in them its seeds, which do not develop without culture." [12]

One passage in the second part of the book seemed particularly arresting. It was a soliloquy spoken by an old astronomer, Bidault-Coquille, who had left his seclusion and his concern with pure science to join in the great fight to save Pyrot, victim of an unjust court: "I am very much afraid . . . that you, Bidault-Coquille, have shown a great lack of understanding of the conditions of the intellectual and moral development of peoples. You thought that social injustices were arrayed on a string like pearls and that all you had to do to make the whole line fall was to pull off one. You flattered yourself that you could establish at one blow justice in your country and in the universe." [13] But, continues Bidault-Coquille, he did not really fool himself—selfishness blinded him: "You said to yourself, 'Here I am, just and courageous once for all. I can repose afterward in the public esteem and the praise of historians.' And now that you have lost your illusions, now that you know it is hard to redress wrongs and that it is a task that must be begun again and again, you are returning to your asteroids. You are right; but return there modestly, Bidault-Coquille!"

France's old enemies read that passage as a confession of folly. Many of France's friends also thought that he had deserted the barricades.[14] Some later critics have agreed; others have tried to show that the passage meant nothing at all. One reviewer said at the time that the old voluptuary had finally realized that he could never live in a world that really enforced equality; some later scholars have excused France's desertion on the ground that he was old and tired.[15] In short, that single passage convinced innumerable readers that France had given up the fight.

Even worse, however, was Part III, in which France morbidly foretold the development of supercapitalism. In the future state that he pictures the masses are so downtrodden that they are neither intelligent enough to revolt nor strong enough to win if they did; the capitalists themselves have become caricatures of caricatures; it remains for a confused anarchist to initiate a series of explosions that reduces industrial civilization to rubble and returns mankind to a rustic, barbarian life. That is not the end. From barbarism men begin to progress. They pass through feudalism to capitalism and so forth, living the life of Sisyphus, acting out the "Eternal Return" with which Nietzsche frightened so many readers at the turn of the century. France even resorted to a blatant technical trick to point his moral, ending his story with the same paragraph he used to describe the coming of the final capitalist civilization. If this were the future France foresaw, his readers asked themselves, then what had happened to the happy socialist future of *Sur la Pierre blanche?* If this were meant as a simple substitute for the socialist utopia France had written of before, he had washed his hands of the human race.

France's attitude had changed, but he had not lost hope.

Bidault-Coquille's soliloquy was not a statement of despair but a demand for humility; "Les Temps futurs" was
not a prophecy, it was a warning. Though disillusioned,
the old astronomer only doubted, as his words made clear,
that social justice could be instituted "at one blow." He
had not really been foolish to plunge into the Pyrot Affair, for, after all, Pyrot had been saved. His crime was
overconfidence, and he was pleading guilty. Having lost
some of his optimism during the three harsh years since
he had published *Sur la Pierre blanche*, France now felt
that the triumph of socialism was far from certain. If
socialism were defeated, though, what then? The history
without end that he called "Les Temps futurs" was his
answer. That defeat, however, was no more certain than
the victory he had so confidently expected in earlier days.
France took a hard look backward and got a glimpse
of reality. Once his inventory was complete, he started
forward once more.

L'Île des pingouins was finished by the end of 1907;
"Les Temps futurs," the concluding and most unsettling
part of the book, was published in a newspaper in December of that year under the title "L'Histoire sans
fin." [16] Early in 1908 France finally published the *Vie de
Jeanne d'Arc* that he had been working on for years. It
gave his readers only the barest clues to his political development, but the clues were there, particularly in the
preface, which France dated February, 1908. Most of that
preface he used to defend the interpretation he was about
to present and to discuss the attitudes of earlier generations toward his heroine. He devoted several pages, however, to an analysis of nationalism, and in those pages,
published less than two months after he had given his

readers "L'Histoire sans fin" to contemplate during the Christmas season, France restated his belief in the triumph of socialism. After discussing the surge of patriotism that was produced by the Revolution, he went on to say that since then the capitalist regime had produced imperialism, colonialism, and the armed peace; more important, capitalism had produced the workers' international, and financial cosmopolitanism.

> Today, as two thousand years ago, to discern the future one must examine not the powerful enterprises of the world but the confused movements of the laboring masses. The nations will not indefinitely support this armed peace, which is such a burden to them. We are seeing every day the organization of the universal community of labor.
>
> The warm human charity that was formed in the Latin conscience of Epictetus and Seneca was extinguished for many centuries by European barbarism, but it has been relighted in the greatest hearts of modern times. In it I discern the coming of the future union of peoples. I believe in that union. And it is vain to argue that I am misled by the illusions of dream and desire: it is desire that creates life, and the future is careful to realize the dreams of philosophers.[17]

Not that war had already been banished from the human scene; for, he added, the growing industrial and commercial rivalry of his day foreshadowed a European or a world war. He was still emphasizing the hardships of the struggle, though he was still convinced it would end in victory.

In a preface published later in that same year, 1908, France again made it clear that although he was more cautious he still foresaw a socialist future. Introducing a book that showed how a collectivist society might operate, he argued, as he had before, that capitalism, by fostering the concentration of wealth and the development of great trusts, was leading directly to collectivism. "Nevertheless, how much time and effort the birth of the future society is going to cost! I believe that Monsieur E. Héberlin-Darcy has accomplished a good and useful task in tracing a general sketch of this society, which we expect to bring more reason and more justice into the world; its realization we announce as historically inevitable." [18]

France once again accented his skepticism in the short stories that he wrote during the two years from early in 1908 through the spring of 1910. Two of these brief compositions, both written in 1908, express a thoroughly cynical outlook. The first was a "Dialogue aux enfers," which appeared as the preface to a new edition of Molière's *Le Misanthrope*. The dialogue, a discussion between a curious abbé and a gentleman ghost, both occupants of hell, ends in a partial agreement:

> L'ABBÉ DOUILLET: I quite fear that human beings have only one choice—to be scoundrels or to be ridiculous.
> L'OMBRE: You see clearly, Father: like me, you hate men.
> L'ABBÉ DOUILLET: No! I scorn them.[19]

Such feelings match those France showed, though perhaps not so strongly, in parts of *L'Île des pingouins*. The other work of 1908, *La Comédie de celui qui épousa une femme muette*, told the story of a judge who employed a doctor to cure his wife's dumbness, only to end by hiring the same doctor to ease a complication that arose from the operation: he would be driven mad by his wife's chatter, the judge said, unless the doctor took steps to deafen him. As usual, France took advantage of every opportunity to ridicule judges and justice. The hero admits, for instance, that deafness will be no disadvantage to him on the bench, since, to avoid hearing lies, he never listens to the testimony anyhow.[20] Though Rabelais contributed the plot, the play is filled with typically Francian irony; throughout it is a profession of total skepticism.

The same skepticism, with a good deal less of the comic element, appeared in the stories France published next. "Les Sept Femmes de la Barbe-Bleue" is the title of both the first story and the volume, published in 1909, in which it appeared. The tale, pleasant and full of local color, is a mock attempt to rehabilitate Bluebeard, whom France depicts as the victim of an unjust legend. This story and the other three in the book all contain allusions to political questions and sly attacks on all sorts of sacred cows. The most important of these political barbs are in "La Chemise," a retelling of the old tale of the shirt of a happy man. A king seeks that shirt when his physician prescribes it as the cure for his ills; the king's men search far and wide, but, of course, they fail, for the happy man they find has no shirt. In this story France used his old weapons, irony and ridicule, against governments and financiers, and he again attacked Socialists who would betray their comrades to win themselves prestige.[21] Readers unaware of France's other activities might have found in this acerbic sketch of Socialist sinners evidence that France had left the party, but he always attacked traitors or self-seekers, never the party as a whole. Again, he stressed the points he made in *L'Île des pingouins;* again, his remarks were demands for simon-purity, not attacks on socialism.

For those who still doubted, France proved his continued devotion to the cause by continuing to sign petitions, speak at rallies, and write propaganda. In 1907 he supported a petition on behalf of the hapless Armenians and in 1908 he accepted the honorary presidency of a society for the protection of Congo natives.[22] He defended an anarchist who was embroiled with the government of Switzerland; he belonged to a committee planning the dedication of a monument to the famous anarchist Louise Michel (whose poetry France had once admired); he told a society organized to bring great art to the masses that he was "more than ever attached" to the socialist doctrines he had embraced, and added that he believed nothing could stop the development of a "society better ordered than ours." [23] He defended jailed labor leaders; he assailed "parliamentary impotence" and said that the French parliament was just a feeble reflection of the power of wealth.[24] So he stayed active, fighting, although he indicated more than once that he expected the battle to last a long time, the victory to be costly.

In the spring of 1909, just before *La Barbe-bleue* was published, France sailed for Buenos Aires, where he was to give a series of short lectures on Rabelais. The Rabelais lectures had no political importance, but he also gave, in Montevideo and Rio de Janeiro, a talk on Auguste Comte, and, in São Paulo, another on Pierre Lafitte, Comte's successor as high priest of the positivist religion Comte had founded. The lectures on Comte and Lafitte were delivered, somewhat apologetically, before audiences made up of members of the Comtist flock. In describing his reasons for remaining outside the fold despite his great respect for Comte and the Comtist philosophy, France made a profession of unfaith that would hold, for him, against any creed. It probably explains better than any other single statement why he could never have become a fanatic, socialist or otherwise: "I am not virtuous enough to believe and to profess the religion of humanity [positivism]. I lack the courage to renounce the fantasies, the caprices, of the individual conscience. I love my errors. I do not want to renounce the delightful liberty to lose my way, to lose my self, to lose my soul." [25] His lack of a creed did not prevent him, however, from believing in the peace to come for the same reasons he had given, in almost identical words, five years before, in *Sur la Pierre blanche*: "Universal peace will be realized someday, not because men will become better (one cannot hope that that will happen), but because a new order of things, a new science, a new set of economic necessities, will impose on them the pacific state as in other times the very conditions of their existence placed them and kept them in a state of war." [26]

While he was in Argentina, France delivered another public speech that showed more clearly than anything else he had done since he wrote *L'Île des pingouins* that he had not given up his hopes for a better future. His audience was composed of young men, so he gave them advice. Study science, he said, in order to be free from the servitude of ignorance and error; but keep your dreams.

> Oh! Do not lose, at the touch of arid reality, the divine gift of dreams.
> Earlier you told me that I had lost my illusions. Were you really serious, were you really convinced of it?

Didn't you say to yourselves, "He's no longer young, we must treat him as a serious man; let's tell him he has no more illusions, that will flatter his vanity"? Well, my friends, you made a mistake. I have illusions. Perhaps they are not those of my youth, but I still have lovely illusions. . . . I believe in love, I believe in beauty, I believe in justice; I believe, in spite of everything, that in this world good will win over evil and that men will create God.

Do as I do. Guard your illusions carefully, dear friends; what good will your science be if you lack the fertile illusions of truth, beauty, and love!

Dream! Without dreams there is no science, there is no wisdom. Dream! Your dreams will not be vain. Slowly, but always, humanity realizes the dreams of the wise.

Dream! Do not fear utopias when they are generous. Love justice. Love truth.

Oh! Above all do not be prudent, do not be moderate. Believe. Dare.[27]

When France returned to Paris from South America, he returned to disaster. He had spent sixty years building a mental scaffolding just strong enough to keep him from falling into despair. By 1908 one pillar of that structure, his political hope, had shown its power to withstand buffeting, but political disappointments probably mattered very little to France in comparison with the destruction of his love.

France had lived and worked for nearly twenty years under the critical eye of Mme de Caillavet. His feelings toward her were always mixed. He loved her, but he let her browbeat him. She was the third woman to play a large part in his life. His mother had dominated his childhood world, but long before she died her jealous guardianship had aroused in him an irritation that weakened his love. He had loved his wife, but she soon pushed her sovereignty past the limits he would tolerate. Mme de Caillavet, his intellectual equal, was better equipped than either of the others to hold her place, but finally she too fell a victim to the fate apparently destined for France's women. Symptoms of his rebellion appeared even in the great days of *Le Lys rouge* and the conquest of the Academy: he tried to evade her attempts to keep him working, he objected when she accused him of being lazy, he resented her very effective efforts to keep him from talking to pretty girls. As the years went by his restlessness increased. By 1908 everyone who frequented the Caillavet salon could see that France was chafing under the dictation of his no longer young nor beautiful mistress.[28] In 1909, when he was invited to lecture in South America, he jumped at the chance to escape. Mme de Caillavet desperately joked about the "madman" who was going to the "antipodes to live upside down in company with savages, apes, and parrots," but she did not try to stop him.[29] His departure upset her terribly; then he compounded the injury by carrying on a flagrant and scandalous love affair with a Parisian actress who was traveling to Buenos Aires on the same ship. Reports that France had married reached Paris, and France never bothered to deny them; in fact, he never wrote at all, and Mme de Caillavet depended on his valet for news of her wandering lover. Beside herself, she turned on the gas in her bathroom and tried to commit suicide. She was saved, but her health was ruined. When France returned, he made matters worse by trying to belittle the importance of his escapade. Reunited, they traveled south together, but her illness grew worse. Against her doctor's orders, they returned to Paris, and there, on January 12, 1910, she died.

France was desolate. At first he broadcast his grief, then he concealed it. On the day his mistress died he wrote to the doctor who had attended her: "You knew this admirable woman long enough to realize how great is my loss. My life is ended." To Marie Scheikévitch, a young friend of Mme de Caillavet's, France said, "Ah! Madame, it is a dead man you see! I am more dead than she is." Mme Scheikévitch said that he was completely broken with grief. Mme Fernand Gregh, who went home from the funeral with France, remembered his plaintive cry: "I have had two women who made of me what they wanted and made up for my lack of will, my mother and Mme Arman [de Caillavet]; now they have both left me. What do they want me to become?" Mme Jeanne Maurice Pouquet (then Mme Gaston de Caillavet), the dead woman's daughter-in-law, believed that France's grief was "deep and sincere," but she thought it was "not of long duration." France did not like, she said, "to nurture painful memories." [30]

France's personal physician, Paul-Louis Couchoud, not only describes France's grief but introduces one of the factors that caused Mme Pouquet, and many of France's early biographers, to doubt its extent: "I saw him a great deal in those days, partly as his physician but mainly as his mourning companion. He went for days without eating, without even getting up. He abandoned himself to his grief, to his remorse, to a somber taste for death. He discussed the philosophic convenience of suicide. Where could he find the nurse of the spirit he so urgently needed? The gods sent him Mme Bölöni." [31] The gods also sent him Laura Gagey, Emma Laprévotte, and sundry other women with "sympathetic souls." France, aged sixty-six, took advantage of his new freedom. Mme Bölöni (the Hungarian writer Sándor Kémeri) with Dr. Couchoud, accompanied France to Italy in the spring following the winter of his ordeal. According to her account, he enjoyed the trip thoroughly; she says once that he seemed "young." [32] During the next three years France traveled even more than he had during his days with Mme de Caillavet, visiting his beloved Italy, the Low Countries, Germany, Austria, Russia, and even North Africa, as well as various French provinces. On all of those journeys he had pleasant companions, sometimes young ladies, sometimes old friends, usually both. All the time he worked at his novels, but during his periods in Paris he found the opportunity to indulge in a serious affair with Mme Pierre Gagey (the Laura mentioned above), to steal a mistress from the Danish critic Georg Brandes, and to take into his home as servant and companion Mlle Laprévotte, who had been one of Mme de Caillavet's personal maids.[33] Mme Gagey, herself only thirty-five or so, gave macabre proof that France was still attractive: when she came to feel that he no longer wanted her, she committed suicide by taking an overdose of sleeping pills.

France seemed to be reveling in an old man's paradise, but he was, at least partly, playing a role. On his trips he carried tiny notebooks in which he kept a record of each day's activity and the thoughts that crossed his mind. In all those diaries—there are nine of them—he wrote not a word about his traveling companions or his new-found loves; instead, he wrote of sorrow:

Naples, March 22.—At Pausilippe, at Casella's museum, I saw nothing but her.

March 26, 1910.—I travel well without her, because she taught me how to travel. . . .

Verona, April 17.—These things, now that she is no more, these things of Italy have lost for me, not their beauty, but their intimacy and a familiar charm that I will never find again.

July, 1910.—I wait for her. I am more desolated: I no longer wait for her.

What astounds me about her is that she has not done the impossible, that she has not returned; what astonishes me is that she is like the other dead.

[*Toward the end of 1910.*]—The mutability of my mind.—I sorrow for her always; I never regret in the same manner.

Le Guérinet, April 12, 1911.—The first sunshiny days, she won't see them.

Saturday, March 30, 1921.—Depart noon the 16th.— The Bordeaux line that I traveled so many times with her. . . .

March 18, 1913.—Six o'clock, arrived at Florence. At eight, in the dining room at the City Hall, where I ate during my visit to Italy, ceilings from the end of the sixteenth century. . . . What a time I had dining there with her! Old things last; old people, no.[34]

She was gone. Gone, too, was France's daughter, for they no longer met. She had divorced Captain Mollin in 1905. In 1908 she remarried, against France's wishes. For some unknown reason he severed relations completely.[35]

While France's personal life disintegrated, he began to feel that somehow his literary reputation was in decline. His biography of Joan of Arc, a historical work very much à la Renan, presents Joan as a simple maid, unbalanced, ignorant, and naïve, who was used by a priest or priests unknown for ends quite beyond her understanding. France undoubtedly expected to be attacked by Catholic and nationalist reviewers, but men he might have expected to be friendly were almost as harsh. Several historians who were just as anticlerical as France pointed out that even though his interpretation of Joan's life might be brilliant and solid he was a bungling amateur when it came to the management of scholarly apparatus. The errors they found, as France said in the preface to a later edition of the book, were minor and did not affect the validity of his interpretation; and, he might have added, those errors were at least partly the fault of his secretary, who had been trusted to check the references, rather than his own.[36] Nevertheless, those criticisms hurt. And, of course, Catholics and nationalists attacked him with violence.

Not long after that setback France began to notice that a rising tide of nationalism was undermining his influence among younger writers. He had always had "disciples," and he was still interested in new performers on the literary scene. Mme de Caillavet had encouraged that interest, as her preface to Proust's work indicated. For long years France had welcomed aspiring artists and writers to his study at the Villa Saïd, where he lived surrounded by his huge collection of books, antiques, and sculpture. They had come as well to the salon over which he presided. In the fall of 1907 he tried to save the famous literary group called L'Abbaye (it included such neophytes as Georges Duhamel and René Arcos) from foundering by letting the group publish something he had written; his gesture did not help, but it shows that he still understood that to be called "maître" obligated him to something more than personal excellence.[37] Despite such gestures, however, his more passionate rivals, men like Péguy and Barrès, were attracting the favor of the new generation. In 1911 France let one of his characters voice the new attitude that threatened his position: "It is not your skepticism that disgusts me with you, even though it is quite out of fashion (because since the national revival one is no longer skeptical in France) . . . but your lack of taste, the bad odor of your ideas, the inelegance of your doctrines." [38] For many years the elegance of France's prose had been enough to win him pardon for the "inelegance" of his doctrines, but as the tide of nationalism rose the importance of doctrine increased; the young literary set no longer was so willing to tolerate the "bad odor"—the bad political odor—that an earlier generation had found not only tolerable but attractive.

France no longer graced the platform at every big Socialist political gathering, but he had not lost interest in the fate of his comrades. Just two weeks after he returned from South America to face his dying mistress, he took time to write a moving letter asking mercy for Francisco Ferrer, a Spanish Socialist who had been convicted —unjustly, France argued—of helping to organize riots in protest against conscription in Barcelona. Ferrer was executed, despite the efforts of France and other French liberals, early in October, 1909.[39] Another defeat had been registered.

Then, on May 28, 1910, less than four months after the death of Mme de Caillavet, France made his greatest speech. On that night he addressed a meeting of the Association Générale des Etudiants de Paris; it was the only public speech he was to make in 1910.[40] Whatever his personal feelings may have been, and his diaries give ample proof that he was in the depths of depression, his speech was not that of a reactionary, a cynic, or even a pessimist.

Just as he had as far back as 1899, when he first began to consider himself a socialist, France told his listeners that in spite of violence and brutality the one power that governs the world is thought: "It creates, it preserves, and it transforms. To think is the essential act—all other actions have durable effects only when they are subordinate to thought." [41] He expressed his long-standing respect for the work of the philosophes of the eighteenth century; the *Encyclopédie*, he said, marked "a new era of civilization." [42] And the progress the writers of that work foresaw, he said, has been continuous: "Humanity acquires little in each generation; but that little is much, because it is added to that which has been acquired previously and helps to make the condition of man from day to day better and less harsh. This progress in morals can be followed through time; without doubt there are regressions, there are halts; but in the long run we gain in knowledge, in wisdom, in power." [43]

In the summer of 1910 France began a thirty-month period of serious writing during which he finished two of the three or four of his works that seem most likely to survive. In one of these, *Les Dieux ont soif*, he again toyed with the pessimistic, skeptical philosophy that had made *L'Île des pingouins* such a puzzle to his Socialist friends.

The central character in this novel of the Revolution is Evariste Gamelin, a mediocre painter who becomes a juryman on the Revolutionary Tribunal. The innocent and ignorant monk, the bourgeois who profits while men struggle for their ideals, the pragmatic girl who makes the best of every situation—all are there, along with the aristocrat, Brotteaux des Ilettes, who has usually been taken to be France's mouthpiece. Whereas the hero, Gamelin, maintains that the germ of virtue is planted by the Supreme Being in every man, Brotteaux says that virtue is inculcated by parents who beat their children enough to "drive virtue up their backsides." [44] As for the methods used by the leaders of the Revolution to produce a virtuous citizenry, Brotteaux finds them unsatisfactory: "I like our simple theophages, who know neither what they say nor what they do, better than these mad bunglers of the law, who guillotine us to make us virtuous and wise and to get us to adore the Supreme Being, who has made them in his own image. . . . It would be better to . . . govern men as they are and not as one would like them to be." [45] Throughout the book France treated the idea that men are innately good with utter contempt, but that was not the whole message of the book, for he could understand the actions of those "mad bunglers" without changing his opinion of their madness.

Brotteaux was not France's only self-projection.[46] Gamelin, the idealist fighting for a better world, undoubtedly exhibits traits that France was able to see in himself. He had, after all, been an avid Dreyfusard, ready to believe that the injustice of the world could be done away with "at one blow." Gamelin is a sympathetic character despite his fanaticism. France's involvement becomes quite apparent toward the end of the novel, when Gamelin, appalled at the acts he has committed in the name of the Revolution, justifies himself by saying that the men who come after him will hold his name in infamy, but they will owe him their freedom.[47] The whole book is a condemnation of the violence and the fanaticism of the jurors on the Revolutionary Tribunals, yet in one passage France defends those same men, not on moral grounds but on the basis of his opinion of humanity: "They were men, neither worse nor better than the others. Innocence, most often, is a piece of good fortune, not a virtue: whoever might have agreed to put himself in their places would have acted as they did and accomplished these trying tasks as badly as they did." [48]

France condemned the men of the Revolution not only for their use of violence, that is, for the things they did, but also for their failure to do more. In one of his strongest indictments of the "revolutionary metaphysic" taught by Robespierre, France included a paragraph in which he bitterly attacked the Jacobins' support of vested interests, particularly that of property ownership.[49] But that attack seems to have passed almost unperceived. The book was called reactionary, and France complained that Socialist critics never understood it.[50]

Even Jaurès, least violent of revolutionaries, did not understand France's message. In *Les Dieux ont soif* France again used, more subtly, the trick of the repeated paragraph that was so obvious in *L'Île des pingouins*. The heroine's farewell to her lover, spoken in the next to last paragraph of the novel, is an exact repetition of an earlier paragraph. In the first part of the book she was saying good-by to another man, on another night, but the second incident is exactly like the first, down to the last comma.[51] To Jaurès, the philosophy this implied meant a constant repetition of "the same temptations, the same deceptions, and the insipid monotony of beginning over and over again." [52] For him, such a philosophy was too bleak. "Is this the last step of thought and the last word of the mind? As for me, I have another view of the far-off depths of reality and of the far-off distance of things." [53] But so did France. That he chose to end a book about the Revolution by returning to its beginning does not mean that he believed such a cycle was inevitable; it might mean as well that he saw that cycle as the just punishment for the men of the Revolution, who had failed to change the world because they imitated the violence of the regime they wanted to destroy. The century that followed that bloody revolution had been, after all, something very like the future France suggested. Revolution had followed revolution, but, from France's point of view, all those revolutions were like their prototype: they had been violent, and they had failed. He obviously dreamed of another kind of revolution that would not fail, a revolution that would break the monotony of new beginnings and weary repetitions of futile struggles.

In his next work, *La Révolte des anges,* France again was too subtle; again he disconcerted his more doctrinaire comrades, although this time he made his theme far more explicit than it had been. He was firmly opposed to violence, no matter how justified it might seem; it appeared to him to be self-defeating. In *La Révolte des anges,* France showed the angels victorious over the "ignorant and vulgar demiurge" he preferred to call Ialdobaoth instead of Jehovah. At the last minute before the final battle, however, Satan calls off the fight because "war engenders war, and victory, defeat." Satan's vision was bleak: "God vanquished would become Satan, Satan victorious would become God. Destiny spare me that dreadful fate!" [54] For men may as well keep their ignorant, jealous, violent God unless they are willing to listen to the friendly demons—Dionysius, Apollo, and the Muses

—who would tell them the whole truth. "The victory is Mind and . . . it is in ourselves that we must attack and destroy Ialdobaoth."

Critics, both hostile and friendly, have called Satan's renunciation a profession of extreme conservatism, either pure cynicism or a call for a moral revolution that is no more than a pious wish.[55] But, as Jean Sareil has recently pointed out, Satan did not really renounce his victory, nor did he confess that the battle had been futile.[56] He will not, he says, become a new God, a new tyrant. "I love the earth, *where I have done some good*, if such a thing is possible in this world where beings subsist only by murder. Now, *thanks to us*, the old God has been dispossessed of his terrestrial empire and everyone who thinks on that globe disdains him or ignores him." (Italics added.) Satan renounces not the end—freedom—but one means to that end—violence. At the same time he claims that his cause has progressed, that the tyrant has lost the loyalty of the best of his subjects. The battle will continue, but the mind, not the sword, is the weapon that will bring the victory.

II

Even in the heyday of his Socialist activity, the time during which he wrote *Sur la Pierre blanche*, France forbade himself to have faith in the perfectibility of society; yet he fought for improvement, as he saw it. In the books he wrote from 1907 through 1912 he emphasized his reservations, but he did not let those reservations affect his public attitude toward socialism. In 1910, stricken by the death of his mistress, he almost completely withdrew from public life. In that year he spoke on only one famous occasion. Beginning in 1911, however, he gradually returned to the arena, and by 1914, when the war began, he was again thoroughly involved in public affairs. That he spoke less often between 1906 and 1912 than before does not alter the fact that when he spoke he spoke as a Socialist, and he spoke with ardor. He was the same anticlerical propagandist, the same baiter of the bourgeoisie. On purely political matters he remained as intransigeant as always. The only noticeable difference was his new insistence on the hard struggle that he believed would necessarily precede the victory of socialism.

In his books he added one new reservation that was not apparent in most of his public speeches. He insisted that the triumph of socialism would not be enough. As he had shown in *Les Dieux ont soif* and *La Révolte des anges,* a change of men in power, or even a change in institutions, would not guarantee the triumph of virtue. Moreover, he began to emphasize his abhorrence of violence. But men could change for the better—that would come, however, only when institutional change, brought about by peaceful means, had made it possible. France the Socialist, whatever reservations he had, was still a militant. He wanted, however, to fight only injustice and greed, not another people who happened to live on the other side of an arbitrary political border. Increasingly he was coming to believe that the greatest struggle he could enter was the struggle for peace.

France had been a critic of the military mind and all its works since the days of Boulanger, but that antimilitarism took on new importance after 1900. To hate the army for its pomp and sham, its cruelty and its medieval political outlook, was one thing when peace seemed assured, another when war threatened to come at any moment.

France first attacked militarism in 1892, long before he became a socialist. The strain of pacifism that ran through most socialist thought undoubtedly helped to bring him into the movement, for his hatred of violence was as strong during the Affair as it had ever been. While the fight for Dreyfus was in progress France had the opportunity to observe the upright bearing of Colonel Picquart, whose military ideas of honor and duty made him the rock upon which the Dreyfusards could build their case, but that performance weighed little against the stubborn clannishness of the General Staff. France wanted to make the army miserable, and he yearned to put an end to war. His membership in the Socialist party gave him dozens of opportunities to work at both projects.

In 1900 the most vociferous opponents of international war were members of the Socialist parties and the anarchists. Benoît Malon, long the editor of the *Revue socialiste* and one of the most respected figures in the French socialist movement, had predicted in 1890 in his *Le Socialisme intégral* that a new war was coming that would make the wars of Caesar and Napoleon seem small, and he had insisted that only socialism triumphant could prevent the holocaust. Nevertheless, in his castigation of the warlike bourgeoisie he had made it clear that "menaced republics" should arm to defend themselves against aggressive monarchies, and had carefully distinguished between the armaments of a "free people that is vigilant and the vicious chancelleries that conspire." [57] By 1906, however, a great many Socialists refused to make that distinction, and the question of Socialist action in time of war became a major issue in party councils. Some Socialists wanted to rebel; others thought it would be better to postpone the revolution until peace had come again; all of them agreed that one of the major aims of the party should be the preservation of peace, whatever they might do in case of war.

During these years of increasing fear Anatole France used every opportunity to push the antimilitaristic policy of the Socialists. In 1899, when Urbain Gohier, an erratic gadfly with a penchant for unrestrained invective, was tried for writing a violent anti-army pamphlet, France helped celebrate Gohier's acquittal. Later that year he devoted part of an installment of his "Histoire contemporaine" to propaganda for the Socialists' plan to substitute a national militia for the standing army, but indicated that he thought the conservatism of the public would prevent its accomplishment for a long while. In a subsequent novel, the *Histoire comique*, he insisted that if men so desired they could rid the planet of war simply by re-organizing society. Whether they would do so or not, said France's spokesman, Dr. Trublet, one could not know. "Perhaps this world is irremediably bad." [58]

Two years later, however, France was becoming more optimistic. The publication of *Sur la Pierre blanche* signaled a serious change in his opinions on the subject of war. In the *Histoire comique* he had left it up to men to prevent war if they wished, by positive action; now he was willing to predict that society would be remade and wars would end, whether men like it or not. That was the gist of the famous paragraph quoted earlier: "Universal peace will be realized someday, not because men will become better (one cannot hope for that), but because a new order of things . . . will impose upon them a state of peace." Writing an essay a few months later for an album of contributions by eminent artists and literary figures that was to be sold for the benefit of victims of the Russo-Japanese War, France repeated that paragraph almost verbatim.[59] In an autobiographical sketch he wrote for his German publisher in November, 1904, he put his belief more simply, using for the first time a motto that he was to repeat again and again: "The union of workers will bring peace to the world." [60]

To France peace had become the end to be sought, the union of workers the means to that end—he did not, like his comrades, see peace as a pleasant by-product of a socialist victory that was in itself the primary good to be achieved. Most of the antiwar speeches France made during the years before 1914 indicate that peace was his foremost concern, but one in particular, given at the Sorbonne in honor of Tolstoy, makes it explicit. After praising Tolstoy as an artist, France praised him as an enemy of war. "On that grave question," said France, "the gravest of all, each must take a stand." [61] He went on to indicate that much as he sympathized with Tolstoy's desires, he could not agree with Tolstoy on the methods most likely to bring peace into being. Peace would not come at the call of weak men who lament, he said: sighs would not bring it; only greatness and strength could put an end to war. "War will not end because it is cruel; nature is itself insensitive and cruel, and we depend on nature; war will not end because it is unjust, because nothing proves that our ideas of justice and goodness will someday be realized; it will end when the political and social causes that have made it possible cease to act. These causes are autocracy, industrial competition, and the oppression of the laboring class." [62]

Throughout the period from 1906 to 1914 France followed diplomatic developments with concern. When war seemed to have been averted by a small margin, as at the time of the Algeciras Conference, he accused governments in general and the French government in particular of having brought the country to the brink of war only to be forced to accept peace by the pressure of public opinion. He considered labor unrest the main factor in preventing war in 1906.[63] Despite his fear that diplomatic blunders could start a war, however, he never indicated until around 1911 that he really thought war was imminent.

France had almost completely withdrawn from public life in 1910, but in the following year he began to make himself heard once more. Gradually he increased the frequency of his public appearances; gradually he began again to sign petitions and to write letters to newspapers. He resumed his efforts in all the fields he had cultivated so actively in earlier days, but the struggle for peace was his main theme.

The Conference of Algeciras, held in 1906, was supposed to have settled Franco-German differences over Morocco, a territory that both considered ripe for annexation, by giving the French certain occupation rights but leaving the country nominally independent, as the Germans demanded. In May, 1911, the settlement broke down, and French forces entered Fez, a city outside their jurisdiction under the treaty terms, to "preserve order." The Germans reacted by sending a gunboat to Agadir. Belligerent talk was the order of the day, but by November the matter was settled by agreement.[64]

Anatole France spoke at a celebration commemorating the first International Peace Conference of The Hague on June 28, 1911, while the incident was unfolding. On that occasion he simply repeated his old belief that wars would end someday because new circumstances would end the situations that produced them.[65] Before the incident was over, however, he wrote the following in a personal letter: "The act of Algeciras, like Cunégonde, has been violated repeatedly, and like Cunégonde it was made expressly for that. We violated it and aren't satisfied, and the Germans say to us: since you have committed an act of violence, give us a gift. It makes one think of the underworld of the Bois de Vincennes. And I see a great many Frenchmen who want to fight Germany over this. I am hearing said this year all I heard said in 1870; I hear the same follies, the same idiocies, and, more absurd than other people, I'm surprised—as if I had been able to believe that humanity, which has hardly been modified in two thousand years, had changed in forty. In reality, the Germans must be afraid of war, and I wouldn't fear it if we weren't playing the game of the English." [66]

As things went from bad to worse France continued to insist that the peace was in danger.[67] Most other Frenchmen thought so, too, and most of them thought that something had to be done to prepare their country for the coming test. Nationalist sentiment swept the land during the days immediately after the Agadir incident, and vast numbers of Frenchmen, including a great many who had been peaceably inclined in the past, began to consider war with Germany not only inevitable but desirable.[68] The nationalist attitudes France had seen developing among the young intellectuals only a few months before spread rapidly, until observers began to recognize a "new" nationalism. What had been a minority attitude rapidly gained respectability after 1911. Good republican politicians who would never have dared to wave the flag a few years earlier suddenly began proclaiming their undying patriotism. Bellicosity was rife. The danger that produced this nationalist revival was emphasized in February, 1913, when the Germans increased the size of their army by about 15 per cent, making it half again as large as that of France. The French government, swept along by the wave of chauvinism that had overwhelmed the country, decided that the term of compulsory military service had to be raised from two years to three. The first step in this direction could be taken without the passage of a new conscription law, for the law of 1905 allowed the government to postpone the discharge of a class finishing its two-year term when "circumstances appeared to warrant" such action. Louis Barthou, who had recently succeeded Briand as premier, considered that circumstances so warranted, and held the class of 1910 in service for an extra year.

Whatever the merits of this move, and it had much to recommend it, Socialists and pacifists absolutely refused to approve it. The best alternative they offered was the old militia idea, dressed up for the occasion and ably defended by Jaurès in his famous book, *L'Armée nouvelle.*[69] Jaurès demanded that conscripts be kept in training only six months, then discharged. No permanent army need exist, he argued. Instead, reservists could be assigned mobilization posts, and could keep their equipment in their homes. In the event of invasion, citizen-soldiers living near the frontier could hold back the enemy while their comrades answered the call to arms. Clearly, such a militia would be useless for aggression, but Socialists were interested only in defense. Believing that the three-year law would serve the interests of capitalists and imperialists, and that it would tend to provoke war rather than preserve the peace, they campaigned to prevent its passage. Their representatives in the Chamber pulled parliamentary strings and made violent speeches; agents of the labor unions who had been called up propagandized against the law within the army just as if they were still on the outside working for the CGT; throughout the country soldiers rioted, singing the "Internationale" and demanding their discharges.[70] The demonstrations were either ignored or dispersed, and on July 19, 1913, the law was passed. Socialist orators continued to denounce the new law in flaming terms at every political meeting.

France, back on the platform increasingly often after his near-absence of two or three years, was in the vanguard of the agitators. He attacked the three-year-law from every angle. He argued that it "profoundly affects the intellectual and economic life of the country [and] can even bring about a regression in French civilization." [71] He considered the law another piece of evidence to prove that the country was run solely in the interests of powerful minorities that desired war. In a newspaper interview he obliquely warned the government that if the present policies were to continue, rebellion was certain to result. "Present events [the army riots] are the necessary and inevitable product of governmental action—action that is brutal, clumsy, and useless! . . . As long as a retrograde government attempts to organize the national defense under the inspiration of a financial, clerical, and reactionary oligarchy; as long as a government takes the advice and receives the support of these people, it will not be obeyed willingly by the masses, which, in a democracy, are the only force upon which one may rely. All the measures taken for the purpose of establishing the national defense will be vain if they are not in harmony with the true sentiments of the worker and peasant proletariat. One can therefore affirm that at the moment the government itself is throwing the country into a disorder for which it alone is responsible." [72]

France was quoted as saying that he had recently talked over the situation with a minister in the government and had warned him that the administration must change its policies or face even more violent antimilitarism. Since his warning had not been heeded and the government had continued its reactionary policy, France said, now all the advice he could give his political friends could be summed up in one word: "Disappear!" Upon looking over the notes his listener had taken, France asked the reporter to erase the last word and make his advice to the politicians read, "Foutez le camp!" (a vulgarism for which a far too polite translation might be "Scram!").

France, and the Socialist party, opposed the three-year law because they hated the army, which they considered a nest of reactionaries; because they were profoundly antiwar; and because the militia they offered as a substitute might well be under their control instead of under that of the government. The very popularity of the militia idea shows, however, that Socialist opposition to war was limited, that even Socialists were willing to fight if attacked, and that many Socialists were, despite their pacifism, committed to some system of national defense. Their aim was to reorganize the army along the lines laid down by Jaurès, but, since that failed, they had to argue that the defense establishment provided by two-year conscription was good enough. This was hard to prove—especially hard to prove because it was quite probably wrong, and evidence to prove that it was wrong was plentiful. The logical point on which to base demands for a return to the old system was, therefore, obvious. If war were not coming, then there was no reason for preparation.

"It is certain," France told a reporter, "that Germany has no desire for war and no intention of attacking France; her action after the Casablanca and Agadir affairs proved that, for if she wanted war, either of those incidents gave her the opportunity of forcing France to declare it, and she did not take that opportunity. But if the French government continues its provocative policy, if the nationalist reactionaries obtain so complete a control of the political machine as to make Germany think that war is inevitable, there may be another Agadir incident with a less happy ending." [73]

France's continued insistence that the responsibility for provoking war would lie entirely on the French government was not just a rationalization for propaganda purposes; it reflected his genuine belief in the peaceful intentions of the Germans. Traveling in Germany in July, 1913, he sent his friend Dr. Couchoud a postcard that read as follows: "I have found a Germany active, rich, joyous, pacific, which has a holiday air every day. The blindness of the French is terrible." [74] There was another Germany he had not found—a Germany active, rich, joyous, strong, adventurous, and not very careful. Moreover, he had forgotten that Germany had friends to the south who might be willing to produce another Agadir incident even if the nationalists of France did not.

In August, 1913, France discussed the growing danger to peace in an article he wrote for the *English Review*. He said that there were two kinds of people who believed that the war in the Balkans would spread: cowards and crazy men. Courageous minds, he said, did not resign themselves so easily; they thought that war could and must be avoided. The French government, carried along by "the wave of nationalism that is now sweeping the ruling class," had made mistakes, but it sincerely did not want war. Passage of the three-year conscription law was not a bellicose action, he continued: "In the minds of its most energetic promoters, in the thought of the clericals and reactionaries who proclaim it necessary for the security of the nation, it is a response to preoccupations of a social nature rather than to thoughts of national defense. It is the first step in an attempt to establish a backward organization of society. It is directed at least as much against the French proletariat as against eventual invaders." [75] Supporters of the law simply wanted to militarize the nation to make it more easily governable, he argued; if this were not their aim, they would accept Jaurès' proposal for a "nation armée." Any movement of opinion directed by industrial and financial interests, he believed, could not be truly bellicose, because the financiers knew that war would cost them dearly. The cosmopolitan interests of financiers guaranteed the future union of peoples. Though national hatreds still existed, peoples should put them aside, for war profited nobody. (He cited, approvingly, Norman Angell's famous book, *The Great Illusion*, in which this argument had been most strongly presented.) In any case, he concluded, the masses in France were pacifist, and it would be dangerous to wake them too suddenly from their dream of universal peace.

In his attacks on clericals and capitalists France showed that he considered the battle for the preservation of peace the gravest struggle of all, but he still found the energy to continue his old battles against all sorts of oppression.

Though he spent most of his effort in antiwar propaganda, he also attacked his enemies on other fronts.

Clemenceau's fall from power had not put a stop to his policy of harsh repression of labor agitation. Strikes, riots, and demonstrations still occurred frequently, and the government still dealt roughly with men it considered troublemakers. France, asked for his aid in one of the ever-recurring incidents in this ceaseless struggle, responded enthusiastically and was rewarded with enthusiastic praise. Three labor militants jailed for participating in various demonstrations went on a hunger strike in July, 1911, because the officials of the Santé prison treated them not as political prisoners but as common criminals. France, asked to intercede in their behalf, wrote a letter and took it himself to the office of *La Bataille syndicaliste*, one of the newspapers supporting the prisoners. He associated himself with the protest, he said, with all his heart: "It is odious, it is iniquitous, that political convicts should be treated as convicts in common law. It is shameful for the republic that in France, as in Russia, prisoners should be forced to go on hunger strikes to gain respect for their honor and their rights." [76] On the following day *La Bataille syndicaliste* carried a worshipful account of France's visit to its office. The story ended with this comment: "At a time when from every side people are trying to discredit syndicalism, to distort its thought and its effort and to blacken the names of its militants, it is comforting to see a man of the great worth of Anatole France, so superior to all the questions of shop and of party, come to affirm his sympathy with our movement and his esteem for our comrades who are so often the victims of calumny. That is why we thank him with all our hearts." [77]

France came to the aid of another prisoner in Decem-

ber of that year. Gustave Hervé had finally been jailed
for writing one of his violently antipatriotic articles.
Asked to contribute a letter to a crusade organized to demand freedom for Hervé, France praised the prisoner and
poured scorn on the government: "Hervé is imprisoned
for having expressed his thoughts, and we think ourselves
a free people! . . . When we have finally become wise
and just we will know how to listen even to that which
displeases us, and we will punish no one for having spoken
according to his conscience." [78]

The Hervé case brought to a head a growing protest
against the government's steady and effective use of the
so-called "lois scélérates" that made possible, among other
things, the conviction of press offenders. A group of intellectuals asked Premier Raymond Poincaré to amnesty
everyone who had been convicted on such charges, but
Poincaré politely told them to bring individual cases to
his attention and he would see what could be done. The
advocates of amnesty began organizing mass demonstrations, and Socialist deputies prepared to introduce an
amnesty bill in the Chamber. Poincaré stood firm, where-
upon a Committee of Action for Freedom of Opinion was
formed. The committee reported that one hundred and
twenty-five press offenders had been convicted in Paris
alone since 1907, and started a newspaper campaign for a
general amnesty. The committee's first major project was
a mass meeting held February 21, 1912. As honorary
president for the occasion, the group chose Anatole
France. He could not be present, but he sent a letter of
regrets that proclaimed once more his indignation at the
continued enforcement of the "lois scélérates." [79]

Convicted labor agitators and press offenders were not
the only prisoners to attract France's attention. He also

had become interested in the plight of a soldier named Rousset who had been convicted under questionable circumstances of murdering a fellow prisoner in an army disciplinary barracks. A committee was formed to assure justice, and France was prominent among the signers of the manifesto published by that group.[80]

The campaign for the rights of oppressed nationalities was still going on. France paid tribute to Pierre Quillard, editor of *Pro Armenia*, when Quillard died, saying that his loss was a public misfortune. He took part in a protest against alleged Russian atrocities in Persia, and he also spoke in honor of the new republic of China.[81]

He also continued his old war against the church. Along with Combes and Jaurès, he was named an honorary president of a congress of the Fédération des Jeunesses Laïques, and in a letter accepting the honor protested that despite the separation law the clergy had been able to keep complete freedom without losing any of its privileges. "United with the militarist party, it can undertake anything, dare anything. If we do not watch out, a criminal government and an imbecile parliament will deliver the republic into its hands." [82]

In May, 1914, the struggles in which France was engaged coalesced into one great campaign to win a Socialist victory in the quadrennial parliamentary election. The great issue for pacifists, Socialists and others as well, was the three-year conscription law; they demanded that it be repealed and promised that a victory for opponents of the law would be a victory for peace. The Socialist party opened its election drive at a meeting of the fourteenth section of the Federation of the Seine on March 14. Jules Guesde, presiding, told the audience that their "great friend" Anatole France could not attend though his spirit was with them.[83] Bracke, another party luminary, said that he had visited France, who was sick. Then Marcel Cachin read a letter the ailing comrade had written in support of the Socialist candidate running in that district: "We need such men to fight the business patriots and furious conservatives who, if we let them do it, are going to ruin France by dissipating all her forces, all her human and material resources. . . . Finance, army: they have compromised all they have touched. May the popular will throw them out of power! May healing socialism come! Socialism, comrades, is science and reason, order and peace, justice for all and the public wealth. Yes, wealth; for it means expanded production and the just distribution of the fruits of labor."

As the campaign progressed, a complication arose. Jean Allemane, leader of a dissident Socialist fraction that had split off from the unified party in 1913, threatened to destroy the Socialist-Radical alliance in his district. He would thereby assure the election of a conservative candidate, who was the very deputy who had introduced the three-year law in the Chamber. In the first round of the election, held in April, the Radical candidate, Hyacinthe Loyson, had run third, the Socialist candidate fourth, and Allemane fifth. The Socialist was retiring in favor of Loyson, but Allemane insisted on remaining in the race. Allemane's party, however, agreed to withdraw his candidacy on condition that either Anatole France or Ferdinand Buisson, an eminent Radical, would take his place. France and Buisson refused to run, and urged Allemane to get out of the race and assure the victory of the Left. France pointed out that he was a member of the Socialist party, and to run would be to commit "an act of grave indiscipline." Allemane stayed on the ballot.[84]

France and other Socialists, true to their alliance, campaigned for Allemane's Radical opponent. At a rally held to support Loyson, France laid down the qualifications he believed voters should look for in a candidate.[85] A good candidate should favor, he said, first, the passage of an income tax law; second, repeal of the three-year law; third, the adoption of proportional representation; and fourth, anticlerical action. In speaking of the reform of electoral procedures, France said that better still would be the reform of the electors, but for that he prescribed heavy doses of propaganda. As for the three-year law, Socialists certainly did not want to be Germans, but they did not want to be Cossacks either.

Despite the efforts of the Socialists, Allemane took just enough votes away from Loyson to allow the conservative candidate to win. In other districts Socialists did better, but they still lacked the parliamentary votes they would need to repeal the three-year law.[86] It hardly mattered, for the struggle for peace had failed.

III

Upon the outbreak of the First World War France remembered the many warnings he had sounded: "I despair at these terrible events, but I am not surprised." [87]

In September, 1914, the Germans bombarded the Cathedral of Reims. The destruction of this symbol of national glory, for centuries the place where French kings had been crowned, could not be pardoned. Perhaps because he was asked to do so, perhaps because he was himself so thoroughly imbued with pride of history and pride of nation, France joined publicly in the chorus of

protest. His letter, published by the erstwhile antipatriot
Gustave Hervé in his left-wing newspaper, *La Guerre
sociale*, might have been expected to win universal praise.
Instead, it unleashed an uproar of abuse.

France opened his letter by calling the enemy "barbarians" and saying that the name German had become
"execrable to the whole thinking universe." [88] He exhorted French soldiers to fight the war "without mercy,"
bue he added that when the war ended, French mag-
nanimity would come into play: "We will not soil our
victory with any crime, and on their territory, after we
have vanquished their last army and reduced their last
fortress, we will proclaim that the French people admit
to their friendship the beaten enemy." What this fierce
septuagenarian intended to do to implement the victory
was not clear, but that he hated less than totally was only
too obvious. The Catholic deputy Albert de Mun wrote
that France was part of a defeatist plot: "We must cut
it short quickly." Maurras, voice of the royalist *Action
française* and darling of the extreme nationalists, said that
France's "atrocious folly [and] cruel philanthropy"
would lay the basis for a new war. He suggested that the
Germans be made to obey for a century or two, then one
might see whether it would be possible to accord a smile
to the *serviteur*. Clemenceau, no friend of Mun and
Maurras, joined the outcry, insisting that if he were silly
enough to take any account at all of such remarks about
"friendship" he would be able to see in them nothing less
than treason against the nation. *L'Humanité* tried to
rescue France by arguing that he was just as patriotic as
M. de Mun, but the damage had already been done.[89]

France made things worse by trying to explain what
he had meant. In another letter to *La Guerre sociale*, pub-

lished five days after the first, he assured his readers that he wanted victory just as much as anyone, and added that when the victory had been won the French should demand from the Germans "every reparation, every restitution due, all the necessary guarantees." Maurras registered the appearance of the new letter, casually mentioning that by "necessary guarantees" he understood the dismemberment of Germany. The uproar was not finished, however; menacing letters continued to come to France. Desperate, the old man compounded his folly:

> To the Minister of War,
>
> Mr. Minister,
>   Many good people find that my style is worth nothing in time of war.
>   Since they could be correct, I am ceasing to write, and I have no function.
>   I am no longer very young, but my health is good. Make of me a soldier.
>
> Very truly yours,
Anatole France

His letter was printed in *Le Matin,* a major newspaper, on October 1, 1914. *Le Temps* published an editorial entitled "Closed Incident." France's gesture honored him, this newspaper said, but he should continue to write. Write he did. From then until the beginning of 1917 a stream of treacly propaganda poured from his pen.[90]

A reporter from *Le Petit Parisien* found him at home in his country house near Tours a month after the "Closed Incident." France told him: "I suffered cruelly from these things, I swear it, and I still feel a profound pain when I think that, according to certain commentaries, one could believe that I did not entirely share in the unanimous ardor that has pitted civilization against barbarism." [91] The rest of the interview was full of bellicose "jusqu'au-boutisme"—the war must be fought to its bitter end. Writing to a friend, France fervently hoped that the interview would cut short a painful "misunderstanding." [92] He was rejected for military service a few days later. One news writer wondered whether he hadn't suspected that might happen.[93]

Letters and articles that made clear his patriotic position began to appear shortly after the interview. "I have no enemies save those of my country," he wrote. Then he wrote more remarks about barbarians; an appeal against German vandalism; demands that the German military machine be crushed at any sacrifice; a letter to an American Socialist for reproduction in America, written at the request of the "grosses légumes" (big shots) at the Quai d'Orsay, in which he asserted that one could not even speak of peace until the German army was destroyed.[94] In a personal letter to a friend he could trust he stated: "I doubt less than ever our victory, which is the most imperious moral necessity of modern times." [95] In an article for a Russian-language newspaper published in Paris he wrote: "Friends, we will fight this war, which we did not want, to the end; we will pursue our terrible and beneficent work to its entire accomplishment." [96] This was reprinted in *Le Temps*.[97] Some of these articles that were published in book form and sold for the benefit of wounded soldiers won fulsome praise from reviewers.[98] One writer spoke of the great emotional impact of these "inflamed pages in which this great writer, expressing the sentiments of every Frenchman, affirms the imminent and brilliant triumph of justice and civilization against brute force and barbarism." [99] A second patriotic volume, a reprint of an article France wrote for *Le Petit Parisien* in November, 1915, was published in July, 1916.[100] Even at his worst, however, France never completely disavowed his first disastrous letter. He never called for extermination of the Germans; he always wanted to "crush" the "military power" of the enemy.

During 1916, however, Anatole France gradually left the camp of the "jusqu'auboutistes." Personal worries added to the pains he suffered over the public tragedies of the day. Shortly before the war he had installed Mlle Laprévotte in his villa as mistress and housekeeper. She had accompanied him to his new country estate in the early days of the war and had become a permanent fixture in his life. Most of his friends seemed to think the arrangement was scandalous (not because the two were not married but because she was a servant), but at least one observer thought her "simplicity and goodness made her worthy of the handsome position that M. France was to assure her later." [101] Whatever her qualities, France was satisfied with her, and her welfare was important to him. In February, 1916, she had to undergo a surgical operation, and France was seriously worried.[102] Her recovery was slow.

France's own health was poor. To Couchoud, his physician and friend, he wrote in May or June, 1916, that he was tortured "perpetually" by pains in his chest. "It would be easy for me to feel nothing more, easy above all if some wise friend would indicate to me the sure means of a quick deliverance. I am ashamed to complain. Pardon me." [103]

In another letter to Couchoud he showed another source of his despair: "Bring me some words of wisdom soon. My reason abandons me. What kills me is not so much the cruelty of men, but their stupidity. Everything I hear, everything I read, is truly stupid. I have lived too long." [104] In July, 1916, he wrote that recent offensives seemed to have produced no great result and commented favorably on an article in *l'Humanité* in which the writer demanded that the Allies pose their conditions for peace.[105] Six months later he had lost all hope of victory: "I don't believe that the Briand ministry can surmount the insurmountable difficulties of a terrible situation. I don't believe either that new war leaders . . . will assure us victory. It is too late: too many mistakes have been made." [106] At about this time, he later said, he came to know that the Austrians had made peace propositions. Because these were kept secret by the government, he ceased to publish his patriotic articles and to make his patriotic speeches. "From then on," he wrote, "I kept silence, not wanting to make myself an accomplice of covetous or fanatical men who continued a war that no longer seemed to me necessary." [107]

Late in 1916, having withdrawn from the ranks of the "patriots," Anatole France began to go into opposition. He used his influence to help obtain the Nobel Prize in literature for Romain Rolland, whose "above the battle" attitude had earned for him the almost unanimous contempt of Frenchmen.[108] Sterner "defeatists" soon heard that France had rejoined the pacifist fold.[109] Earlier in 1916 he had criticized neither the objectives of the war nor the justice of the struggle but only the way the war was being fought. In February, 1917, however, he broke the truce he had made with his society. Answering a friend who had asked whether he thought the Allies dared conclude a "peace without victory," he wrote as follows: "Peace without victory, is that contentment? Peace without victory, it is bread without yeast, stew without wine, perch without capers, mushrooms without garlic, love without quarrels, camel without humps . . . sausage without mustard; in fact, it's something insipid. . . . Ah! That good taste must be praised that has made us choose a well-made peace, perfectly formed, plump, wealthy, bringing us honor and profit, in fine, a peace with victory. As a matter of fact, that charming peace may be a while in coming. But we are in no hurry! The war is costing France only ten thousand men a day." [110] That letter was circulated far and wide in manuscript, with France's blessing. It was finally printed, with the last line cut by the censor, in a Paris left-wing newspaper; then a Swiss review printed it in full. [111] The French editor triumphantly commented in his introduction that "M. Bergeret is not dead!"

Sometime in 1916 Paul Vaillant-Couturier and Raymond Lefebvre, two young French Socialist intellectuals, visited France and asked him to join a group dedicated to the reconciliation of men of letters in the warring countries. [112] France did not accept the invitation until early in 1917. In February of that year he gave Lefebvre his "complete" adhesion, but in March he explained to Henri Barbusse, another of the organizers, that although he would help plan the project, he would allow nothing to be published about his participation until the war had ended. By June of 1917, however, France had relaxed his caution enough to publish a letter protesting wartime censorship in a new international socialist review, *Les Nations*. He praised the new journal for its attacks on censorship and warned that governments must be absolutely sure of their genius to "deprive themselves thus of all counsel, of all light." [113] *Les Nations*, apparently one of the first projects undertaken by the Barbusse-Vaillant-Lefebvre group, included among its French contributors not only France and its founders, but also Sévérine, Jean Longuet, Charles Rappoport, Jean Goldsky, and Boris Souvarine—all well-known members of the extreme Left, some of them definitely revolutionary. Simply by associating himself publicly with these writers France was defying the "patriots." The English contributors, most of them Fabians, may have taken away the curse: H. G. Wells, Norman Angell, Ramsay MacDonald, and G. B. Shaw were among them. France was still cautious, but he was returning to his old political haunts.

Even though he limited his criticisms in order to avoid any public commitment to "defeatism," France continued in his personal letters to attack the French government and to question the motives of all the Allied powers. In a letter of October, 1917, for example, he deplored the failure of the French government to take advantage of rumored German peace offers. "That refusal," he said, "will cost the world plenty of disasters and a great many miseries." [114] He even went so far as to write a letter of condolence to Joseph Caillaux, the once respected but then notorious former premier, when Caillaux was to be prosecuted for what amounted to aiding the enemy. [115] He also came to the aid of Rappoport, one of his good friends, who was arrested in March, 1918, on the ground that he had made "defeatist" statements at a meeting. When Rappoport's case was tried in July, France wrote a letter of reference for him, but the letter apparently contained nothing to disturb unduly the vigilant supporters of war "jusqu'au bout." [116] In public France was still a patriot. When he was asked to write a letter to be read at a French art festival in Buenos Aires in August, 1917, he still praised the victors of the Marne and called French soldiers the defenders of a country that had been unjustly attacked.[117]

France has been accused of cowardice for his failure to add his voice to the growing chorus of demands for immediate peace.[118] Certainly there were men who risked a great deal by speaking their minds; certainly France followed the course of prudence. In his defense it can only be pointed out that if he had publicly affirmed his "defeatist" convictions he might well have been arrested, and he was old and infirm, in no condition, physically or mentally, to feel the need for a sojourn in jail. Rumor had it that Clemenceau himself was ready to act against France if the old man said "a word too much," and, given the character of Clemenceau as the scourge of the fainthearted, the rumor was probably true.[119]

Puttering about, carping at the government, writing his memoirs, suffering pains in his heart, watching the world pursue its "stupid" business—these were France's activities during the last years of the war. Only one thing happened to give him hope. By January, 1918, he had already returned to his old conviction that only universal revolution would bring eternal peace. In the old days, before the war, the revolution had been a dream. After 1917 the dream seemed to be taking on the shape of reality. In Russia, the land of the tsars, a new nation was coming into being—a nation created in the name of the working class.

5
The "Bolshevik"
(1917–1924)

Communists have made a minor saint of Anatole France, while some of their enemies have carefully minimized the extent of his relations with the party. Neither attitude is justified: the Communist activities of France's last years fit in logically with his lifelong political and philosophical convictions, and when they ceased to fit he reluctantly altered his conduct, not his convictions.

I

France was an old friend of the Russian worker. He had propagandized for the Russian revolutionaries in 1905 and had served on several committees organized to help the persecuted or the destitute of prewar Russia. His efforts had not gone unnoticed. In 1917, probably shortly after the February revolution, France received from Vladimir Burtsev, a leading member of the Social Revolutionary party of Russia, a telegram from Petrograd saluting the "Voltaire of our days." France replied with a "salute to free Russia, which from the first hour of its sublime liberation turns its faithful thought toward France." [1] He remained a warm partisan of the Russian Revolution after the Bolsheviks seized control and, with occasional misgivings, he supported the Soviet regime until he died.

When Burtsev's telegram came, however, the war was not yet over. As always, France's supreme concern was the establishment of peace. His letters of 1918 show that more and more he was becoming convinced of the validity of the Leninist theory that imperialism was the major cause of modern war. In January, 1918, he said in a letter to a friend that if the length of the war were left up to the generals and armies, it could last quite a while, but if it should depend on the statesmen of England and Germany, the war would never end: "Germany is demanding colonies that England will not give her any more than England will give Mesopotamia to Turkey." [2] In another letter he said that England was succeeding in fulfilling its ambitions in Turkey because Russia was out of action and in German hands: "Thus the two imperialisms will share Asia. . . . Only universal revolution, only the revolt of peoples and the success of socialism will bring universal disarmament. This horrible war is pregnant with three or four others just as horrible. That is the frightful truth. I hasten to add that my firm hope is that socialism will be at the very least strong enough in the most civilized countries to assure a truce to unhappy humanity." [3] Later in the year France wrote that he believed the new regime in Russia to be "solid and durable"; England and France would not be able to destroy it.[4] The revolution would spread, he believed, to the lands of the victors, though it would come last to France, which had "only a small, disorganized proletariat." Concluding, he said that Marx, "a man of rare genius," had predicted all this in 1871.

In the midst of this relative optimism, however, he was still far from happy. As the victory came closer, life became easier, and the seventy-four-year-old Socialist was suspicious; this new prosperity might be dangerous: "Workers and employers, small and big merchants, want to hear nothing said about peace. . . . In America, Wilson is judged not bellicose enough. The Germans and their allies can't continue to fight any longer; they are exhausted. Perhaps we will be obliged (who knows?) to give them new forces so they can continue the war, the blessed war. I am desolated by what I see." [5] France's vague hopes were never realized, but things never turned out quite as badly as he had feared they might.

Jaurès, the man who personified socialism for Anatole France, had been murdered on the eve of the outbreak of World War I. The trial of the assassin, postponed for nearly five years and finally held early in 1919, was an outrage that provoked France to new heights of fury. France was asked to testify, probably as a character witness since he certainly had no direct knowledge of the circumstances of the shooting, but he had to refuse because of illness. He was suffering from persistent headaches that prevented his traveling to Paris from La Béchellerie, his Touraine estate.[6] He did, however, write what amounted to a delayed obituary of Jaurès that *l'Humanité* published during the trial.[7] In it France quickly reviewed Jaurès' life and character, and then discussed the great orator's position on war: "He dreaded war for his country and for humanity. He did not fear it, neither for his fortune nor for his ideas. He foresaw, to tell the truth, that victorious France would pay with her liberty for the triumphs of her arms; but he knew also that she would not be held to the terms of the ransom for long, and that the Revolution, breaking out first in the defeated nations, would soon carry its flames to the homes of the victors. He knew that this war would not be a game for princes . . . or a great adventure . . . but that, born of industrial rivalries never known until our times . . . , it would be social, and that after the almost universal effort of the soldiers would follow the universal efforts of the workers. Events have shown that he was right." No one could believe, France continued, that the human floods raised by such a tempest would simply go back into their former beds. The victors as well as the vanquished had lost so much that work could no longer follow the prewar pattern. Jaurès knew well, France said, that a war of the people would be the harbinger of socialism, yet he tried to prevent the war. He was not willing to pay with the lives of men for the victory of his ideas.

That memorial, written while Jaurès' killer was in the dock, tells as much about France's ideas as it does about those of Jaurès. France believed that the triumph of socialism was near, yet he could praise Jaurès, so easy to praise for so many other things, for preferring peace and a later triumph to war and immediate victory. France sought change, but he still put peace ahead of revolution. Violence might be inevitable, but it must be delayed as long as possible.

France's memorial barely touched on the trial then in progress. Apparently the outcome seemed certain. The killer's guilt was not open to doubt. He had been captured at the scene of the crime, and had confessed. But the jurymen were not Socialists, and when the defendant pleaded his patriotism he was acquitted.

The Socialists took the decision in amazingly docile fashion. *L'Humanité* rumbled in heavy headlines, and called for an orderly demonstration. France was back on the front page immediately, and his tone was menacing:

> The assassin of Jaurès has been declared not guilty.
> Workers, Jaurès lived for you. He died for you!
> A monstrous verdict proclaims that his assassination was not a crime.
> That verdict makes you outlaws, you and all those who defend your cause.
> Workers, wake up!

This manifesto was published in *l'Humanité* on Friday, April 4, 1919, and reprinted, under an even bigger headline on Sunday, April 6, the day set for the protest march.

The demonstration went off quietly. France was very much in view. Apparently his headaches were not bad enough to keep him away from an affair like this one. He began the day attending Mme Jaurès at her home in Paris, "the little house in the impasse de la Tour," [8] with several other old friends of her celebrated husband. *L'Humanité* made a good deal of France, "délicat et familier," chatting in a low voice, telling stories of his days at Jaurès' side. France received an "indescribable ovation" as he left the house. He walked at the head of the procession to a square in which a bust of Jaurès had been placed, and there he helped some old soldiers pin their medals on the bunting that was draped under the bust. "Then, during the ovation the veterans gave him as they filed past in precise order crying 'Vive la France!', our great master and friend answered: 'Non! "Vive l'Internationale!" ' And, quite moved, he embraced Paul-Boncour, who was hardly less shaken himself." [9] The story, probably colored by the enthusiasm of the reporter from *l'Humanité*, shows France's standing with the Socialists. But "Vive l'Internationale" fitted well with the frame of mind he had displayed in his message to the workers two days earlier.

Jaurès had been not only his friend but also one of the very few men he had ever truly respected. For fifteen years, from 1899 to 1914, Jaurès had been the chief leader of the political movement in which Anatole France had placed whatever faith he had in the future of mankind. He had never criticized Jaurès, and had praised him often. On the other hand, he had constantly insisted that justice was unknown in his country. Now the man he admired above all his generation had been "outlawed" by the so-called justice he abhorred. Little wonder that he was moved to anger. The patriotism the jury had approved was, to France, the nationalism that fomented hatred and war.

The revolution Anatole France expected had not yet come in France, and the nationalism he found so vicious was, it seemed, stronger than ever. Whenever he spoke he attacked this bête noire. During these years he spent a great deal of his time at La Béchellerie. He was there when he was invited to speak at the congress of the unions of public school teachers that met in Tours in August, 1919.

"Make hatred hated!" [10] That phrase, the theme of his talk, has been grist for the mills of his left-wing admirers; it is almost always cited when the memory of his last years is recalled. The speech opened a scheduled debate on educational reform. France's thesis was simple: the task of schoolteachers was to form a generation that would be free of the prejudices of nationalism, and thus to prepare the way for universal peace. In passing, he struck most of the chords in the Socialist repertoire: "Victors and vanquished are sunk side by side in a common misery, still exchanging looks full of hatred! . . . You must change primary instruction from top to bottom in order to produce workers. There is no place in our society for anyone but workers. . . . No more industrial rivalries, no more wars: work and peace. . . . A new order of things is arising. . . . However sorely stricken through the fault of their blind or wicked masters, mutilated, decimated, the proletariats remain erect; they are going to unite to form from now on only a single, universal proletariat, and we will see accomplished the great Socialist prophecy: 'The union of workers will bring peace to the world.' " He asserted that only the awakening of new minds would prevent the downfall of civilization. He poured anathema on imperialism, and he charged that the peace had consecrated the social and moral disorder created by the war; he insisted that human beings can be changed more by changes in education than by variations in the air and food provided by their environments. But he said nothing of revolution. He still hoped for a peaceful victory.

During the weeks before the national election of November, 1919, France's statements showed that he still believed a bloodless revolution was possible. He refused on grounds of poor health to become a Socialist candidate himself, but he attached a ringing statement of Socialist faith to his letter of regret: "I believe that only socialism has the capacity to create a stable order, guarantee universal peace, emancipate the human conscience, and renew secular civilization at last by founding it no longer on the economic exploitation of the masses but on the unlimited powers of collective work and free exchange." [11] He ended by applauding in advance (it was the best time —there was nothing to applaud when the ballots had been counted) "the Socialist victories which will assure humanity, after so much unmerited suffering, a happy future."

In private France was not so confident of this particular victory. He wrote to a friend to tell him that things were so confused in Paris that it was impossible to know what was happening, but that things seemed to be going "as badly as possible." He continued: "The worst is not the electoral defeat of the Socialists, which is to be expected. Well-being and ruin don't depend on assemblies. But what frightens me is the public spirit, fallen into a dreary egoism, and Europe, which is foundering in barbarism." [12]

From the point of view of the Left, public affairs were indeed in a parlous state. The Bloc national, a temporary union of nationalist parties, was quick to take advantage of the near panic that fear of Bolshevism had produced in the French public.[13] The bloody "man with the knife between his teeth" glared down everywhere from posters paid for by the powerful Union of Economic Interests. The Radicals refused to ally themselves with the Socialists. Moreover, a new election law militated against a victory of the disorganized Left. The new strength gained by the Socialists after the war was, as the election was to show, not yet enough to compete with that of the traditional parties. Socialists, however, fought hard to discredit the forces of the Right.

France, despite his pessimism, contributed two more statements to the Socialist campaign. The first was the election appeal of the Clarté peace group, a newly formed organization of intellectuals devoted to preserving the world from war.[14] That appeal was signed by France and Henri Barbusse, whose antiwar novels had made him the natural choice to lead Clarté. The second was an open letter to one of the Socialist campaign committees. It made clearer France's ideas on the question of revolution by ballot versus revolution by violence.

> The Socialists present themselves alone, without alliances, to the French people because they alone are innocent of the crimes and errors of old societies. They alone think creatively, and they alone have the ability and the will to organize society.
>
> Let us not close our eyes to reality. The class struggle will end only when classes disappear; classes will melt into one only when labor is imposed upon everyone without distinction, and when political institutions are brought into harmony with economic necessities.
>
> Nothing will prevent the inevitable and necessary revolution that is already being accomplished under your eyes. But it depends upon you, Citizens, whether that revolution is carried out in order and peace. The revolution will be kind to those who guide and support it, but it will break the foolhardy who violently oppose its majestic march.
>
> We are order and peace.[15]

The rest of that letter was spread far and wide in *La Feuille commune*, a journal that carried news of the labor movement during a strike that shut down every newspaper in Paris. It condemned the current regime for making a "disordered, insidious, unfinished" peace and for attempting to crush the Russian Revolution. "That regime," he concluded, "is condemned; it is collapsing into the abyss it has hollowed with its own hand. In its hate of socialism, it has prepared its own future. What is socialism? The universal conscience."

France had correctly prophesied the outcome of the elections. The Socialists were roundly defeated; though the Bloc national did not get an actual majority of the votes cast, the new system of proportional representation was so constructed that the Rightist alliance got a majority in the Chamber of Deputies. For the first time since the eighteen-seventies, the French were governed by a really reactionary parliament—the Chambre bleu horizon, nicknamed after the uniforms worn by the army it so warmly supported.

France continued his political activities after the election and on through 1920, ringing the changes on themes he had stressed during the campaign and pleading the causes of new victims of interclass or international conflicts. He had signed, just before the election, a protest against the enforcement of a claim against Germany: the Germans were required by the peace treaty to deliver huge quantities of livestock to the victors, but the protestors claimed that enforcement of this agreement would mean death for 600,000 children left without milk. After the election he signed another appeal on behalf of Germany, this one dealing with the rights of German soldiers still held as prisoners of war. He spoke at a meeting of the Ligue des Droits de l'Homme in February, 1920, to protest against pogroms that had broken out in Eastern Europe. He was, as usual, ready to defend any Socialist who fell afoul of the law; he bitterly denounced the government when Raymond Lefebvre, the young firebrand who had visited him with Vaillant-Couturier during the war, was prosecuted for writing an article that the government claimed was an incitement to the assassination of the president of the republic. A little later he and Barbusse asked the Ligue des Droits de l'Homme to attempt to save another writer, the Hungarian Socialist Andreas Latzko, who had been condemned to death by the Horthy regime.[16]

On May 1, to help celebrate the annual Socialist show of power, France urged: "Proletarians of all countries, unite to bring about the reign of peace and abundance in all the world." [17] For, he argued, if the present order, or rather "the present disorder," were to continue much longer, everyone would "perish in a frightful ruin."

Russia continued to attract his attention. In August, 1920, the French government recognized Wrangel, the general who then appeared to be the best hope of the beaten Russian aristocracy, as the rightful governor of Russia. France was stirred to make a new appeal to the proletariat. This "policy of the capitalists, soldiers, and diplomats," who stirred anew the fires of war in Russia just at the time the English were coming to an agreement with the Red forces, he condemned as the prelude to a new and horrible outbreak of hostilities.[18] Only the French proletariat, not "as a rule" strong in government circles, could, he thought, prevent a new war. He urged Frenchmen to "save the peace of the world!"

France spent most of these two years, 1919 and 1920, receiving friends, refurbishing his country house, and carefully revising his old novels, changing an adjective here and an adverb there. He also had the Villa Saïd, his house in Paris, redecorated. He had intended to move

back to Paris permanently, but he found that he preferred the charms of Touraine. Emma Laprévotte gradually recovered from her ailments and continued to serve
as his hostess and companion. In August, 1920, France
suffered a mild stroke that left him paralyzed for a few
days.[19] Facing the fact that Emma would be ignored by
any court that probated his will, France decided, at the
age of seventy-six, to marry her in order to assure her
future security. The informal wedding was held at the
city hall in Tours on October 11, 1920. Several of France's
good friends attended, and a delegation of young Socialist women came with armloads of roses to present to the
bride. France thanked these women for the tribute, vow-
ing that he would continue to his last day to do what he
considered to be his social duty.[20]

The gift of flowers was only one of many compliments
paid by the Socialists to their "great master" during the
early postwar period. The Socialists not only gave France
plenty of room to present his views in *l'Humanité*, but
also praised him regularly. Introducing the story of his
refusal to run for office, *l'Humanité* called him "our
illustrious comrade." On September 18, 1920, *Floréal*
("the weekly illustrated paper of the world of labor")
devoted two pages to a feature story on France that was
a model of hero worship. When he married, *l'Humanité*
covered the modest festivities in full detail and spoke of
him as "our friend." In a story about the efforts of the
"merchants of the four seasons" (street peddlers) to
lower their costs by buying in common, *l'Humanité* mentioned that these were the men "whose adventures and
misadventures our master Anatole France has described to
us." The story was headed "Crainquebille at the Labor
Exchange," in reference, of course, to France's famous

tale of a peddler in the toils of the law. France's friendship for the proletariat obviously was accepted and returned by Socialist editors, either out of a genuine sense
of comradeship and recognition or because they thought
France was valuable to the cause and wanted to use him
to the maximum. One of France's friends and biographers,
recalling this period in France's life, said that the old man
received "thousands" of letters testifying to his influence.[21]

During this period France sympathized openly with
Bolshevik Russia; he even wrote to a young friend that
he had always admired Lenin and was "now a Bolshevik
in heart and soul." [22] He spoke most often, however,
about the "peace of the world" that would be brought
about by the "union of workers." He argued that only
socialism could bring order and justice, but he apparently
still thought, or hoped, that the triumph of socialism
could be managed without violence, if only the bourgeoisie could be persuaded to give in gracefully. His most
outspoken plea for action, the statement he made urging
the workers to "wake up" after the acquittal of Jaurès'
murderer, was issued in the heat of the moment, and in
later pronouncements he emphasized, as he always had
before, the possibility of peaceful revolution, the idea
that violence was a last resort.

II

The French Socialist party split in two on December 29,
1920.[23] No one was surprised. The Bolshevik Revolution
had brought vast numbers of new recruits into the French
Socialist party, and most of them were "Bolsheviks," con-

vinced that there was only one way—the Russian way—
to bring about the triumph of socialism. When the war
ended, confusion reigned. Some national parties attempted
to revive the Second International, but it had been mor-
tally wounded when its members cooperated with their
respective governments at the outbreak of the war. The
most radical Socialists everywhere pressed for union with
the Russian-organized, Russian-dominated Third International. In 1920 a French delegation went to Russia to
investigate. From Moscow came a letter stating the conditions under which the French party would be allowed
to join the International of the Bolsheviks. These conditions were harsh. Léon Blum, speaking for a large minority, urged delegates at the party congress at Tours in
December, 1920, to demand better terms. He deplored
the control that the Central Committee of the International would exercise in France and refused to accept the
International's demand that a secret, illegal directing committee be formed. Most important, he insisted that Socialists could never refuse to defend their country in time of
war. The moderates lost. Three thousand delegates voted
to accept the Moscow letter, and only a thousand followed Blum. The minority left the congress to form the
Parti socialiste français and to remain in the Second
International. The majority stayed to become the French
section of the Communist International (SFIC).

The Communists immediately opened a campaign to
recruit the undecided and to bring the dissenters back
into line. Rappoport, now a member of the propaganda
committee of the Communist party, set out to take his
friend Anatole France with him into the new organization. On Sunday, January 9, 1921, he paid the old writer
a visit at the Villa Saïd.

Rappoport, France and his wife, and two couples who were close to France, M. and Mme Jacques Lion and M. and Mme Michel Corday, spent the afternoon together. Lion, the ardent admirer who had already begun his collection of *Franciana*, left in that collection a written account of the day's most momentous event:

> On Sunday, January 9, 1921, Suzon [Mme Lion] and I went to pay a visit to M. and Mme France, who were leaving the next day for Antibes with M. and Mme Corday, who also were there.
>
> After a little while Rappoport arrived. Conversation on current events. All of a sudden the following dialogue took place (I did not miss a word, being seated just in front of M. France):
> —RAPPOPORT: "Monsieur France, will you give me fifty francs? It's for a good work."
> —M. FRANCE . . . addressing Emma [Mme France]: "Tico, give Rappoport fifty francs."
> (Emma got up, and came back with a fifty-franc bill.)
> —RAPPOPORT: "Thank you, Madame, thank you, Monsieur France, it's for the party, it's for the good cause."
>
> That little incident passed almost without notice. We spoke of other things.

On the following Tuesday *l'Humanité*, inherited by the Communist majority of the old party, featured a two-column front-page story headed "Anatole France affirms his solidarity with the party." [24] The article said:

> We did not doubt a single instant that our great friend Anatole France, whose enthusiastic admiration for the Russian Revolution we know, sympathized

completely with the Party which represents the Communist International in France.

We are, nevertheless, infinitely happy to learn that the illustrious writer, whose friendship for Jaurès has never been questioned, is bent on making these sentiments of solidarity known to the Socialist public that he loves so much.

May Anatole France receive here the expression of our joy. May he know that in our present difficult circumstances, his noble manifestation brings us precious comfort.

To our detractors we are proud to say that we are still, enlightened by the experience of the war and the Russian Revolution, the party of Jaurès *with Anatole France!*

And we hope that if there are some comrades who are still hesitating and looking for the path of duty, the act of Anatole France will show them which way they should turn.

Later that week *l'Humanité* published a list of people who had contributed for "the development of the Socialist party (SFIC)." [25] France, with his fifty-franc donation, headed the list. The incident thus ended was what has become known as France's "adhesion" to the Communist party. Later events were to clarify its meaning.

France was not particularly active in politics in 1921. His health was bad, and he spent most of his working hours completing *La Vie en fleur*, the last of his volumes of fictionalized memoirs of his childhood. Though the book is largely about his earliest years, he expressed some of the opinions of his old age in various passages and shed some light on the philosophical basis of his political action.

If it did nothing else, *La Vie en fleur* added more evidence to indicate that his socialism was not based on shallow optimism; he was still a skeptic. In July, 1921, he wrote: "I have perceived, after long observation . . . that desire embellishes the objects to which it lends wings of fire, and that satisfaction, most often deceptive, is the ruin of illusion, the only true good of men; satisfaction kills desire, which alone gives charm to life." [26] In September he found occasion to write that men, driven to murder by necessity since life began, are subject to an eternal law that forces them to kill in order to live.[27] But he still foresaw the end of his own civilization, which he believed would be succeeded by a culture so different that the art and the thought of the past would be ignored.[28] At the end of his book, in a postface that was first published on September 21, 1921, he again referred to the need for illusion: "I love the truth. I believe humanity has need of it; but certainly mankind has a much greater need for lies, which flatter it, console it, give it infinite hopes. Without lies, humanity would perish of despair and boredom." [29]

The few political acts France did perform in 1921 proved that despite his infirmities he was as militant as ever. Twice he signed, in company with Barbusse, manifestos issued by the directing committee of the Clarté group. The first of these, published in the group's bulletin, *Clarté*, on July 21, 1921, was a violent protest against a new press law proposed by the government. Under the terms of this bill anyone who wrote or spoke anything that tended to persuade soldiers to fail to fulfill their duties would be liable to a fine of 20,000 francs. Such a law would be a travesty of democratic rule, the protest said: "The bourgeois dictatorship is getting heavier, more odious." The second manifesto, which appeared in *Clarté* on September 23, 1921, was a plea for aid to famine-stricken Russia.

On another occasion France and Barbusse addressed a recruiting letter for Clarté "To the Intellectuals of Latin America." Though it is quite possible that Barbusse wrote the letter, France usually knew what he signed, and this letter included some strong statements. It began with a plea that Latin American intellectuals leave their ivory towers and take part in public affairs. Old moral ideas were artificial and unjust, it continued, but they were moral laws; now the world was ruled by the law of the strongest, which had taken on the form of the rule of money. "Our epoch is . . . an epoch of economic parasitism. The well-being and the lives of individuals and nations are at the mercy of that monster, money; all misery, all suffering, all wars have, it is generally agreed, an economic cause." [30] It was not enough just to know this, the letter said, nor simply to say that the remedy lay in a new social order that would bring equality and justice. "One must share this belief with everyone; . . . ideas are the roots of acts. . . . We have founded the Clarté group to diffuse, to teach as an exact religion, a doctrine that bares the abuses and brings to light the principles of justice." The authors thoughtfully concluded with detailed instructions on the method of forming new branches of Clarté.

France spoke for himself alone on October 31, 1921, when he wrote a letter entitled "Anatole France to the People of America" asking them to prevent the execution of Sacco and Vanzetti, the Boston anarchists whose fight for life made headlines all over the world for nearly a decade.[31]

Then, on December 10, 1921, France spoke not only to America but to the world, from the platform upon which he had just been awarded the Nobel Prize for literature. After expressing his thanks to the judges who had chosen to honor him, he made a frankly political speech. One paragraph contained the gist of his thought: "The most horrible of wars has been followed by a treaty which is not a treaty of peace but a prolongation of the war. Europe will perish of these things if reason does not enter into its councils." [32] As one of his biographers has remarked, most Frenchmen did not speak of the Treaty of Versailles in such harsh terms in December, 1921: France was confirming his reputation as an aged *enfant terrible* and expressing the views of his left-wing comrades.[33] (He had said much the same thing a few weeks earlier in the columns of *Clarté*, which by then had switched its allegiance from pacifism to communism.[34]) *L'Humanité* praised his speech as "true thought" expressed in words that were "courageous and firm." A month after the award had been made, the literary critic of *l'Humanité*, discussing a book of anecdotes about France that had just been published, re-emphasized Communist gratitude for France's support, saying that only a strong idea could win the approval of such a great skeptic.[35]

France appeared more often on the political stage in 1922. In January he publicly defended the two ex-ministers, Caillaux and Malvy, who had been convicted of aiding the cause of "defeatism" during the war, and joined a committee formed to press for the release of Jean Goldsky, the newspaper editor who had been convicted and condemned to eight years in prison on a similar charge. A little later he wrote the preface to a brochure that was part of the campaign to aid the hungry children of Russia.[36]

In February he received a warm tribute from the group that included his oldest friends and fellow crusaders, the Ligue des Droits de l'Homme. The Ligue, veteran of hundreds of battles in defense of civil liberties since it had been formed to serve the needs of the Dreyfusards, held a banquet in France's honor on February 18, 1922. Tributes came from several quarters, along with the expected new attacks from the press of the Right. In *l'Humanité* the praise France received that day carried a hint of trouble to come, although probably not many people could read the signs. Under the heading "Salute to Anatole France" the Communist paper announced the banquet, and added:

> Doubtless Communists will not be very numerous at this demonstration, but they are determined to proclaim here that Anatole France is not only an admirable writer, the best worker in the French language since Flaubert, but a good citizen.
>
> Raised in the romantic and Parnassian doctrine of art for art's sake, Anatole France did not believe he would lower himself by mixing in the battles, often vulgar and always passionate, of the market place and the city. After having been an ardent Dreyfusard, he did not fear to declare himself a Socialist; he did not fear, more recently still, to attest his spiritual sympathy for the hated movement of which Lenin is the soul. In the twilight of his life, no longer expecting any personal gain from men, he does not harbor an old man's useless regret for the dead past, but he has hopes for a better future that he willingly visualizes in the form that, since Marx, communism and the proletariat have given them.
>
> Anatole France, we salute you!

In his speech at the celebration France recalled old struggles and then passed on to the new. He spoke of the cases of Caillaux, Malvy, and Goldsky, and condemned the government for persecuting such men. He then protested the imprisonment of André Marty, a naval officer who had led sailors of the Black Sea fleet when they refused to fire on Red Army troops during the Allied expedition against the Bolsheviks. Stupidity and blindness still characterized the rulers of France, he said, but force could never prevail against the current of the times. "I may wonder, with my friends the Socialists and Communists," he said, "whether the end of that regime is not approaching." [37] He concluded by arguing that modern life bound all nations so tightly together that only true peace, the peace that was in men's hearts, could rid the world of its miseries.

During the next few days France's name was in almost every Paris newspaper. Maurras reiterated in his royalist gazette, *L'Action française*, his old claim that France was really a split personality, an aristocrat who had been led astray. *Le Populaire de Paris*, under the political direction of Blum and the Socialist party, printed France's entire speech (it was long) with warm approval.[38] *L'Humanité* published long excerpts on the day after the banquet, identifying France as "the writer who so greatly honors the field of letters" and the "citizen who always claims his place in the vanguard, in arms against injustice and inequality."

The day after that *l'Humanité* published another article on the banquet, a long, highly significant column by Amédée Dunois, general secretary of the paper. Dunois recalled the days of his youth and spoke of the tenderness with which he still viewed the Ligue des Droits de

l'Homme "despite all its errors and all its faults." [39] It
brought to his mind, he wrote, the intoxicating days when
he was twenty, fighting for truth and justice. Now the
Ligue had paid tribute to one of its earliest members.
"[Anatole France] we know truly appreciated that
salute. We know it because our old master, if he does
not himself belong to the Communist party (he belongs
to no party), strongly desires to be the friend of those
who represent a little in France the great Russian idea.
. . . They said of him twenty years ago that he was nothing but a great nihilist. The great nihilist has become a
great believer. . . . Anatole France has the right to call
himself our friend: he has this in common with us, *that
he believes in the proletariat.*" The remark of the previous
week about France's "spiritual sympathy" with the Communists had been confirmed. He was not a member of the
party at all, but only a fellow traveler.

A month later France himself demonstrated that despite
his friendliness toward the Communists he had not the
least idea of the premises on which their party was built.
In March, 1922, the press reported that the Soviet government was about to hold a mass trial of members of
the Russian Social Revolutionary party.[40] The Social
Revolutionaries, notorious for their lavish use of terror-
ism against the tsarist regime, had always been champions
of the peasantry. Some of them had supported Alexander
Kerensky's attempts to keep Russia in the war. They
were sworn enemies of the Bolsheviks, who based their
program, if not their power, on the industrial proletariat
and had taken Russia out of the war. Tolerated or hunted
down individually until 1922, the Social Revolutionaries
finally faced complete extinction.

Anatole France, in the habit of protesting whenever he scented injustice, telegraphed the Soviet government: "In the name of humanity, in the name of the superior interests of the world proletariat, do not carry out against political adversaries acts which could be interpreted as vengeance. You could by doing so prejudice irreparably the great cause of the liberation of the workers of the world." [41]

Retaliation was not particularly swift, but it was harsh. Boris Souvarine, one of the firebrands of the French Communist party, was serving as the delegate from the Directing Committee of the SFIC to the office of the International in Moscow when France's telegram arrived. A month elapsed before his reply was printed in Paris. He wrote that France, "prey to an indulgent eclecticism," had been led astray by rumormongers. [42] The Revolution had defended itself by force of arms for five years, he continued, so naturally there were dead on both sides. "Anatole France cannot be ignorant of that." The Social Revolutionaries were not simple militants; they were "adventurers" who had committed sabotage, assassination, espionage, treason, and chicanery. The issue seemed to be somewhat more complicated than France had thought.

Despite his chastisement, France was still allowed to maintain good relations with the Communists. In June, 1922, he signed, with a number of other writers, not all of whom belonged to the party, an appeal to the French government on behalf of Maxim Gorki, who had asked permission to reside on French territory while recuperating from an illness. [43] Gorki returned the favor early in July by writing to France asking him to send a new appeal to the Soviet government in favor of the Social Revolutionaries, some of whom were still being tried. [44] Gorki

included a copy of the letter he himself was sending.
France replied as follows:

> Dear Citizen Gorki,
>
> I am sorry that I am not very well acquainted with
> the great affair concerning which you ask my aid, and
> have not been able to follow, step by step, the debates
> in the trial of Revolutionary Socialists now going on
> in Moscow.
>
> Like you, however, I believe that the men before the
> bar have in their time sincerely served the cause of the
> liberation of the Russian people. Like you, I believe that
> their condemnation would weigh heavily on the destiny
> of the Soviet republic.
>
> It is with all my heart, Dear Gorki, that I adhere to
> the appeal that you have addressed to the Soviet gov-
> ernment, one of whose members, I am told, is acting
> as prosecutor at the trial.[45]

Sobered by Souvarine's denunciation, France had composed a masterpiece of tact, as the next day's Communist
reaction showed. *L'Humanité* published his letter "in
favor of the Russian Social-Counterrevolutionary agents
of the Entente," and pointedly praised his "wise reserve."

Two weeks later France again made himself thoroughly
popular with the Communists. He had always tried to be
useful to his literary friends (and satellites), devoting
articles to their latest works while he was critic for *Le
Temps* in the eighteen-eighties, later writing laudatory
prefaces and occasional reviews. When Michel Corday
published *Les Hauts fourneaux*, a Marxist muckraking
tract, France wrote a review of the book that would have
done justice to the most agile of professional propagandists. He used the occasion to declare once more his

hatred for bourgeois society and to strike yet another blow for peace. In a long letter published on the front page of *l'Humanité* on July 28, 1922, he announced that at last he knew the causes of the World War. From Corday's book, he said, one learned that, as some had suspected, the war "was essentially the work of men of finance; that it was the industrial chiefs of the different states of Europe who from the first wanted it, made it necessary, provoked it, prolonged it." After quoting a few paragraphs from the book, France declared: "Thus, those who died in that war did not know why they died. It is the same in all wars. . . . They believed they were dying for their fatherland; they were dying for big business." Turning to another point, he said that the book showed that the newspapers, in the hands of rich industrialists, were responsible for the senseless hatred of other peoples that first became known in France during the war. Such hatred he called a "strange mania," arguing as he had before that because peoples are composed of individuals, most of whom did not want the war and most of whom were innocent of all responsibility for it, that hate was incomprehensible: "To hate a people is to hate opposites—good and evil, beauty and ugliness."

Needless to say, France's implication that the book threw new light on the causes of the war was ridiculous; France himself had blamed war on big business long before the World War began. The Communists, however, presumably were less interested in originality than in orthodoxy, and this was orthodoxy. The letter was reprinted in *Avanti*, the Communist journal in Milan, and a few months later *l'Humanité* began to run *La Vie en fleur*, France's latest volume of childhood memories, as a daily serial.[46]

France cemented his return to good grace in November, 1922, when the Communists celebrated the fifth anniversary of the Bolshevik Revolution. On the front page of *l'Humanité* he published a "Salute to the Soviets" that the editors called an offering of "inestimable value" by "our greatest writer." [47] France began by telling how the makers of Russia's revolution brought a "new spirit" to menace the powers of injustice and oppression. Then, with evident satisfaction, he recalled that the Red Armies had crushed the "hordes of bandits" sent by the governments of Europe to stifle them. The Soviet Revolution, he said, produced for the first time a government of the people and by the people. "Born in indigence, growing in the midst of famine and war, how could the Soviets have accomplished their grand design and realized true justice? At least they have posed the principle. They have sown the seeds which, if destiny smiles, will be spread throughout Russia and perhaps one day will fertilize the whole of Europe." He still refused to call the Soviet treatment of the Social Revolutionaries "justice," but he no longer condemned, he forgave. Apparently he could feel once more that he was in harmony at the same time with the creators of the new world and the promptings of his own conscience. He was to have two months to enjoy that state of affairs.

L'Humanité was always in the thick of a battle: at the end of November, 1922, the campaign for the release of André Marty reached a crescendo. To the Communists, Marty was a new Dreyfus, though more legalistic Frenchmen probably thought there was at least one difference—Dreyfus had never broken a law, just or unjust, whereas Marty undoubtedly had. In any case, the Communists, with full backing from the Socialists and other antimilitarists, argued that the amnesty pronounced some months before in favor of the enlisted mutineers should have included the officer Marty as well. To put new force into the campaign, Victor Méric, one of the regular writers of *l'Humanité*, planned a series of protest articles that would be written by various intellectuals.[48] One of the first on his list, of course, was Anatole France, whose response was one guaranteed to stir hatred in the hearts of patriots.

> IT IS FINE FOR A SOLDIER TO DISOBEY CRIMINAL ORDERS. That is what Marty did.
>
> A court-martial could not absolve him without condemning those who ordered him to act as a scoundrel by violating the most sacred laws. That condemnation was necessary.[49]

In the following paragraphs, France argued that by excepting Marty from the general amnesty the government held him up for admiration. He concluded by saying:

> MARTY IS TODAY THE MOST POPULAR MAN IN FRANCE.

Méric's campaign continued through December as intellectuals, some respected, some unknown, some Communists, some not, followed France's lead.

On December 2, 1922, *l'Humanité* published France's preface to a new French edition of Jack London's revolutionary novel, *The Iron Heel*. The book was far from optimistic; London predicted a centuries-long struggle between the working class and the "Iron Heel" of the plutocracy. France's preface was as pessimistic as the book it introduced. He criticized Socialists for allowing their party to crumble into factions, and he said that the war had killed spirits just as it had killed bodies. The struggle would continue, however, and someday there would be battles as bloody as those described by London. Some people doubted that such "indescribable" horrors could be produced in France, he said, but they should recall the horrors of the June Days of 1848 and the suppression of the Paris Commune in 1871: "Anything is permitted against the poor." But the great power of the "Iron Heel," a power greater than most Socialists realized, would, he said, be crushed in the end.

While Méric organized his band of littérateurs and France fulminated at the inept politicians of his government, Leon Trotsky, in Russia, pondered the desirability of intellectuals as allies in the class war. A number of French Communists had not paid much attention to the conditions laid down by Moscow for their acceptance by the Third International. Pacifists and patriots, for example, tended to ignore Moscow's high regard for the Red Army and its distaste for other peoples' nationalism. Veteran liberals disregarded the demands of party discipline. In December, 1922, a dispute on tactics between the Executive Committee of the International and the leaders of the French party was laid before the Fourth World Congress of the International for decision. Trotsky's committee on French Communist affairs seized the opportunity to clarify the nature of the duties of members of the International.

Trotsky's "Resolution on the French Question," passed easily by the Congress, ended all discussion of the rights of national parties against the Executive Committee. The resolution affirmed the superior authority of the Committee and explained in detail what was and what was not permitted.[50] It stated that the Ligue des Droits de l'Homme was "an organization of bourgeois radicalism" to which no Communist could belong. It said that no Communist could remain a member of the Masonic order. In its most sweeping blow, the resolution required all party "intellectuals" to break every tie with the bourgeoisie and submit themselves to party discipline. That section of the resolution put an end to Méric's campaign for the mutineer Marty, which was an affair of intellectuals that frankly included members of the liberal bourgeoisie; when Méric complained, he was expelled from the party. With him went a number of other pacifist writers and professors. L.–O. Frossard, general secretary of the party, was a Freemason; he resigned his office and quit the party rather than undergo the penance imposed.[51]

No one better fitted the Communist definition of "intellectual" than Anatole France. France had thrown his weight behind the Communist cause, but he certainly had not submitted to discipline. He had not actually attacked the Russian government but he had intervened in favor of the Social Revolutionaries and had been rebuked harshly for his pains. He had retreated, but not without a certain reluctance, as his letter to Gorki and his later "Salute to the Soviets" showed. He had accepted honors from that organ of bourgeois radicalism, the Ligue des Droits de l'Homme. He had, finally, been associated with intellectuals like Méric who were now outside the pale. None of these things had been forbidden, of course, and only the letter about the Social Revolutionaries had been publicly condemned. France's conduct was, in general, very like that of other members of the party who ignored the orders from Moscow. The Fourth World Congress, however, had punished Communists of that kind by expelling them, or at the very least, by ordering them to submit to discipline. In the eyes of the International, anyone who failed to take orders was really an enemy of the working class.

Dunois, who had been on the winning side in the party struggle, attempted during the first few days of the new regime to clarify France's status. In a front-page article headed "A Formal Denial," he told the readers of *l'Humanité* on January 1, 1923, that bourgeois journals had reported that France would be invited to stop calling himself a Communist. The report, Dunois stated, was not true. Perhaps not; but France stopped anyhow.

France quit writing for *l'Humanité* and switched his collaboration to *Le Quotidien*, a new Paris journal controlled by the non-Communist Left. In an interview that appeared in that paper on March 11, 1923, two months after the "purge," France delivered an indirect insult to his old comrades. He told the reporter: "Your enterprise —to create a journal in which there will be no false news— is magnificent. I want to make it known that I am with you with all my heart." In the same interview, however, he defended the Soviets once more, arguing that, after all, France had had its own revolution. But his two-year fellowship with the Communists was over. He had learned, along with many other more experienced politicians who had not been able to conceive of an enemy to the Left, that the Communists tolerated no dissidence once a decision had been made. Minorities not only were to be voted down, they were to be forbidden to exist.

III

France, old and feeble, made his last appearance as an orator at a celebration of the centenary of one of his literary idols, Ernest Renan, in March, 1923. The ceremony, organized by a number of anticlerical and republican groups, was actually a counterdemonstration against the official fête held the week before at the Sorbonne. There Renan had been more vilified than glorified: speakers like Maurice Barrès, no internationalist, turned the meeting into an attack on Renan's lukewarm patriotism and decidedly cool skepticism.[52] For France, the second ceremony was an opportunity to pay a last tribute to a man and thinker he adored. He asserted that Renan, despite his refinement and his dilettante air, was not an aristocrat but a lover of the people.[53] Obviously, France was pleading his own case as well. Only a few passages in his speech touched on contemporary politics; in these he said that what would have hurt Renan about the World War was that it had been followed by a treaty that did not put an end to war and was "only the organization of disorder, hate, discord, and misery in unhappy Europe." Commenting on Renan's prediction that nations would die and be replaced by a European federation, France reiterated his hatred of nationalism. He did not mention communism at all.

L'Humanité reacted with a straight news story in which a number of France's statements were quoted.[54] The story exuded an air of patronizing superiority that contrasted noticeably with the admiring tone of the report published in the Socialist *Populaire*. The real Communist reaction was made clear, however, in an editorial article, "Renan et nous," written by Dunois. Like Barrès, Dunois could not abide Renan's skepticism. He did not attack France directly, but he made a point of saying that he hoped people would stop calling Renan a "friend of the people." Renan, like Voltaire, destroyed more than he created, Dunois argued. Renan ended as a nihilist, and nihilism was a doctrine of decadence and despair. What workers needed, Dunois recalled from his study of Marx (and, no doubt, from Trotsky's recent reminder), were thinkers who taught not how to understand the world but how to change it. The dead need not be attacked; the target of these remarks was Anatole France.

France continued, despite this rebuff, to act as an advocate of the proletariat. In one of his last published articles, written for a newly founded left-wing review, France warmly praised the second volume of Corday's impassioned exposé of the alleged warmongers in big business and enlarged upon his own regret at having turned patriotic at the beginning of the war. France said that during the war he had suspected that the great industrialists were responsible for the carnage then going on, but that he had lacked both the courage and the knowledge to tell the truth. "I even let myself make little speeches to soldiers living or dead," he said, "and I regret that as the worst act of my life." [55] All Europe "is threatened with destruction in the great slaughters that are being prepared." But there was hope for the future: "The progress of the proletariat cannot be denied. In France, where it is less numerous than in the other countries of Europe, its divisions and its troubles prevent it from acting." The German proletariat, however, held out the hand of peace. And there was one other hope: nations were dying, to be replaced by a United States of Europe.

Foreign war might be followed by civil war, but one could not be sure. "Therefore," he concluded, "we must not despair of the future of humanity."

In May, 1923, he had an opportunity to reiterate his pacifist message when he was invited to send a letter of welcome to the American "Good-Will Delegation," a group of women who came to France to deliver in person the money collected by popular subscription for the rebuilding of the devastated areas of the country. His text was simple. After giving thanks for the aid they brought, France told them that women, having more courage than men, must save humanity:

> You are the ones who must attack the monster that devours us, the ones who must make war on war, a war to the death.
>
> From this time forward, hate war with an inextinguishable hate.
>
> Hate war in contemplating its crimes; hate war even as you see it in the ornaments of triumph, the palms of victory. May your hate be mortal; may it kill war.[56]

He concluded by predicting once again that the grandchildren of his generation would see the "Universal Republic."

France was by then seventy-nine, and ailing. On June 3, 1923, Georges Pioch, a minor poet and pacifist who left the Communist party as a result of Trotsky's purge, acted as his spokesman when a statue of Jaurès was unveiled at Carmaux. Pioch read a typical Francian denunciation of the warlike bourgeoisie. As might be expected, France was incensed by the French occupation of the Ruhr valley, occasioned by a German default on reparations payments, and he asserted that the nation was on the brink of war. This memorial celebration was followed by another, the next day, at Toulouse. Again France sent greetings, this time emphasizing the need for a union of the parties of the Left. *L'Humanité* quoted a few of France's more inflammatory remarks in its story of the Carmaux gathering, calling his speech a "courageous page, worthy of a great writer." [57]

Six months later France had a fainting spell that lasted an hour and a half. Both *l'Humanité* and *Le Populaire* ran short reassuring notices when it became clear that the stroke had not been fatal.[58] The patriarch of letters was to live long enough to savor the joys of two grand celebrations in his honor.

France's status as the greatest living French writer was almost undisputed. Among his fellow writers there were some who demurred, but two public opinion polls had given him the palm late in 1923. His reputation was reason enough for all Paris to celebrate his eightieth birthday. *Paris-Soir* was first to announce plans for paying homage to the old master, and that newspaper's display of testimonials was most impressive. *L'Humanité* managed, however, to get in the Communist salute early by printing its story on the eve of the anniversary. That salute took the form of a "Letter from Crainquebille to Anatole France." It was homage, but it was also a rebuke. Crainquebille recalled himself to France, saying that he still thought of France as his patron and defender. But, he inquired, what is all this "magic of style" that everyone praises?

> Me, I find frankly that you tell the truth, that you speak straight out, . . . that you have always been on the side of justice, that you have never practiced hy-

pocrisy. . . . An innocent man is condemned. You are
for him. What's his name? Dreyfus, Zola, the man-
with-the-knife-between-his-teeth? It doesn't matter,
you are with him to the end. . . .

But one question: I just want to know—after all, it's
quite simple. If something happened, you understand,
something, well, you would be for us, wouldn't you?

France might have been embarrassed if he had been forced
to answer that question, for that *something* was, of course,
revolution.[59]

In a way, however, France did answer the question.
As elections drew near once more, the parties of the Left
organized to unseat the nationalist government. All except the Communists joined in the Cartel des gauches.
Socialists were willing to ally with bourgeois parties in
order to defeat the Right; the Communists were not.
France had written his answer to Crainquebille even before he saw the article that asked his attitude on that important "something," for he supported not the Communists but the Cartel des gauches.

Half the front page of the April 16, 1924, issue of *Le
Quotidien* was devoted to birthday praise of Anatole
France; a third of page two, headed "Le Civisme d'Anatole France," was given to excerpts from France's past
speeches that, in general, tended to support the Cartel
des gauches. The speeches quoted were made in 1902 and
1905; the paragraphs selected contained France's old attacks on nationalism. The last citation, from a campaign
speech made just before the elections of 1902, was highly
appropriate to the electoral situation twenty-two years
later: "You are not going to drown your votes in the
clouds of a liberalism that respects every oppression and

every iniquity. You will give them to the candidate—
Radical, Radical-Socialist, or Socialist—who supports true
liberty, the kind that recognizes no liberty against itself."
In view of France's earlier endorsement of *Le Quotidien*,
it is almost certain that he approved the use of this quotation. *Le Quotidien* ran this one paragraph again, in a
front-page box, on the day of the elections.[60]

Meanwhile, *Clarté*, the erstwhile pacifist, now Communist, journal, was making sure that its readers understood that France was no longer a member of the Clarté
group that had once been so proud to have his support.
On May 1 *Clarté* printed a story commemorating France's
jubilee, and headed it: "Let Us Keep Our Distance." The
writers of *Clarté* lumped France and Barrès as bourgeois
apologists, saying that France was a "precious skeptic."
At roughly the same time the Socialists and the Fédération des Jeunesses Laïques et Républicaines were defending France against such charges; the journal of the
Fédération called him a "man of action whose skepticism
covers profound convictions that have been shown each
time he has had to prove his energy and his civic courage." [61] The only people who agreed with the Communists of *Clarté* in their estimate of France's skepticism
were the extreme reactionaries who called Orleanists
"canaille" and insisted that France was an unstable cynic
under the influence of Jews.[62]

Both the reactionaries and the Communists were beaten
soundly at the polls, and France's three parties of "true
liberty" won a majority of the seats in the Chamber of
Deputies. France joined in the jubilation:

> I salute this great victory.
> France has just manifested her will to peace.

I do not believe—I have said it often—that war must be an eternal human necessity.

I wish for, I hope for, I foresee a future of peace and concord between peoples of equal culture.

Let us prepare that desirable peace. . . . In reality, if one wants peace, one must prepare for peace.

Such is our desire, such is our care, such should be our work.

Let us work for universal peace. And is it not a task worthy of the greatest souls and the fiercest prides? The Rome of the Caesars tried to do this when it was the queen of the universe. May the Europe of the present accomplish it! [63]

The victory of the Left was probably as good a birthday gift as France could have received, but, after the homage of his anniversary celebration and the triumph of his side in the elections, yet another day of glory remained. He had spent his birthday in seclusion; now a group of friends organized a new ceremony at which he might appear. On the day of the new fête—May 24, 1924 —both *Le Populaire* and *Le Quotidien* ran front-page notices about the celebration to be held that afternoon; *l'Humanité* gave it a paragraph in its weekly column of literary "petites nouvelles." The hall chosen for the celebration was the Trocadero Theater, a hallowed place for Anatole France, the scene of many meetings of Socialists, pacifists, and protectors of the allegedly innocent. The hall was filled. François-Albert, senator and president-elect of the League for Education, a predominantly Socialist group, presided; Léon Jouhaux, long-time leader of the non-Communist part of the French trade-union movement, brought greetings from the workers; Alphonse Aulard, then the most respected historian of the

French Revolution, praised France's historical sense.[64] The two newspapers of the non-Communist Left gave admiring reports of the occasion and made big news of France's only statement of the day, one that was short and political: "What the French people has done in the past few days [the elections] is a great thing. But let us not sleep on our victory; let us not forget that we have promised to provide peace—that first—peace and an amnesty. Because if we do not accomplish the acts that the electors expected of us, that their vote has dictated to us, we will not be forgiven." That was France's last public statement. True to form, he used his rapidly failing strength to rasp out not a song of triumph but a call to hard work. Even *l'Humanité*, voice of one of the parties vanquished in the election, had to approve France's remarks.

The Communists had more to say, however, of France's association with the Cartel des gauches than of his plea for peace and an amnesty. After a few sarcastic remarks on François-Albert's eulogy of France's literary genius and philosophical lucidity, *l'Humanité* commented:

> Alas! It is quite true that this man of good will considers his own enthusiasms with irony. And it is only too true that he accepts public felicitations meant for the "precursor, the artisan," of an electoral success due to the confusion, the skepticism, that reigns in France just as in the "political thought" of Anatole France.
>
> Thus, the master writer who once was believed an "internationalist" and a "Communist" offers a little of his prestige to the bourgeoisie "of the Left"! [65]

Crushed at last by the various ailments that had attacked him in his old age—neuritis, rheumatism, hardening of the arteries—France found himself, toward the end of September, 1924, unable to leave his bed. He declined rapidly; he ate very little and slept almost constantly. Once he spoke: "So this is what dying is! It takes a long time." [66] He smiled at the little group of friends who stayed at his side. On the afternoon of October 12 he slipped into unconsciousness. Occasionally he murmured a word: "Mama . . ." Just before midnight he died. He was buried on October 18, after a pompous state funeral.

Conclusion

In some countries literature and politics are related only indirectly, but in France writers traditionally lend whatever prestige they can command to parties or political ideas. In doing so they immediately raise two questions: Are they sincere, or are they just selling books and asking for praise? And do their war cries attract any attention, influence any votes, or are they so much wasted ink? Neither of these questions can be answered with certainty, but both demand consideration.

Sincerity is both difficult to prove and greatly overrated. In these post-Freudian years it is a commonplace that everyone's motives are mixed, and it is only too easy to show that world-renowned statesmen as well as petty politicians do not act purely out of disinterested patriotism. Barring cases of blatant hypocrisy, it is better to let the motives lie and discuss the achievements. Certainly this study makes it clear that Anatole France thirsted for glory, and he could be accused of using politics to bolster his always shaky sense of his own worth. I have argued that his move toward political radicalism in 1888 and the years following was conditioned, if not caused, by various events in his personal life. Still, the path he took in those years and during the rest of his days was not the path of least resistance. The arbiters of taste in that era were the Brunetières, not the Ravachols and their supporters. Moreover, the relative coolness of France's attachment to the Left, marked by his continued skepticism, weakened the acclaim he won from his political allies. A glory hunter would have done better to go the whole distance. When France joined the socialist band, he undoubtedly was seeking companionship and approval as well as justice for the poor and the persecuted, but he could have taken easier ways. Emotional needs may have made him a militant, but what counts is what he fought for, not why he fought.

But did France's thirty years of propagandizing serve any purpose? There is no sure way to judge. All one can do is point out that his support was much in demand. Presumably the people who asked him to make a speech or write a letter of protest thought he was worth something in the struggle. Presumably the people who decorate today's letterheads with famous names know what they are doing, and there is no reason to suppose similar action was less effective fifty years ago.

France worked for causes. When they triumphed, he shared the credit; when they failed, he shared in the defeat. It is no more possible to parcel out credit to propagandizing intellectuals for their individual efforts than it is to judge the parts played by individual soldiers in vast battles. Each one does what he is fitted to do under the circumstances that prevail; some stand out more than others; but armies, not individuals, win or lose the wars. France deserves no credit as a strategist, for he was not a pioneering political thinker. He deserves instead whatever credit belongs to the man who does what he can to further the cause that he thinks is just.

France chose, finally, to fight as a socialist, but the cause in which he was enlisted was far older than socialism. In his time France was the major representative of the philosophical tradition of skeptical humanism, a tradition of profound skepticism coupled with sympathy and hope for humanity. Montaigne, one of the founders of the tradition, expressed its basic premises in one sentence: "After all, it is setting a very high price on one's conjectures to burn a man alive for them." [1] Skepticism, yes; irony, yes —but in the interest of saving human lives.

Developed by Montaigne and Rabelais, carried on by such luminaries as Voltaire and Renan, the tradition of skeptical humanism has never been popular with zealots. It is conservative in its caution, yet conservatives distrust it because it dares to question. It is liberal in its humanitarianism, but apostles of change seldom like to be reminded that they may be wrong.

France's defense of that tradition has won him many enemies. Before he died he was under attack from critics of the Right as a traitor to his nation, a subverter of morals, a dangerous radical. The old attacks continued after his death. He was even blamed for his country's defeat in World War II. Jean Dutourd, a Gaullist intellectual, writing in 1957 of the "sniveling humanitarianism of the Moderate Left," identified that wicked doctrine with the "paltry Bergeret who talks smoothly to us of freedom and justice but who has done everything to disarm France." [2]

The Left has been only a little more friendly. An

obituary that appeared in *La Vie ouvrière* a few days after France died gave him credit for sympathizing with the workers, but said that his lack of a doctrine made him weak and vacillating. Marcel Cachin, writing in *l'Humanité* at about the same time, said much the same thing. More recently, in a highly laudatory anniversary article published in 1954, *l'Humanité* rehabilitated France by the simple expedient of speaking of him as if he had been a dedicated orthodox Communist. Socialists have generally been kinder when they bothered with France at all, but their criticism has been quite superficial.[3] France's political opinions have found little echo: he was not a "pure." This is the century of the doctrinaire, and skepticism is in bad odor.

The literati are not immune to politics, and the same urge for militance and doctrinal purity has influenced criticism for many years. Mme Tison-Braun has not completed her work on "la crise d l'humanisme," and it is not easy to see what her conclusion will be. Nevertheless, the surge toward militant faith that she sees as beginning in the 1890s is by no means dead. The communism of the 1930s was part of it, as was the vogue of existentialism after World War II; the current reawakening in theology is another symptom. Buffeted by crisis after crisis, generations of intellectuals have taken up the quest for certainty. Among recent literary greats perhaps the only one who might be said to continue the humanist line is Albert Camus, and his life of intellectual agony and political ambiguity is excellent evidence of the difficulty that faces a man who tries to maintain the integrity of that tradition. It is no coincidence that Voltaire's reputation has slipped at the same time as that of Anatole France. Simple changes in taste undoubtedly influence standings in the literary hierarchy, but so do other things: in the past three or four decades critics holding fashionable political or philosophical positions were almost sure to find Voltaire's politics and France's books irritating in the extreme.

Yet skepticism has its virtues.

If it is not constructive, as has been argued *ad nauseam*, it is at least sane. If, in the hands of a Voltaire or an Anatole France, it saps the foundations of old institutions, it is dangerous only to hypocrisy and injustice. Living, useful institutions cannot be destroyed by the weapon of doubt.

It has positive aspects. Remarking on the effects of a certain bloody revolution, someone once said that he saw the broken eggs, all right, but where was the omelet? Skeptics like Anatole France seldom lose sight of the eggs; they "vacillate" because they lack the fanatic's ability to concentrate on the end while ignoring the means. Such an attitude always irritates the fanatic, but it may, if expressed often and loud enough, save a life or open a prison door. It may even save the fanatic's edifice from tumbling down, for reason that is tempered with mercy is tougher building material than reason pure. Finally, the skeptical humanist does, after all, work for a better world, as France did, even though he thinks perfection is unattainable and progress is slow.

France was not typical of the intellectuals of his time. Though he was sometimes inconsistent in his actions, France remained a skeptic, attached to a kind of liberalism that was centuries old, while most of his fellow intellectuals left both skepticism and liberalism behind. His magnificent popular success indicates that the ideas he expressed were widely shared in his society. Skeptical humanism still lived, even though the intellectual vanguard had abandoned it. For thirty years France used his talent and his fame in the struggle to preserve that beleaguered tradition.

Notes

1. The Conservative (1844–1888)

1. Works on France are plentiful. The best general biography is that by Jacques Suffel, *A.F.* (Paris: Editions du Myrte, 1946). Much more detailed for the period it covers is Edwin Preston Dargan's excellent *A.F.: 1844–1896* (New York: Oxford University Press, 1937). The best book on France's childhood, one used by every scholar who works on A.F.'s youth, is Georges Girard's *La Jeunesse d'A.F.: 1844–1878* (Paris: Gallimard, 1925). Marie-Claire Bancquart's *A.F. Polémiste* (Paris: Nizet, 1962) touches on a great many things treated in this study, but her approach differs so completely from mine that I have not attempted to discuss her arguments. Both Dargan's and Suffel's books include bibliographies that together contain most of the important material. France's fictionalized memoirs (*Le Livre de mon ami, Le Petit Pierre, Pierre Nozière*, and *La Vie en fleur*) all are mines of information, but it is not always easy to separate fiction from fact. Throughout this book I use the memoirs as sources, but with extreme care. For an extended discussion of the memoirs as sources see Dargan, pp. xx–xxvi.

2. For particulars on Mme France not discussed in the works cited above, including her first marriage, see Suffel, "Autour d'A.F.: Documents inédits," *Mercure de France*, CCCX (Oct. 1, 1950), 248–65.

3. Noël France was born François-Noël Thibault; "France," the Angevin diminutive of François, was his nickname. He used France over his bookshop, and gradually the Thibault fell into disuse. His son, Anatole-François Thibault, followed parental practice. For details on Noël France, see Georges Huard, "Le Père d'A.F., François-Noël Thibault, libraire et éditeur (1805–1890)," *Bulletin du Bibliophile*, new series, 4th year (Mar. 1, 1925), 121–29; see also Suffel, *A.F.*, pp. 7–10, and Dargan, pp. 8–9.

4. A.F., *Œuvres complètes illustrées de A.F.*, ed. L. Carias et G. Le Prat (25 vols.; Paris: Calmann-Lévy, 1925–1935), III (*Le Livre de mon ami*), 221. (This collection will be cited hereafter as *O.C.*; the particular book cited in the *O.C.* will be indicated by title where necessary, as has been done here.)

5. Jean-Jacques Brousson, France's secretary for a time just after the turn of the century, quotes his master as saying that she tucked him into bed every night until he left home, married, at thirty-three—*A.F. en pantoufles* (Paris: G. Crès, 1924), pp. 221–22. Unfortunately, the memoirs of France's associates usually suffer from fictional touches as much or more than do his own, but the associates do not admit it. The book cited here is not fully trustworthy, nor are most others of its type. I use them with the same care I do those of France himself; on occasion, they are helpful. Dargan, pp. xxvi–xxix, discusses them in detail, but here, I think, his cautions are too weak; I trust these authors far less than he does, and have acted accordingly.

6. *O.C.*, XXIII (*La Vie en fleur*), 412.

7. André Vandegans, *A.F.: Les Années de formation* (Paris: Nizet, 1954), is the standard work on the years immediately after A.F.'s graduation; I follow it gratefully.

8. Suffel, "A.F., maître d'école," *Le Soir* (Brussels), Sept. 2, 1950; *O.C.*, III (*Les Désirs de Jean Servien*), 109–36. Suffel proves that France was at the Institut Sigisbert Pompée, and A.F. puts Jean Servien through difficulties that are universally accepted as his own.

9. Letter, F.-N. Thibault to the Comte de Chambord, Oct. 6, 1862, quoted in Girard, pp. 21–24.

10. The following discussion of France's aesthetic, religious, and philosophical development is essentially a summary of the

authoritative treatment by Vandegans in Part II of his study of A.F.

11. "Bibliographie," *L'Amateur d'Autographes* (Mar. 16, 1869), 90–91, quoted in Vandegans, p. 75.

12. *L'Amateur* (Mar. 16, 1869), 93, quoted in Vandegans, p. 81, n. 3.

13. "Les Livres," *Le Bibliophile français* (Feb., 1872), 48, quoted in Vandegans, p. 105.

14. "Les Romanciers contemporains," *Le Temps*, Nov. 24, 1875, quoted in Vandegans, p. 106.

15. Voltaire, quoted in Walter L. Dorn, *Competition for Empire, 1740–1763* (The Rise of Modern Europe; New York: Harper & Brothers, 1940), p. 211.

16. E.g., in *Méditations sur les ruines de Palmyre*, cited in Vandegans, p. 67.

17. O.C., I, 156, cited in Vandegans, p. 68.

18. Flammarion, *La Pluralité des mondes habités*, 10th ed., p. II, quoted in Vandegans, p. 91.

19. O.C., VII, 430, quoted in Vandegans, p. 95.

20. "Note sur la querelle des Imaginaires," *Œuvres de Jean Racine*, V (Paris: Lemerre, 1875), 104, quoted in Vandegans, p. 99; for his decision that Darwin's theory was not proved, see his "Les Origines humaines. I. La Terre," *La Musée des deux mondes*, I (July 15, 1873), 46.

21. Brousson, p. 192.

22. *Ibid.*, pp. 192–93.

23. Vandegans, p. 21; "Denys," *La Gazette rimée*, No. 2 (Mar. 20, 1867), 28–30; "Varus," *La Gazette*, No. 5 (June 20, 1867), 75–78; on the fate of *La Gazette*, L.-X. de Ricard, "Petites mémoires d'un Parnassien," *Le Temps*, Dec. 7, 1898.

24. Vandegans, pp. 21–22; bulletin de souscription, photocopy in Bibliothèque Nationale, Franciana, June 14, 1868 (original in Bibliothèque de la Ville de Paris). Franciana is a huge collection of loose-leaf scrapbooks made by one of France's greatest admirers, Jacques Lion, and since his death placed in the Periodical Room of the Bibliothèque Nationale. Because it is arranged chronologically, I refer to it by date rather than volume and page. It contains clippings, autograph letters, dinner programs, and all sorts of miscellaneous matter concerning A.F.

25. *L'Amateur* (July 1–16, 1868), 177, quoted in Vandegans, p. 22.

26. Vandegans, p. 22.

27. Fernand Calmettes, *Un Demi-Siècle littéraire: Leconte de Lisle et ses amis* (Paris: Librairies-Imprimeries réunies, 1902), pp. 296–97; he describes the political climate *chez* Leconte de Lisle on pp. 121–33.

28. Quoted in Vandegans, p. 29. On political affairs at this time, see Charles Seignobos, *L'Evolution de la 3ᵉ République: 1875–1914*, Vol. VIII of *Histoire de France contemporaine depuis la Révolution jusqu'à la paix de 1919*, ed. E. Lavisse (10 vols.; Paris: Hachette, 1919–1921), pp. 62–75.

29. *Le Rappel*, Sept. 17, 1869, cited by Vandegans, p. 29. Vandegans gives a good deal of weight to France's decisions to write for journals of various political complexions as evidence for his own political attitudes; I consider this evidence dubious, because it seems quite likely that in 1869 and 1870 France, in need of money all the time and really not very politically minded, would have written for whoever was likely to pay him.

30. Jan. 7, 1870; photocopy in B.N., Franciana; quoted in Vandegans, p. 31.

31. Professor Vandegans takes great pains to present all the arguments for and against France's authorship (p. 3, n. 1); he decides affirmatively, as do I.

32. Aug. 19, 1870, quoted in Vandegans, p. 33.

33. Vandegans, p. 34; Michel Corday, *A. F. d'après ses confidences et ses souvenirs* (Paris: Flammarion, 1927), pp. 51–52; A.F., "La Vie littéraire," *Le Temps*, June 26, 1892, and Dec. 9, 1888 (*O.C.*, VI, 611).

34. Letter, A.F. to Mme J. Charavay, Mar., 1871, quoted in Girard, p. 199; letter, A.F. to F. Calmettes, May 3, 1871, quoted in Vandegans, p. 35.

35. Letter, A.F. to Chas. Asselineau, May 4, 1871, quoted in Vandegans, p. 35.

36. Letter, A.F. to E. Charavay, June 4, 1871, quoted in Girard, p. 208.

37. *O.C.*, III, 164–65.

38. Sand to A.F., Apr. 26, 1876, quoted in Suffel, *A.F.*, p. 76; Taine to A.F., n.d. [Jan., 1876], quoted in Jeanne Maurice

Pouquet, *Le Salon de Madame Arman de Caillavet* (Paris: Hachette, 1926), pp. 60–61.

39. Girard, p. 233; Vandegans, p. 45.

40. On his misadventures in love, see Vandegans, pp. 45–46.

41. Letter of Comtesse de Martel (Gyp), quoted in Pouquet, p. 57, n. 1.

42. *Cf.* Vandegans, pp. 260–61, on France's switch from poetry to prose.

43. Dargan, p. 250; Flaubert to A.F., Mar. 7, 1879, quoted in Suffel, *A.F.*, pp. 96–97.

44. Brousson, p. 352; award quoted in Suffel, *A.F.*, p. 99.

45. France collected many of these columns to make four volumes numbered in series, each entitled *La Vie littéraire*, which were published in 1888, 1890, 1891, and 1892. Jacques Suffel edited a fifth volume, *La Vie littéraire, V*e *série* (Paris: Calmann-Lévy, 1949). France used parts of various columns in *Le Jardin d'Epicure* (1894) and in other books, often revising them before including them in volumes. I cite from the original newspaper column and include in parentheses references to the same column as it appeared in *O.C.* if it was included in a collection.

46. Virginie Demont-Breton, *Les Maisons que j'ai connues*, Vol. II: *Nos Amies artistes* (4th ed.; Paris: Plon, 1927), pp. 155–58.

47. In *Le Livre de mon ami, O.C.*, III, 343–66.

48. Suffel, *A.F.*, pp. 119–30, is the best account of A.F.'s life in the salons; Mme Pouquet's book is the major source.

49. Letter, n.d., quoted in Pouquet, p. 49.

50. *O.C.*, III, 365

51. *Le Temps*, May 22, 1888 (*O.C.*, VI, 453).

52. *Le Temps*, Oct. 30, 1887 (*O.C.*, VI, 296).

53. *Le Temps*, Sept. 4, 1887.

54. *Le Temps*, May 23, 1886 (*OC.*, IX, 433).

55. *Le Temps*, Mar. 11, 1888 (*O.C.*, VI, 476–77).

56. *Le Temps*, Apr. 24, 1887 (*OC.*, VI, 115).

57. *Le Temps*, Sept. 5, 1886.

58. *Ibid.*, Dec. 12, 1886.

59. *Ibid.*, June 13, 1886.

60. *Ibid.*, Sept. 19, 1886 (*O.C.*, IX, 405–07).

61. *O.C.*, VI, 326 (Mar. 2, 1890).

62. *Le Temps*, Oct. 29, 1888 (*O.C.*, VI, 5).

63. *Le Temps*, July 18, 1886.

64. *L'Univers illustré*, July 24, 1886, p. 466 (quoted at length in Charles Braibant, *Du Boulangisme au Panama: Le Secret d'A.F.* [Paris: Denoël et Steele, 1935], pp. 72–74).

65. *Le Temps*, Mar. 6, 1887 (*O.C.*, VI, 80).

66. *L'Univers illustré*, Aug. 8, 1885, pp. 498–99.

67. *Le Temps*, Oct. 31, 1886.

68. *Ibid.*, Aug. 15, 1886 (*O.C.*, X, 431–32).

69. *Le Temps*, Aug. 3, 1890.

70. *L'Univers illustré*, Mar. 31, 1883, p. 494; see also Aug. 25, 1888, p. 531.

71. *Le Journal des Débats*, Mar. 5, 1884; not published in book form.

72. *Le Temps*, Mar. 20, 1887 (*O.C.*, VI, 86).

73. *L'Univers illustré*, May 4, 1889, p. 274.

74. *Le Journal des Débats*, Mar. 16, 1884.

75. A.F., *Clio* and *The Château de Vaux-le-Vicomte*, trans. by W. Stephens (London: John Lane, 1923), p. 218.

76. *French Poets and Novelists* (London: Macmillan, 1884), pp. 102–03.

77. *L'Univers illustré*, Sept. 18, 1886, p. 594 (quoted in Braibant, p. 39). Here I depart radically from Braibant's interpretation; he failed to notice the difference between attacks on the "Red" city council and the conservative national government, and thus saw France as more liberal than he really was.

78. Barrès, "Les Hommes de la Jeune France. XIII. A.F.," *Jeune France*, V (Feb. 1, 1883), 589–610; Lemaître, "A.F.," *Revue politique et littéraire*, 3rd series, X (Sept. 12, 1885), 322–30; both these articles are summarized in Suffel, *A.F.*, pp. 121–22.

79. Quaesture du Sénat, extract from *arrêt* of Dec. 1, 1884, B.N., Nouvelles acquisitions françaises 13121, f. 134.

80. *Le Temps*, Dec. 19, 1886 (*O.C.*, VI, 32).

81. Louis Barthou, "A.F., commis-bibliothécaire au Sénat," *Revue de Paris*, CLXXXV (Dec. 1, 1924), 484.

82. Quoted *ibid.*, pp. 485–86.

83. Letter, Mme de C. to A.F., 1888, quoted in Suffel, *A.F.*, p. 160, n. 1.

84. The description of France's domestic difficulties that follows is based on information to be found in Pouquet, p. 57, n. 1

(a letter from Gyp to Pouquet, n.d.); Pierre Calmettes, *La Grand Passion d'A.F.* (Paris: Seheur, 1929), p. 47; *O.C.*, XI (*Le Mannequin d'osier*) and III (*Le Livre de mon ami*); and Dargan, pp. 204–06 and 380–84, where may be found the best and fullest study of France's married life.

85. Eighth year (October, 1885), pp. 529–35.

86. Letter, Mme de C. to J. Lemaître, n.d., quoted in Pouquet, p. 45; also Pouquet, p. 57.

87. Letter of Sept., 1887, quoted in Pouquet, p. 55.

88. Aug. 2, 1888, quoted in Suffel, *A.F.*, p. 152. (Suffel printed a number of extracts from this correspondence, which until recently was thought to have been destroyed.)

89. N.d., quoted *ibid.*, p. 153.

90. Suffel (ed.), *A.F. par lui-même* (Ecrivains de toujours; Paris: Seuil, 1954), p. 179.

2. *The Anarchist (1888–1898)*

1. *Le Temps*, Oct. 29, 1888 (*O.C.*, V, 5).

2. Suffel, *A.F.*, p. 152, and *A.F. par lui-même*, pp. 33–35.

3. *Le Temps*, Sept. 9, 1888 (*O.C.*, VI, 557).

4. For background on the Boulanger crisis, see Adrien Dansette, *Le Boulangisme* (Paris: Fayard, 1946).

5. *Le Temps*, July 18, 1886.

6. July 24, 1886, p. 466.

7. *Le Temps*, May 8, 1887 (*Vie litt.*, V, 31–35), and July 3, 1887.

8. *L'Univers illustré*, Dec. 17, 1887, p. 807.

9. *Ibid.*, May 5, 1888, p. 275.

10. J. and J. Tharaud, *Mes Années chez Barrès* (Paris: Plon, 1928), p. 170.

11. Letter, A.F. to Mme de C., Paris, n.d., quoted at length in Pouquet, pp. 82–83. This letter is the only piece of evidence with which to date the beginning of France's close association with Boulanger. Braibant dates it between Dec., 1887, and Apr. 1, 1889 (p. 90); Suffel says 1888 (*A.F.*, p. 165). It was written, how-

ever, after France had stayed at Capian with Mme de C., hence, late in September or early in October at the earliest; but Boulanger had been absent from Paris from Aug. 27 to Oct. 8; it is most unlikely that France dined with him on the day after his return, which was a Tuesday; ergo, the letter was probably written after Oct. 9, and certainly before the end of November, when Mme de C. returned to Paris.

12. Pouquet, p. 87.

13. Letters quoted in Pouquet, pp. 87–90; Dansette, p. 252.

14. Letter, n.d. [Jan. 30, 1889], quoted in Pouquet, p. 90.

15. Jacques Roujon, *La Vie et les opinions d'A.F.* (Paris: Plon, 1925), p. 27. This book, based partly on reminiscences the author got from his father, who knew France well, is not entirely reliable, but there is no reason to doubt the existence of the rumor; as for its truth, it seems unlikely, but Boulanger promised anything to anybody—and why shouldn't he have made A.F. a minister?

16. Feb. 9, 1889, p. 82, quoted in Braibant, p. 104.

17. Roujon, p. 27.

18. Braibant, pp. 90–96.

19. *Ibid.*, p. 101.

20. N.d., quoted in Pouquet, p. 95.

21. Letter, n.d., Mme de C. to friend, quoted *ibid.*

22. Letter, n.d., quoted *ibid.*, p. 96.

23. P. Brucker, "À propos d'un roman de *La Revue des deux mondes*," *Etudes religieuses, philosophiques, historiques et littéraires* (Dec., 1889), quoted at length in Suffel, *A.F.*, pp. 173–74.

24. *O.C.*, I, 249 (*Noces corinthiennes*, preface).

25. The description that follows is drawn largely from Dargan, pp. 393–97.

26. Marie Scheikévitch, *Time Past: Memories of Proust and Others*, trans. by F. Delisle (New York: Houghton Mifflin, 1935), p. 72; quoted in Dargan, p. 395.

27. Scheikévitch, pp. 76–77, describes M. Arman's character and his place in the household.

28. Myriam Harry, *Trois ombres: Huysmans, Lemaître, France* (Paris: Flammarion, 1932), quoted in Dargan, p. 395

29. Pouquet, pp. 78–82.

30. Because of this, I do not use these articles after 1890 as sources for A.F.'s opinions, except when his authorship is beyond doubt. Cf. Dargan (pp. 288–89), who takes the same course.

31. Pouquet, pp. 97–99.

32. Fernand Gregh, *L'Âge d'or. Souvenirs d'enfance et de jeunesse* (Paris: Grasset, 1947), p. 158.

33. Dargan, pp. 389–91.

34. *Ibid.*, pp. 380–83; Pouquet, pp. 122–24.

35. See, e.g., in "Vie litt." columns in *Le Temps*, on science: Dec. 1, 1889, Apr. 27, 1890 (*O.C.*, VII, 427–33), May 8, 1892 (*O.C.*, IX [*Jardin d'Epicure*], 430–31; on justice, Dec. 1, 1889; on emotions, Mar. 20 and May 8, 1892; on knowledge, June 15, 1890 (*Vie litt.*, V, 78–86), Nov. 8, 1891 (*Vie litt.*, V, 326; *O.C.*, IX, 455), May 8, 1892 (*O.C.*, IX, 430–31); on necessity for ignorance, Jan. 24, 1892 (*Vie litt.*, V, 126–35; *O.C.*, IX, 409); quotation, Feb. 5, 1893 (*O.C.*, IX, 424–25).

36. *O.C.*, VII, 63–71.

37. "Revue littéraire: À propos du *Disciple*," *Revue des deux mondes*, CCII (July 1, 1889), 222, 216, 220.

38. Also in *O.C.*, VII, 71–77.

39. Dargan, pp. 358–66, gives an excellent account of France's relations with the Symbolists; H. Mondor, *L'Affaire du Parnasse* (Paris: Editions Fragrance, 1951), covers another facet of the problem.

40. The original article was a "Vie litt." in *Le Temps*, Mar. 27, 1887; the pruned version is in *O.C.*, VI, 92–101.

41. *Le Temps*, Jan. 15, 1893 (*Vie litt.*, V, 270–78).

42. Dargan, pp. 354–56, summarizes the development of France's attitude toward Zola.

43. *Le Temps*, Sept. 4, 1887 (*O.C.*, VI, 213).

44. *Le Temps*, Apr. 20, 1890 (*O.C.*, VI, 355).

45. *Le Temps*, June 26, 1892.

46. *Le Temps*, Aug. 19, 1888 (*O.C.*, VI, 515–25); Nov. 25, 1888 (*O.C.*, VI, 603–08); Mar. 2, 1890 (*O.C.*, VI, 328 ff.).

47. Also in *O.C.*, VI, 15–22.

48. *Le Temps*, Jan. 19, 1890 (*O.C.*, VII, 247–56).

49. *Le Temps*, Mar. 30, 1890.

50. *L'Univers illustré*, Sept. 21, 1889, p. 595, quoted in Braibant, p. 107.

51. *Le Temps*, Nov. 18, 1888 (*O.C.*, VI, 595–602); Renan had written two sequels to the play, both published, shortly before this article was written, in his *Drames philosophiques* (Paris: Calmann-Lévy, 1888).

52. *Le Temps*, Oct. 11, 1891 (*O.C.*, IX [*Jardin d'Epicure*], 421–22); see also Jan. 31, 1892.

53. *Le Temps*, Nov. 16, 1890 (*O.C.*, IX, 445–46).

55. *L'Univers illustré*, Mar. 9, 1889, p. 147.

56. *Ibid.*, Feb. 22, 1890, p. 115.

57. *Ibid.*, Aug. 23, 1890, p. 531.

58. *Le Temps*, Sept. 7, 1890.

59. *L'Univers illustré*, May 17, 1890, p. 306.

60. May 4, 1890 (*O.C.*, VII, 365).

61. On charity hospitals, "Vie à Paris," *Le Temps*, Apr. 4, 1886; on physician, *L'Univers illustré*, Aug. 8, 1885, p. 498.

62. *L'Univers illustré*, July 12, 1890, p. 434, quoted at length in Braibant, pp. 187–88.

63. *L'Univers illustré*, July 26, 1890, p. 466.

64. *Ibid.*, Sept. 26, 1890, quoted in Braibant, p. 186.

65. "Vie à Paris," *Le Temps*, Mar. 21, 1886.

66. Paul Louis, *Histoire du socialisme en France* (5th ed.; Paris: Rivière, 1950), pp. 257–58; for details on the Clichy affair and other anarchist activities discussed in this chapter see Marius Boisson, *Les Attentats anarchistes sous la Troisième République* (Paris: Editions de France, 1931).

67. Also in *Vie litt.*, V, 136–43.

68. Quoted in Seignobos, p. 175.

69. *L'Univers illustré*, quoted in Braibant, pp. 213–14.

70. *Le Temps*, June 26, 1892.

71. *Ibid.*, July 3, 1892.

72. See the summary of criticism in Dargan, pp. 486–87.

73. *Le Temps*, Jan. 22, 1893 (*Vie litt.*, V, 279–85).

74. D. W. Brogan, *The Development of Modern France (1870–1939)* (London: Hamish Hamilton, 1940), pp. 268–85, gives the best short summary of the Panama affair.

75. *L'Echo de Paris*, Mar. 15, 1893 (*O.C.*, VIII, 365).

76. *L'Echo*, Mar. 22, 1893 (*O.C.*, VIII, 335).

77. *L'Echo*, Mar. 29, 1893 (*O.C.*, VIII, 354).

78. *L'Echo*, Apr. 5, 1893 (*O.C.*, VIII, 380).

79. *L'Echo*, Apr. 5, 1893 (*O.C.*, VIII, 384).
80. *L'Echo*, Apr. 12, 1893 (*O.C.*, VIII, 392).
81. *L'Echo*, May 3, 1893 (*O.C.*, VIII, 414).
82. *L'Echo*, June 14, 1893 (*O.C.*, VIII, 492).
83. *L'Echo*, July 19, 1893 (*O.C.*, VIII, 325).
84. *L'Echo*, July 19, 1893 (*O.C.*, VIII, 322).
85. *O.C.*, VIII, 327–39.
86. Cf. Braibant's discussion of *Opinions*, pp. 226–65.
87. *O.C.*, IX, 106–07.
88. Dargan, pp. 528–29.
89. *Ibid.*, pp. 513–28; Suffel, *A.F.*, pp. 215–24.
90. New York: Pyramid Books, 1959.
91. Dargan, pp. 596–97.
92. *Ibid.*, p. 600; the story of France's election told here follows Dargan, except as otherwise noted.
93. Gregh, *Âge d'or*, pp. 176–77.
94. Beginning Apr. 21, 1896, in *L'Echo de Paris*.
95. His last "Courrier de Paris" appeared on Sept. 20, 1896.
96. Dargan, pp. 593–95.
97. Archag Tschobanian, *L'Arménie: Son histoire, sa littérature, son rôle en Orient* (Paris: Mercure de France, 1897), quoted in A.F., *Vers les Temps meilleurs: Trente ans de vie sociale*, ed. Claude Aveline and H. Psichari (3 vols., one more in prep.; Paris, Emile Paul, 1949–), I, 4–5. (Hereafter cited as *Trente ans.*)
98. *L'Echo de Paris*, Mar. 16, 1897 (*O.C.*, XI [*Le Mannequin d'osier*], 364–65).

3. The Crusader (1898–1906)

1. Micheline Tison-Braun, *La Crise de l'humanisme*, Vol. I: *1890–1914* (Paris: Nizet, 1958).
2. *Ibid.*, p. 90.
3. *Ibid.*, p. 69, n. 1.
4. Michel Décaudin, *La Crise des valeurs symbolistes: Vingt ans de poésie française, 1895–1914* (Toulouse: Privat, 1960), pp. 128–40.

5. *Ibid.;* this is one of Décaudin's major conclusions.

6. Jan. 15, 1900, quoted in Tison-Braun, p. 133.

7. On the Dreyfus Affair, see Joseph Reinach, *Histoire de l'Affaire Dreyfus* (7 vols.; Paris: Fasquelle, 1901–1911); Guy Chapman, *The Dreyfus Case: A Reassessment* (New York: Reynal & Co., 1955); Louis Capéran, *L'Anticléricalisme et l'affaire Dreyfus, 1897–1899* (Toulouse: Imprimerie régionale, 1948); and Maurice Baumont, *Aux Sources de l'Affaire: L'Affaire Dreyfus d'après les archives diplomatiques* (Paris: Les Productions de Paris, 1960). Reinach was a Dreyfusard leader; Chapman, whose study is the most comprehensive recent effort, whitewashes the generals; Capéran is a Catholic apologist, but his study is still excellent; Baumont stresses certain complex details.

8. *France since 1789* (New York: Harper & Row, 1963), p. 258.

9. Also in *O.C.*, XII (*L'Anneau d'améthyste*), 15–22.

10. *L'Aurore*, Nov. 23, 1897.

11. Maurice Barrès, in *Mes Cahiers*, Vol. I: *1896–1898* (Paris: Plon, 1929), pp. 224–31, reports a conversation of Dec. 7, 1897, that shows that France was still uncommitted at that time.

12. Marcel Proust, *Correspondance générale*, ed. R. Proust and P. Brach, Vol. III (Paris: Plon, 1932), p. 71.

13. Gregh, *Âge d'or*, pp. 290–92.

14. France, *Trente ans*, I, 10.

15. *L'Echo de Paris*, Feb. 15, 1898 (*O.C.*, XII, 154).

16. *L'Echo de Paris*, Mar. 22 and 29, 1898.

17. *Ibid.*, Mar. 29, 1898.

18. *Ibid.;* this part of the dialogue is reproduced, with the names of the speakers changed, in France's *Pierre Nozière*, *O.C.*, X, 390–94 (the passage quoted here is on p. 391).

19. *L'Echo de Paris*, Mar. 29, 1898 (*O.C.*, X, 394).

20. *L'Echo*, Apr. 5, 1898 (*O.C.*, XII, 126–27).

21. *L'Echo*, May 24, 1898.

22. France, *Trente ans*, I, 12.

23. *Ibid.*

24. *L'Echo de Paris*, Nov. 22, 1898 (*O.C.*, XII, 183–90).

25. *L'Echo*, Nov. 29, 1898 (*O.C.*, XII, 257–61).

26. France, *Trente ans*, I, 13.

27. *L'Echo de Paris*, Dec. 27, 1898.

28. July 5, 1899 (*O.C.*, XII [*Monsieur Bergeret à Paris*], 342–45).

29. *Le Figaro*, Aug. 2, 1899.

30. *Ibid.*, July 26, 1899 (*O.C.*, XII, 355 ff.).

31. *Le Figaro*, July 12, 1899 (*O.C.*, XII, 420); and July 19, 1899, reprinted in A.F., *Opinions sociales* (Bibliothèque socialiste; 2 vols.; Paris: Cornély, 1906), II, 172–84.

32. *Le Figaro*, Aug. 9, 1899.

33. *Ibid.*, Aug. 16, 1899 (*O.C.*, XII, 405 ff.). France received at least one letter from Picquart, and Picquart had visited, or was to visit, the Villa Saïd.—Note, A.F. to Mme Louis Havet, n.d., B.N., N.A. fr. 24494 (2), f. 137; visiting card, A.F. to Louis Delaporte, n.d., B.N., Collection Lion, III, 3.

34. Gabriel Monod, review of *Monsieur Bergeret à Paris*, *Revue historique*, LXXVI (July–August, 1901), 379.

35. *Le Figaro*, Aug. 24, 1899.

36. *Ibid.*, Aug. 30, 1899.

37. Note, A.F. to Mme L. Havet; cf. the episode of the "Histoire contemporaine" in *Le Figaro*, Sept. 13, 1899.

38. France, *Trente ans*, I, 36.

39. *Ibid.*, p. 31.

40. *Le Figaro*, Nov. 15, 1899.

41. *L'Echo de Paris*.

42. *Le Figaro*, July 5, 1899 (*O.C.*, XII, 339–45).

43. *Le Figaro*, Aug. 9, 1899 (*O.C.*, XII, 326–27).

44. France, *Trente ans*, I, 27.

45. *Ibid.*, p. 29.

46. *Ibid.*, p. 57.

47. France said often that his participation in the Affair was the occasion for his conversion to socialism; e.g., in France, *Trente ans*, II, 201–02; and *L'Aurore*, Dec. 22, 1903. On his admiration for Jaurès, see, e.g., *La Tranchée républicaine* (Paris), July 25–Aug. 2, 1917.

48. G. Palante, "A.F., peintre social," *La Revue socialiste*, XXXIII (April, 1901), 442–52.

49. France, *Trente ans*, I, 68.

50. Some of the "H.C." episodes in the *Opinions sociales* were not included in *O.C.*, and thus are available only in the newspapers or in the Bibliothèque socialiste edition, cited earlier.

51. Publication began on Apr. 18, 1904, in the first number of *l'Humanité*. While preparing the manuscript for publication in book form, France added several fairly long passages that had not appeared in the newspaper; this final draft was published on Feb. 2, 1905. Citations refer to the definitive edition, as reprinted in *O.C.*, XIII.

52. *O.C.*, XIII, 479.

53. *Ibid.*, pp. 483–84.

54. *Ibid.*, p. 540.

55. *Ibid.*, p. 546.

56. The simile is from a "Vie litt." in *Le Temps*, May 8, 1892 (*O.C.*, IX, 431).

57. Cf. Aaron Noland, *The Founding of the French Socialist Party (1893–1905)* (Cambridge: Harvard University Press, 1956), pp. 206–07.

58. Adrien Dansette, *Histoire religieuse de la France contemporaine* (édition revue et corrigée; 2 vols.; Paris: Flammarion, 1951), is the standard account of relations between church and state in France since 1789. For the period up to 1870, Dansette's book has not entirely superseded the work of A. Debidour, *Histoire des rapports de l'Eglise et de l'Etat en France de 1789 à 1870* (Paris: Félix Alcan, 1898). Dansette is a liberal Catholic; Debidour was anticlerical. An excellent summary of the educational struggle between church and state from the Revolution to 1848, discussed below, may be found in Richard Howard Powers, *Edgar Quinet: A Study in French Patriotism* (Dallas: Southern Methodist University Press, 1957), pp. 98–125; a good study of the next few years is presented in Ross W. Collins, *Catholicism and the Second French Republic: 1848–1852* (New York: Columbia University Press, 1923); and the quarrel over education in the early years of the Third Republic is summarized in Brogan, pp. 144–63.

59. Dansette, *Hist. rel.*, II, 296; Brogan, pp. 360–61. The text of the pertinent articles of the law is quoted in Robert David, *La Troisième République: Soixante ans de politique et d'histoire (de 1871 à nos jours)* (Paris: Plon, 1934), pp. 313–14.

60. *Bulletin officiel de la Ligue des Droits de l'Homme*, July 1, 1902, cited in France, *Trente ans*, I, 76, n. 1.

61. France, *Trente ans*, I, 77.

62. *Ibid.*, pp. 82–85.

63. *Ibid.*, p. 94.

64. *Ibid.*, pp. 97–102.

65. David, pp. 330–36; Brogan, pp. 361–65; Dansette, *Hist. rel.*, II, 301–05.

66. *Cahiers de la Quinzaine, XXIᵉ cahier de la IIIᵉ série* (August, 1902), 198–215.

67. *Ibid.*, pp. 207, 214–15.

68. Cf. a similar opinion on this question in Sidney D. Braun, "Péguy and Bernard Lazare: A Common Mystique," *Symposium*, IV (May, 1950), 131–40.

69. *La Petite République*, Aug. 3, 1902, quoted in Romain Rolland, *Péguy* (2 vols.; Paris: Albin Michel, 1944), I, 98.

70. *C. de la Q., XVᵉ cahier de la IIIᵉ série* (May, 1902); and *Iᵉʳ cahier de la IVᵉ série* (October, 1902). (The October number was the first popular edition of "L'Affaire Crainquebille.")

71. France, *Trente ans*, I, 116–20.

72. *Ibid.*, p. 124.

73. "M. Patru, ou la liberté," *L'Aurore*, Dec. 27, 1902 (*O.C.*, XXV, 295–305).

74. France, *Trente ans*, I, 133.

75. René Johannet, in his *Vie et mort de Péguy* (Paris: Flammarion, 1950), p. 125.

76. Dansette, *Hist. rel.*, II, 306–08; David, pp. 316, n. 1, 346.

77. Draft in B.N., Coll. Lion, IV, 21–22.

78. France, *Trente ans*, I, 152–66.

79. The Combes book appeared on Jan. 5, 1904; later the preface was republished as part of France's *L'Eglise et la République* (Paris: Pelletan, 1904), which, in turn, was reprinted in France, *Trente ans*, I, 171–72, and II, 22–42 and 69–72. Citations refer to *Trente ans*.

80. France, *Trente ans*, II, 39–42.

81. Publication details *ibid.*, I, 170, and II, 8.

82. Typed copy of letter, Mme de C. to Henri Monod, Nov. 11, 1903, in B.N., Franciana.

83. For details on the incident described here see Dansette, *Hist. rel.*, II, 313–29; Alexandre Zévaès, *Histoire de la IIIᵉ République* (Nouvelle ed.; Paris: Nouvelle Revue critique, 1946), pp. 245–46; and Brogan, pp. 374–75.

84. The most detailed history of the "Affaire des Fiches" easily available is in David, pp. 370–77; Brogan, pp. 379–87, also is good. Combes told his side of the story in his *Mon Ministère: Mémoires, 1902–1905,* ed. Maurice Sorre (Paris: Plon, 1956), pp. 242 ff.

85. *Bulletin officiel de la Ligue des Droits de l'Homme,* V (Jan. 16, 1905), 1–7.

86. Letter, Reinach to Pressensé, *Le Temps,* Dec. 19, 1904, reprinted *ibid.,* V, 9–10.

87. *Bulletin,* V, 15–19.

88. France, *Trente ans,* I, 175–79; II, 8.

89. Suffel, *A.F.,* pp. 272, 295; letter, A.F. to Dr. Cezaux, Dec. 25, 1902, B.N., Coll. Lion, III, 93–94; Brogan, p. 382.

90. France, *Trente ans,* I, 214–19.

91. *Neue Freie Presse,* Dec. 15, 1904, reprinted in *L'Eglise et la République* as chap. VIII; France, *Trente ans,* II, 55–61.

92. *Neue Freie Presse,* Jan. 5, 1905, published in advance in *L'Eglise et la République* (Jan. 1, 1905) as chap. IX; France, *Trente ans,* II, 67.

93. Paul Grunebaum-Ballin, *La Séparation des Eglises et de l'Etat: Etude juridique sur le projet Briand et le projet du gouvernement,* preface by A.F. (Paris: Bellais, 1905), in France, *Trente ans,* II, 73.

94. France, *Trente ans,* I, 19–20.

95. Maurice Baumont, *L'Essor industriel et l'impérialisme colonial (1878–1904)* (Peuples et civilisations, Histoire générale; 2d ed.; Paris: Presses universitaires de France, 1949), pp. 246–49.

96. France, *Trente ans,* I, 42–50, 71, 113, 138–39, 143–45.

97. See, e.g., *Vie litt.,* V, 10–20.

98. E.g., in "Histoire contemporaine," *O.C.,* XII, 233–34.

99. *Opinions sociales,* II, 120–27.

100. France, *Trente ans,* I, 101.

101. *Ibid.,* I, 183 and II, 117–21; *O.C.,* XIII, 374–75.

102. Félicien Challaye, *Le Congo français: La Question internationale du Congo* (Paris: Albin Michel, 1909), pp. 108–44.

103. In 1902, in *Histoire comique, O.C.,* XIII, 228–32; in 1904, in the *Neue Freie Presse;* France, *Trente ans,* I, 199–204.

104. France, *Trente ans,* I, 205–09.

105. *L'Humanité,* Jan. 24, 25, 26, 27, and ff., 1906.

106. France, *Trente ans*, II, 135–39.

107. *L'Humanité*, Feb. 22, 1906.

108. France, *Trente ans*, II, 151–52.

109. *Ibid.*, pp. 82, 90–93, 128–33; the quotations are from p. 107.

110. *Ibid.*, p. 60.

111. *Ibid.*, p. 132.

112. *Ibid.*, pp. 73–74.

113. For a concise summary of Franco-Russian relations during this period, see Pierre Renouvin, *La Crise européenne et la première guerre mondiale* (Peuples et civilisations, Histoire générale; 3d ed.; Paris: Presses universitaires de France, 1948), pp. 99–106, 131–56; also Brogan, pp. 396 ff., 402.

114. France, *Trente ans*, I, 66.

115. *Ibid.*, pp. 66–67.

116. Nina Gourfinkel (ed.), *Gorki par lui-même* (Ecrivains de toujours; Paris: Seuil, 1954), pp. 42–45.

117. France, *Trente ans*, II, 75.

118. *Ibid.*, pp. 76–83, 85–100.

119. *Ibid.*, pp. 76–79 (Jan. 27, 1905).

120. Resolution passed at meeting Feb. 3, 1905, quoted *ibid.*, p. 88.

121. France, *Trente ans*, II, 101–03, 153–55 (April, 1906), 196–99 (June, 1906).

122. *Ibid.*, pp. 119–20.

123. *Ibid.*, p. 211.

124. Georges Deherme, founder of the U.P. Coopération des Idées, quoted in Université Populaire, Coopération des Idées [A. Kownacki], *Histoire de douze ans (1818–1910)* (Paris: La Coopération du Livre, 1910), p. 7.

125. Edouard Herriot, *In Those Days: Before the First World War*, trans. by A. de Milly (New York: Old and New World Publishing Co., n.d.), p. 148; see also Daniel Halévy, in his preface to Charles Guieysse, *Pages libres: Extraits* (Hennebont: Méhat, 1927), p. 5.

126. Guesde, in interview in *Le Temps*, Apr. 12, 1900; Lafargue, in *Le Socialiste, Organe central du Parti Ouvrier français* (Guesdiste weekly), Mar. 11, 1900.

127. France, *Trente ans*, I, 35 (Jan. 7, 1900).

128. *Ibid.*, p. 81 (Jan. 19, 1902).

129. *Ibid.*, pp. 33, 37, 40, 55, 67, etc.

130. For examples of the arguments, see Kownacki, pp. 15–16, 18–19; and F. Challaye, *Péguy socialiste* (Paris: Amiot-Dumont, 1954), p. 143. On the breakup of the movement, see D. Halévy, "Un Episode," in his *Luttes et problèmes* (Paris: Rivière, 1911); R. Rolland, *Jean-Christophe à Paris: La Foire sur la place* (3d ed.; Paris: Ollendorf, 1908), pp. 215–17; Johannet, *Péguy*, p. 168. Brogan's account (pp. 371–72) is illuminating, but, despite the steady brilliance and accuracy of his book, his interpretation of the demise of the U.P.'s is not entirely correct; he neglects the bourgeois-socialist quarrel. There is no general study on the subject.

131. Kownacki, *passim.*

132. France, *Trente ans*, II, 182–85.

133. Suffel, *A.F. par lui-même*, p. 184.

134. France, *Trente ans*, II, 174 (mid-April, 1906).

4. The Socialist (1906–1917)

1. Georges and Edouard Bonnefous, *Histoire politique de la Troisième République* (4 vols.; Paris: Presses universitaires de France, 1956–1961), I, 34–35; David, p. 406.

2. France, *Trente ans*, II, 222 (article in *Neue Freie Presse*, Oct. 28, 1906).

3. Brogan, p. 423; Bonnefous, I, 19.

4. Edouard Dolléans, *Histoire du mouvement ouvrier* (3 vols.; Paris: Armand Colin, 1936–1953), II (5th ed., 1957), 142–145.

5. Quoted *ibid.*, p. 134.

6. Jules Renard, *Journal, 1887–1910* (Bibliothèque de la Pléiade, Vol. CXLV; Paris: Gallimard, 1960), p. 1095.

7. O.C., XVIII, 78.

8. *Ibid.*, pp. 342, 410 (capitalism); 401 (justice); 240 (statesmen).

9. *Ibid.*, p. 258.

10. *Ibid.*, p. 294.

11. *Ibid.*, p. 356.

12. *Ibid.*, p. 259.

13. *Ibid.*, p. 323.

14. Typical of those who interpret *L'Île des pingouins* as nihilistic is N. Addamiano, *A.F., l'uomo e l'opera* (Padua: Cedam, 1947), p. 290; among France's friends, one who objected to the tone of the book was Jaurès, quoted in Blanche Vogt, "Un Jaurès inconnu," *Les Œuvres libres,* no. 140 (February, 1933), p. 320.

15. The reviewer was René Doumic, in "M. A.F. chez les Pingouins," *Revue des deux mondes,* XLVIII (Nov. 15, 1908), 453; among the critics are Haakon Chevalier, in his *The Ironic Temper: A.F. and His Time* (New York: Oxford University Press, 1932), p. 38, n. 1, and Felix Giovanelli, in his "The Role of Contemporary Events in A.F.'s Works," unpublished Ph.D. dissertation, University of Illinois, 1939, p. 244.

16. *New York Herald* (Paris edition), Dec. 15, 1907 (Christmas number).

17. *O.C.,* XV, 61.

18. Edouard Héberlin-Darcy, *L'Esquisse d'une société collectiviste* (Jussy: Albert Fournier, 1908); preface reprinted in France, *Trente ans,* II, 293–94.

19. *O.C.,* XXV, 353.

20. *Ibid.,* XVIII, 473.

21. *Ibid.,* XIX, 246, 275–76, 291–92.

22. *Pro Armenia,* Aug. 20, 1907, quoted in France, *Trente ans,* II, 231–33; *Le Courrier européen,* Feb. 25, 1908, cited in France, *Trente ans,* II, 237–38.

23. Charles Vuille, *Bertoni, doit-il être expulsé? Lettre ouverte à tous ceux qui voudront bien la lire. Avec deux lettres de A.F.* . . . (n.p., n.d.; France's letter dated Jan. 23, 1907), quoted in France, *Trente ans,* II, 228; *L'Aurore,* June 13, 1907, cited in France, *Trente ans,* II, 230; *l'Humanité,* Apr. 6, 1908, quoted in France, *Trente ans,* II, 244–45.

24. Letter, A.F. to M. Morhardt, Nov. 6, 1908, quoted in France, *Trente ans,* II, 290; *La Revue,* Apr. 15, 1908, quoted in France, *Trente ans,* II, 249–50.

25. *O.C.,* XVII, 272.

26. *Ibid.*, p. 293.

27. France, *Trente ans,* III, 32.

28. Dargan, pp. 386–400; Pouquet, pp. 247–49; Scheikévitch, p. 89.

29. Pouquet, p. 250. For other details, see Pouquet, pp. 250–63; Suffel, *A.F. par lui-même,* p. 84; Jacob Axelrad, *A.F.: A Life Without Illusions* (3d ed.; New York: Harper & Brothers, 1944), p. 359.

30. France to M. Aunis, Jan. 12, 1910, quoted in Pouquet, p. 262; Scheikévitch, pp. 96–97; Gregh, *L'Âge d'airain (Souvenirs 1905–1925)* (Paris: Grasset, 1951), p. 135; Pouquet, p. 263.

31. Preface to Sándor Kémeri [Mme Georges Bölöni], *Promenades d'A.F.* (Paris: Calmann-Lévy, 1927), pp. i–ii; cf. Harry, 219–20.

32. Kémeri, p. 62.

33. Suffel, *A.F. par lui-même,* pp. 93–98; Jean Bouvard, "Les Souvenirs inédits du médecin d'A.F. [P.-L. Couchoud]," *Le Dauphiné libéré* (Grenoble), Mar. 24, 1954, p. 3; A. Rouveyre, "Brandès parmi nous," *Mercure de France,* CXCIV (Mar. 15, 1927), 576–77.

34. France, Carnets, B.N., N.A. fr. 24358–24361; Léon Carias' collection of excerpts from these little notebooks, *Les Carnets intimes d'A.F.* (Paris: Emile-Paul, 1946), contains everything of value in them except notations concerning France's literary work; the entries quoted are all in the published collection, on pp. 88, 85, 87, 110, 86, 97, 90, 90 (in the order quoted).

35. Dargan, p. 384.

36. Suffel, *A.F.,* p. 290; Victor Giraud, *A.F.* ("Temps et visages"; Paris: Desclée de Brouwer, 1935), pp. 206–07, includes a bibliography of several typical reviews; on the secretary, see *O.C.,* XV, 72.

37. Luc Durtain, *Georges Duhamel* (Paris: Cahiers des amis des livres, 4ᵉ cahier, 1920), pp. 9–10.

38. *O.C.,* XXII (*La Révolte des anges*), 300–01; cf. Raoul Girardet, *La Société militaire dans la France contemporaine* (Paris: Plon, 1953), pp. 238–40; and Eugen Weber, *The Nationalist Revival in France, 1905–1914* (Berkeley: University of California Press, 1959), pp. 36–37.

39. France's letter in *Trente ans*, III, 107–8; on the Ferrer case, see *l'Humanité*, July 24, 28, 29, 31; Sept. 3, 4, 5, 6, 12; and Oct. 14, 18, 1909.

40. So said Aveline, after a long search (France, *Trente ans*, I, xlv); another search produced the same result.

41. A.F., *Aux Etudiants: Discours prononcé à la Maison des Etudiants le samedi 28 mai 1910* . . . (Paris: Pelletan, 1910), p. 37.

42. *Ibid.*, p. 34.

43. *Ibid.*, p. 36.

44. O.C., XX, 78.

45. *Ibid.*, pp. 130–31.

46. France once warned his listeners at an informal manuscript reading that they should not make the mistake of taking the opinions of his characters as his own (O.C., XX, 334); it is more important not to forget that he often used more than one character as his spokesman. Giovanelli was the first critic to notice that Brotteaux was not France's only alter ego in *Les Dieux ont soif* (cf. his dissertation, p. 268).

47. O.C., XX, 282.

48. *Ibid.*, pp. 196–97.

49. *Ibid.*, pp. 169–70.

50. Corday, p. 148.

51. O.C., XX, 154.

52. Jean Jaurès, review of *Les Dieux ont soif*, *Revue de l'enseignement primaire*, no. 41 (July 5, 1912), reprinted *ibid.*, p. 355.

53. *Ibid.*, p. 357.

54. O.C., XXII, 322.

55. E.g., Paul Souday, in *Le Temps*, Mar. 26, 1924; Ernest Seillière, *A.F., critique de son temps* (Paris: Nouvelle Revue critique, 1934), p. 215; Carias, *A.F.* (Paris: Rieder, 1931), p. 76; and even Suffel, *A.F.*, p. 325.

56. In his *A.F. et Voltaire* (Geneva: Droz, 1961), pp. 184–86; Helen B. Smith, in her *The Skepticism of A.F.* (Paris: Presses universitaires de France, 1927), pp. 118–19, is the only earlier critic I have found who takes a similar position, even though this interpretation is so obviously correct.

57. *Le Socialisme intégral* (2nd ed.; 2 vols.; Paris: Félix Alcan, 1891), I, 62.

58. On Gohier, see France, *Trente ans*, I, 17; on militia, O.C., XII, 326–27; for Trublet quotation, O.C., XIII, 231.

59. France, *Trente ans*, I, 192.

60. *Ibid.*, p. 214.

61. A.F. and Jean Jaurès, *Deux discours sur Tolstoï* (Paris: L'Emancipatrice, 1911), p. 10.

62. *Ibid.*, p. 11.

63. France, *Trente ans*, II, 163–68.

64. Renouvin, pp. 147–49, 157–61.

65. France, *Trente ans*, III, 149–53.

66. A.F. to P.-L. Couchoud, Paris, Aug. 26, 1911 (photostat in B.N., Franciana).

67. E.g., in a letter marking the tenth anniversary of Zola's death in *Gil Blas*, Oct. 6, 1912.

68. Bonnefous, I, 337–40; Weber, esp. Part Three.

69. *L'Organisation socialiste: L'Armée nouvelle* (Paris: J. Rouff, 1911); this book is analyzed in Richard D. Challener, *The French Theory of the Nation in Arms, 1866–1939* (Columbia Studies in Social Sciences, No. 579; New York: Columbia University Press, 1955), pp. 72–74.

70. Bonnefous, I, 339–42.

71. France, *Trente ans*, III, 203.

72. Interview by François Crucy, *l'Humanité*, May 23, 1913, reprinted in France, *Trente ans*, III, 207–10.

73. Interview in the *Manchester Guardian*, June 26, 1913 (dispatch from Paris correspondent), reprinted in France, *Trente ans*, III, 220.

74. B.N., Coll. Lion, IV, 98.

75. "Pour la Paix," *English Review*, XV (August, 1913), 9, 11; this article also appears in France, *Trente ans*, III, 223–29.

76. France, *Trente ans*, III, 156.

77. *La Bataille syndicaliste*, July 25, 1911.

78. France, *Trente ans*, III, 162.

79. *L'Humanité*, Jan. 19, 21, 28–31, Feb. 14, 21, 1912; France, *Trente ans*, III, 173.

80. *L'Humanité*, Feb. 12, 1912. (Rousset was freed a year later when his appeal was heard.—Jean Grave, *Le Mouvement libertaire sous la 3ᵉ République* [*Souvenirs d'un révolté*] [Paris: Les Œuvres représentatives, 1930], pp. 236–37.)

81. On Quillard, see France, *Trente ans*, III, 170–72; on Persia, *L'Humanité*, Feb. 10, 1912; and on China, *l'Humanité*, Mar. 15, 1912; reprinted in France, *Trente ans*, III, 175–76.

82. *Les Droits de l'Homme* (Paris), Sept. 7 to 21, 1913.

83. *L'Humanité*, Mar. 15, 1914; letter quoted below also printed in France, *Trente ans*, III, 262–63.

84. *Le Temps*, May 4, 1914; *Le Matin*, May 1, 1914; *l'Humanité*, May 3, 1914; letter in France, *Trente ans*, III, 266–67.

85. *Les Droits de l'Homme*, May 16 to 23, 1914; speech also printed in France, *Trente ans*, III, 269–71.

86. Bonnefous, I, 405–06.

87. Letter, A.F. to L. Kahn, Chartres, n.d., in *Catalogue de la Bibliothèque et des correspondances autographes et manuscrits ayant appartenu à M. Léopold Kahn, ami d'A.F.*, preface by D. Halévy (Paris: G. Andrieux, 1935), p. 42 (no. 142).

88. *La Guerre sociale*, Sept. 22, 1914; reprinted in France, *Trente ans*, III, 273–74.

89. Mun, in *L'Echo de Paris*, Sept. 23, 1914; Maurras, in *L'Action française* the same day; Clemenceau in *L'Homme libre* (Bordeaux), Sept. 27, 1914; *l'Humanité*, Sept. 26, 1914.

90. *La Guerre sociale*, Sept. 28, 1914 (reprinted in France, *Trente ans*, III, 275); Maurras in *L'Action française*, Sept. 29, 1914; on the abusive letters, Suffel, *A.F.*, p. 337, and Harry, p. 227; *Le Temps*, Oct. 3, 1914.

91. Oct. 21, 1914.

92. A.F. to L. Kahn, Oct. 22, 1914, in Kahn catalogue, p. 42 (no. 192).

93. *L'Echo de Paris* (Bordeaux edition), Nov. 3, 1914.

94. On enemies, letter, A.F. to G. Hervé, *La Guerre sociale*, Jan. 1, 1915, reprinted in A.F., *Sur la Voie glorieuse* (25th ed.; Paris: Champion, 1916), p. 35; on barbarians, *Voie glorieuse*, pp. 55–71, *passim* (Feb. 1, 1915); on vandalism, *Le Petit Parisien*, Mar. 9, 1915; on German army, letter to editor of *Clarion* (London), Apr. 15, 1915, in *Voie glorieuse*, pp. 75–76. The Quai d'Orsay letter went to [William] English Walling, n.d., in *Voie glorieuse*, pp. 79–82; for remarks about it, see letter J. Longuet to A.F., Chantenay (Seine), Apr. 27, 1915, typed copy in B.N., Franciana; and visiting card, A.F. to J. Lion [Apr. 30, 1915], B.N., Coll. Lion, V, 78.

95. A.F. to J. Lion, La Béchellerie [May 17, 1915], B.N., Coll. Lion, V, 107–08.

96. *Novosti (Les Nouvelles)*, May 1, 1915.

97. May 3, 1915.

98. *Voie glorieuse* (appeared June 4, 1915).

99. *La Liberté*, June 27, 1915.

100. *Ce que disent nos morts* (Paris: Helleu, 1916).

101. E. Wasserman, in J. de Lacretelle, *À la rencontre de France*, suivi de *A.F. vu par un Américain*, par E. Wasserman (trad. de J. de Lacretelle) (Paris: Trémois, 1930), p. 47.

102. Suffel, *A.F.*, pp. 341–42.

103. B.N., Coll. Lion, VI, 80–81.

104. Jan. 6, 1916; B.N., Coll. Lion, VI, 74.

105. Letter, A.F. to L. Kahn [about July 10, 1916], Kahn catalogue, p. 46 (no. 202).

106. Letter, quoted in Suffel, *A.F.*, p. 346.

107. Inscription in Wasserman's copy of *Ce que disent nos morts*, quoted in Lacretelle, *Rencontre*, p. 56.

108. René Arcos, *Romain Rolland* (Paris: Mercure de France, 1950), pp. 52, 167; Arcos cites no source for this information, but Professor William T. Starr of Northwestern University, who has studied Rolland's correspondence, has informed me that the assertion is based on an unpublished letter, R.R. to Mme Louise Cruppi, Dec. 17, 1921, in which Rolland attributes the original proposal of his name to the Nobel committee to A.F.

109. Letter, Dec. 15, 1916, quoted in Romain Rolland, *Journal des anneés de guerre, 1914–1919. Notes et documents pour servir à l'histoire morale de ce temps*, ed. Marie Romain Rolland (Paris: Albin Michel, 1952), p. 1008.

110. A.F. to E. Richtenberger, Feb. 2, 1917, quoted in Suffel, *A.F.*, p. 347; copy in B.N., Franciana.

111. *La Tranchée républicaine*, May 1 to 9, 1917; *Revue mensuelle* (Geneva), No. 190 (June, 1917), pp. 302–03.

112. Vaillant-Couturier, "How A.F. Turned Against the War," *The Nation*, CXX (Apr. 15, 1925), 406–07; Barbusse to Lefebvre, Chartres, Feb. 16, 1916, Archives André Marty, Harvard University microfilm, Roll No. 1, in which Barbusse thanks Lefebvre for informing him of the results of the conference with France, and says "l'adhésion si complète et si effective d'un

homme de l'importance et du rayonment de France est un appoint considérable"; Barbusse to Marty, n.p., Mar. 21, 1917, in which Barbusse explains the conditions governing France's adhesion, indicating that he is still quite pleased with France's conduct. I cite these letters at length in order to dispel the impression left by Vaillant-Couturier, who implies in his article that France's refusal to participate openly in the group during the war was then viewed as unpardonable cowardice. Barbusse and Lefebvre evidently found France's conduct, if not courageous, at least not remarkably pusillanimous. Vaillant's account was written in 1925, after events discussed in the following chapters had estranged him from France.

113. "Pour la liberté," *Les Nations*, I (June 29, 1917), 1.

114. To L. Kahn, Kahn catalogue, p. 51 (no. 215).

115. Photocopy in J. Caillaux, *Mes Mémoires*, Vol. III: *Clairvoyance et force d'âme dans les épreuves, 1912–1930* (Paris: Plon, 1947), facing p. 113.

116. *Le Figaro*, June 4, 1918.

117. *Le Temps*, Aug. 10, 1917.

118. Notably by Rolland, in his *Journal de guerre*, pp. 1824–25.

119. Corday, p. 207.

5. The "Bolshevik" (1917–1924)

1. Manuscript copies of both telegrams in B.N., Coll. Lion, VII, 6.

2. To L. Kahn, n.d., Kahn catalogue, p. 53 (no. 218).

3. To Kahn, Jan. 9, 1918, Kahn catalogue, pp. 52–53 (no. 217).

4. To Kahn, n.d., Kahn catalogue, p. 56 (no. 227).

5. To Kahn, n.d. [Oct., 1917], Kahn catalogue (no. 226).

6. To Kahn, n.d. [Mar., 1917], Kahn catalogue, p. 57 (no. 231).

7. Mar. 26, 1919.

8. *L'Humanité*, Apr. 7, 1919.

9. *Ibid.*; J. Paul-Boncour, *Entre Deux guerres: Souvenirs sur la IIIᵉ République*, Vol. II: *Les Lendemains de la Victoire (1919–1934)* (Paris: Plon, 1945), p. 16.

10. *L'Humanité,* Aug. 9, 1919.

11. *Ibid.,* Oct. 19, 1919.

12. To Dr. Mignon, n.d. [Oct. 24, 1919], B.N., Coll. Lion, VII, 56–57.

13. Brogan, pp. 556–61.

14. *L'Humanité,* Nov. 6, 1919.

15. A.F. to Bracke and to the Comité électoral du troisième secteur de Paris, n.d., in *La Feuille commune* (*Humanité* columns), Nov. 16, 1919.

16. Milk appeal in *Clarté,* Oct. 25, 1919; soldier appeal, *Clarté,* Jan. 10, 1920; pogroms, *l'Humanité,* Feb. 16, 1920; Lefebvre, *l'Humanité,* Mar. 9, 1920; Latzko, *l'Humanité,* Mar. 11, 1920.

17. *Clarté,* May 1, 1920.

18. *L'Humanité,* Aug. 14, 1920.

19. Suffel, *A.F.,* pp. 359–62; *France par lui-même,* pp. 117–19.

20. *L'Humanité,* Oct. 12, 1920.

21. Refusal, *ibid.,* Oct. 19, 1919; François Crucy, "A.F.," *Floréal,* I (Sept. 18, 1920), 757–58; marriage, *l'Humanité,* Oct. 12, 1920; Crainquebille, *l'Humanité,* Aug. 19, 1919; Corday, pp. 67–72.

22. A.F. to P. Calmettes [Jan. 23, 1920], quoted in P. Calmettes, *Grande Passion,* p. 9.

23. Louis, chap. XI; Gérard Walter, *Histoire du Parti communiste français* (Paris: Somogy, 1948), pp. 1–42; A. Zévaès, *Histoire du socialisme et du communisme en France de 1871 à 1947* (Paris: France-Empire, 1947), p. 377; L.-O. Frossard, *De Jaurès à Lénine: Notes et souvenirs d'un militant* (Paris: Nouvelle Revue socialiste, 1930), p. 5.

24. Jan. 11, 1921.

25. Jan. 14, 1921.

26. *O.C.,* XXIII, 482.

27. *Ibid.,* p. 499.

28. *Ibid.,* p. 560.

29. *Ibid.,* p. 564.

30. *Clarté,* June 17, 1921.

31. "A.F. to the People of America," *The Nation,* CXIII (Nov. 23, 1921), 586.

32. *L'Humanité,* Dec. 13, 1921.

33. Suffel, in *A.F.*, p. 362.

34. Nov. 19, 1921; on the political position of *Clarté*, see Barbusse's article "Clarté" in the same issue.

35. *L'Humanité*, Dec. 13, 1921, on the speech; Jan. 19, 1922, on the book.

36. On Caillaux and Malvy, see interview by Philip Carr, *The Observer*, Jan. 22, 1922; on Goldsky, *l'Humanité*, Jan. 22, 1922; on Russia, *l'Humanité*, Feb. 17, 1922.

37. *Le Journal du peuple* (Paris), Feb. 19, 1922.

38. *L'Action française*, Feb. 20, 1922; *Le Populaire*, Feb. 19, 1922.

39. Feb. 20, 1922.

40. Frederick L. Schuman, *Russia since 1917: Four Decades of Soviet Politics* (New York: Alfred A. Knopf, 1957), pp. 12–13, 73, 81, 91, 100, 107, 113–14, 132.

41. *Le Temps*, Mar. 18, 1922.

42. *L'Humanité*, Apr. 26, 1922.

43. *Ibid.*, June 8, 1922.

44. *L'Œuvre* (Paris), July 7, 1922.

45. Manuscript letter in B.N., Coll. Lion, VII, 94–95; published, corrected, in *l'Humanité*, July 11, 1922.

46. *Avanti*, July 23, 1922; *l'Humanité*, Oct. 15, 1922.

47. Nov. 8, 1922.

48. *L'Humanité*, Nov. 6, 1922.

49. *Ibid.*, Nov. 30, 1922.

50. *Ibid.*, Dec. 18, 1922; excerpts in Walter, pp. 121–22.

51. *L'Humanité*, Dec. 29–30, 1922, and Jan. 7, 1923; Walter, p. 122.

52. *Le Temps*, Mar. 12, 1923.

53. *Le Populaire*, Mar. 12, 1923.

54. Mar. 12, 1923.

55. "La Houille rouge," review of book of same title by M. Corday, *La République*, I (Apr. 28, 1923), 5–6.

56. *Le Populaire*, Apr. 16, 1924.

57. At Carmaux, *Le Populaire*, June 4, 1923, and *La Dépêche* (Toulouse), June 4, 1923; at Toulouse, *L'Œuvre*, June 5, 1923, and *l'Humanité*, June 4, 1923.

58. Both Feb. 6, 1924.

59. Polls: *Crapouillot,* Oct. 1, 1923, and *Les Maîtres de la plume,* I (Jan. 15, 1924), 12; *Paris-Soir,* Apr. 16, 1924; *l'Humanité,* Apr. 15, 1924.
60. May 11, 1924.
61. *Le Populaire,* Apr. 17, 1924; *Le Cri des jeunes* (Montpellier), May 3, 1924.
62. [Urbain Gohier,] "A.F. ou 'Monsieur Rance,'" *La Vieille-France,* No. 366 (May 1, 1924), pp. 1–3.
63. *L'Œuvre,* May 14, 1924.
64. *Le Populaire* and *Le Quotidien,* May 25, 1924.
65. May 25, 1924.
66. Suffel, *A.F.,* pp. 372–73.

Conclusion

1. Marvin Lowenthal (ed.), *The Autobiography of Michel de Montaigne* (New York: Vintage Books, 1956), p. 181.
2. *The Taxis of the Marne,* trans. by Harold King (New York: Simon and Schuster, 1957), pp. 55, 85.
3. *La Vie ouvrière,* Oct. 17, 1924; Cachin, *l'Humanité,* Oct. 16, 1924; anniversary article by Jean Fréville, *l'Humanité,* Oct. 20, 1954. For one of the best of the admiring socialist treatments, see the oddly titled work of Axelrad, *A.F., A Life Without Illusions.*

Bibliography

I. WORKS BY ANATOLE FRANCE

A. Manuscripts

France, Anatole. Correspondence. B.N., Nouvelles acquisitions françaises 13121.

———. Carnets. Bibliothèque Nationale, Paris, Nouvelles acquisitions françaises 24358–69.

———. Collection Jacques Lion. Franciana. Loose-leaf scrap-books of clippings and notes, uncatalogued, in Periodical Room of B.N.

———. Collection Jacques Lion. Manuscript letters and drafts of letters of A.F. B.N., Manuscript Room, uncatalogued.

———. Papers of Louis Havet. B.N., Nouvelles acquisitions françaises 24494 (2). Contains letters from A.F. to Louis Havet.

B. Books

Aux Etudiants: Discours prononcé à la Maison des Etudiants le samedi 28 mai 1910. . . . Paris: Pelletan, 1910.

Ce que Disent nos morts. Paris: Helleu, 1916.

Clio and *The Château de Vaux-le-Vicomte.* Translated by Winifred Stephens. London: John Lane, 1923.

Œuvres complètes illustrées de Anatole France. Edited by L. Carias and G. Le Prat. 25 vols. Paris: Calmann-Lévy, 1925–1935. Cited as O.C.

Opinions sociales. Bibliothèque socialiste. 2 vols. Paris: Cornély, 1906.

The Red Lily. New York: Pyramid Books, 1959.

Sur la Voie glorieuse. 25th ed. Paris: Champion, 1916.

Vers les Temps meilleurs: Trente ans de vie sociale. Edited by Claude Aveline and Henriette Psichari. 3 vols., one more in preparation. Paris: Emile-Paul, 1949–.

La Vie littéraire, V^e série. Edited by Jacques Suffel. Paris: Calmann-Lévy, 1949.

With Jean Jaurès. *Deux discours sur Tolstoï*. Paris: L'Emancipatrice, 1911.

C. *Articles, Stories, Poems, and Published Letters*

"L'Affaire Crainquebille," *Cahiers de la Quinzaine* (I^e cahier de la IVe série), Oct., 1902.

"Anatole France to the People of America," *The Nation*, CXIII (Nov. 23, 1921), 586.

"Denys, tyran de Syracuse," *La Gazette rimée*, No. 2 (Mar. 20, 1867), 28–30.

"Les Guérin," *La Revue alsacienne*, 8th year (Oct., 1885), 529–35.

"La Houille rouge," review of book of same title by Michel Corday, *La République*, I (Apr. 28, 1923), 4–6.

"Les Légions de Varus," *La Gazette rimée*, No. 5 (June 20, 1867), 75–78.

Letters. *Catalogue de la Bibliothèque et des correspondances autographes et manuscrits ayant appartenu à M. Léopold Kahn, ami d'Anatole France*. Preface by Daniel Halévy. Paris: G. Andrieux, 1935. (Includes quotations from and summaries of numerous letters from France to Kahn.)

Letter to E. Richtenberger, Feb. 2, 1917, *Revue mensuelle* (Geneva), No. 190 (June, 1917), 302–03.

"Les Origines humaines. I. La Terre," *La Musée des deux-mondes*, I (July 15, 1873), 45–46.

"Pour la Liberté," *Les Nations*, I (June 29, 1917), 1.

"Pour la Paix," *The English Review*, XV (Aug., 1913), 9–15.

Speeches. *Cahiers de la Quinzaine* (XVe cahier de la IIIe série), May, 1902.

Various uncollected speeches, articles, and letters by Anatole France, and interviews of which he was the subject, have been cited from the following newspapers and bulletins (published in Paris unless otherwise noted): *L'Aurore, Avanti* (Milan), *La Bataille syndicaliste, Clarté, La Dépêche* (Toulouse), *Les Droits de l'Homme, L'Echo de Paris, La Feuille commune, Le Figaro, Gil Blas, La Guerre sociale, L'Humanité, Le Journal, Le Journal des Débats, Le Journal du Peuple, Manchester Guardian* (London edition), *New York Herald* (Paris edition), *Novosti (Les Nouvelles), The Observer* (London), *L'Œuvre, Le Petit Parisien, Le Populaire de Paris, Le Quotidien, Le Temps, La Tranchée républicaine, L'Univers illustré.*

II. OTHER WORKS CITED

A. Manuscripts

Archives André Marty, Harvard University. Contains letters by Henri Barbusse and others concerning the foundation of the Clarté group.

B. Books

Addamiano, N. *Anatole France, l'uomo et l'opera.* Padua: Cedam, 1947.

Arcos, René. *Romain Rolland.* Paris: Mercure de France, 1950.

Axelrad, Jacob. *Anatole France: A Life Without Illusions, 1844–1924.* 3d ed. New York: Harper & Brothers, 1944.

Bancquart, Marie-Claire. *Anatole France Polémiste.* Paris: Nizet, 1962.

Barrès, Maurice. *Mes Cahiers. Tome I: 1896–1898.* Paris: Plon, 1929.

Baumont, Maurice. *Aux Sources de l'Affaire: L'Affaire Dreyfus d'après les archives diplomatiques.* Paris: Les Productions de Paris, 1960.

———. *L'Essor industriel et l'impérialisme colonial (1878–1904).* Peuples et civilisations, Histoire générale. 2d ed. Paris: Presses universitaires de France, 1949.

Boisson, Marius. *Les Attentats anarchistes sous la Troisième République.* Paris: Editions de France, 1931.

Bonnefous, Georges and Edouard. *Histoire politique de la Troisième République.* 4 vols. Paris: Presses universitaires de France, 1956–1961.

Braibant, Charles. *Du Boulangisme au Panama: Le Secret d'Anatole France.* Paris: Denoël et Steele, 1935.

Brogan, D. W. *The Development of Modern France (1870–1939).* London: Hamish Hamilton, 1940.

Brousson, Jean-Jacques. *Anatole France en pantoufles.* Paris: G. Crès, 1924.

Caillaux, Joseph. *Mes Mémoires.* Vol. III: *Clairvoyance et force d'âme dans les épreuves, 1912–1930.* Paris: Plon, 1947.

Calmettes, Fernand. *Un Demi-Siècle littéraire: Leconte de Lisle et ses amis.* Paris: Librairies-Imprimeries réunies, 1902.

Calmettes, Pierre. *La Grande Passion d'Anatole France.* Paris: Seheur, 1929.

Capéran, Louis. *L'Anticléricalisme et l'affaire Dreyfus, 1897–1899.* Toulouse: Imprimerie Régionale, 1948.

Carias, Léon. *Anatole France.* Paris: Rieder, 1931.

——. *Les Carnets intimes d'Anatole France.* Paris: Emile-Paul, 1946.

Challaye, Félicien. *Le Congo français: La Question internationale du Congo.* Paris: Albin Michel, 1909.

——. *Péguy socialiste.* Paris: Amiot-Dumont, 1954.

Challener, Richard D. *The French Theory of the Nation in Arms, 1866–1939.* Columbia Studies in the Social Sciences, No. 579. New York: Columbia University Press, 1955.

Chapman, Guy. *The Dreyfus Case: A Reassessment.* New York: Reynal & Co., 1955.

Chevalier, Haakon M. *The Ironic Temper: Anatole France and His Time.* New York: Oxford University Press, 1932.

Collins, Ross W. *Catholicism and the Second French Republic: 1848–1852.* New York: Columbia University Press, 1923.

Combes, Emile. *Mon Ministère: Mémoires, 1902–1905.* Edited by M. Sorre. Paris: Plon, 1956.

Corday, Michel. *Anatole France d'après ses confidences et ses souvenirs.* Paris: Flammarion, 1927.

Dansette, Adrien. *Le Boulangisme.* Paris: Fayard, 1946.

——. *Histoire religieuse de la France contemporaine.* Edition revue et corrigée. 2 vols. Paris: Flammarion, 1951.

Dargan, Edwin Preston. *Anatole France: 1844–1896*. New York: Oxford University Press, 1937.

David, Robert. *La Troisième République: Soixante ans de politique et d'histoire (de 1871 à nos jours)*. Paris: Plon, 1934.

Debidour, A. *Histoire des rapports de l'Eglise et de l'Etat en France de 1789 à 1870*. Paris: Félix Alcan, 1898.

Decaudin, Michel. *La Crise des valeurs symbolistes: Vingt ans de poèsie française, 1895–1914*. Toulouse: Privat, 1960.

Demont-Breton, Virginie. *Les Maisons que j'ai connues*. Vol. II: *Nos Amies artistes*. 4th ed. Paris: Plon, 1927.

Dolléans, Edouard. *Histoire du mouvement ouvrier*. 3 vols. Paris: Armand Colin, 1936–1953.

Dorn, Walter L. *Competition for Empire*. The Rise of Modern Europe. New York: Harper & Brothers, 1940.

Dutourd, Jean. *The Taxis of the Marne*. Translated by Harold King. New York: Simon and Schuster, 1957.

Durtain, Luc. *Georges Duhamel*. Paris: Cahiers des amis des livres, 4e cahier, 1920.

Frossard, L.-O. *De Jaurès à Lénine: Notes et souvenirs d'un militant*. Paris: Nouvelle Revue socialiste, 1930.

Gagnon, Paul A. *France since 1789*. New York: Harper & Row, 1963.

Giovanelli, Felix. "The Role of Contemporary Events in Anatole France's Works." Unpublished Ph.D. dissertation, University of Illinois, 1939.

Girard, Georges. *La Jeunesse d'Anatole France, 1844–1878*. Paris: Gallimard, 1925.

Girardet, Raoul. *La Société militaire dans la France contemporaine*. Paris: Plon, 1953.

Giraud, Victor. *Anatole France*. Temps et Visages. Paris: Desclée de Brouwer, 1935.

Gourfinkel, Nina (ed.). *Gorki par lui-même*. Ecrivains de toujours. Paris: Seuil, 1954.

Grave, Jean. *Le Mouvement libertaire sous la 3e République (Souvenirs d'un révolté)*. Paris: Les Œuvres représentatives, 1930.

Gregh, Fernand. *L'Âge d'airain (Souvenirs 1905–1925)*. Paris: Grasset, 1951.

Gregh, Fernand. *L'Âge d'or. Souvenirs d'enfance et de jeunesse.* Paris: Grasset, 1947.

Guieysse, Charles. *Pages libres: Extraits.* Preface by Daniel Halévy. Hennebont: Méhat, 1927.

Halévy, Daniel. *Luttes et problèmes.* Paris: Rivière, 1911.

Harry, Myriam. *Trois ombres: Huysmans, Lemaître, France.* Paris: Flammarion, 1932.

Herriot, Edouard. *In Those Days: Before the First World War.* Translated by Adolphe de Milly. New York: Old and New World Publishing Co., n.d.

James, Henry. *French Poets and Novelists.* London: Macmillan, 1884.

Jaurès, Jean. *L'Organisation socialiste: L'Armée nouvelle.* Paris: J. Rouff, 1911.

Johannet, René. *Vie et mort de Péguy.* Paris: Flammarion, 1950.

Kémeri, Sándor [Mme Georges Bölöni]. *Promenades d'Anatole France.* Preface by P.-L. Couchoud. Paris: Calmann-Lévy, 1927.

Kownacki, A. *See* Université Populaire, Coopération des Idées.

Lacretelle, Jacques de. *À la Rencontre de France,* suivi de *Anatole France vu par un Américain,* par E. Wasserman (traduction de Jacques de Lacretelle). Paris: Trémois, 1930.

Louis, Paul. *Histoire du socialisme en France.* 5th ed. Paris: Rivière, 1950.

Lowenthal, Marvin (ed.). *The Autobiography of Michel de Montaigne.* New York: Vintage Books, 1956.

Malon, Benoît. *Le Socialisme intégral.* 2d ed. 2 vols. Paris: Félix Alcan, 1891.

Mondor, Henri. *L'Affaire du Parnasse: Stéphane Mallarmé et Anatole France.* Paris: Editions Fragrance, 1951.

Noland, Aaron. *The Founding of the French Socialist Party (1893–1905).* Cambridge: Harvard University Press, 1956.

Paul-Boncour, J. *Entre Deux guerres: Souvenirs sur la IIIᵉ République.* Vol. II: *Les Lendemains de la Victoire (1919–1934).* Paris: Plon, 1945.

Pouquet, Jeanne Maurice. *Le Salon de Madame Arman de Caillavet.* Paris: Hachette, 1926.

Powers, Richard Howard. *Edgar Quinet: A Study in French*

Patriotism. Dallas: Southern Methodist University Press, 1957.

Proust, Marcel. *Correspondance générale.* Edited by Robert Proust and Paul Brach. Vol. III. Paris: Plon, 1932.

Reinach, Joseph. *Histoire de l'Affaire Dreyfus.* 7 vols. Paris: Fasquelle, 1901–1911.

Renan, Ernest. *Drames philosophiques.* Paris: Calmann-Lévy, 1888.

Renard, Jules. *Journal, 1887–1910.* Bibliothèque de la Pléiade, Vol. CXLV. Paris: Gaillimard, 1960.

Renouvin, Pierre. *La Crise européenne et la première guerre mondiale.* Peuples et civilisations, Histoire générale. 3d ed. Paris: Presses universitaires de France, 1948.

Rolland, Romain. *Jean Christophe à Paris: La Foire sur la place.* 3d ed. Paris: Ollendorf, 1908.

——. *Journal des années de guerre, 1914–1919. Notes et documents pour servir à l'histoire morale de ce temps.* Edited by Marie Romain Rolland. Paris: Albin Michel, 1952.

——. *Péguy.* 2 vols. Paris: Albin Michel, 1944.

Roujon, Jacques. *La Vie et les opinions d'Anatole France.* Paris: Plon, 1925.

Sareil, Jean. *Anatole France et Voltaire.* Geneva: E. Droz, 1961.

Scheikévitch, Marie. *Time Past: Memoirs of Proust and Others.* Translated by Françoise Delisle. New York: Houghton Mifflin, 1935.

Schuman, Frederick L. *Russia since 1917: Four Decades of Soviet Politics.* New York: Knopf, 1957.

Seignobos, Charles. *L'Evolution de la 3e République.* Vol. VIII of *Histoire de la France contemporaine depuis la Révolution jusqu'à la paix de 1919.* Edited by Ernest Lavisse. 10 vols. Paris: Hachette, 1919–1921.

Seillière, Ernest. *Anatole France, critique de son temps.* Paris: Nouvelle Revue critique, 1934.

Smith, Helen B. *The Skepticism of Anatole France.* Paris: Presses universitaires de France, 1927.

Suffel, Jacques. *Anatole France.* Paris: Editions du Myrte, 1946.

—— (ed.). *Anatole France par lui-même.* Ecrivains de toujours. Paris: Seuil, 1954.

Tharaud, Jérôme and Jean. *Mes Années chez Barrès.* Paris: Plon, 1928.

Tison-Braun, Micheline. *La Crise de l'humanisme.* Vol. I: *1890–1914.* Paris: Nizet, 1958.

Université Populaire, Coopération des Idées [A. Kownacki]. *Histoire de douze ans (1898–1910).* Paris: La Coopération du Livre, 1910.

Vandegans, André. *Anatole France: Les Années de formation.* Paris: Nizet, 1954.

Walter, Gérard. *Histoire du Parti communiste français.* Paris: Somogy, 1948.

Weber, Eugen. *The Nationalist Revival in France, 1905–1914.* Berkeley: University of California Press, 1959.

Zévaès, Alexandre. *Histoire de la IIIe République.* Nouvelle ed. Paris: Nouvelle Revue critique, 1946.

———. *Histoire du socialisme et du communisme en France de 1871 à 1947.* Paris: France-Empire, 1947.

C. Articles

Barbusse, Henri. "Clarté," *Clarté,* new series, No. 1 (Nov. 19, 1921), 1–2.

Barrès, Maurice. "Les Hommes de la Jeune France. XIII. Anatole France," *Jeune France,* V (Feb. 1, 1883), 589–610.

Barthou, Louis. "Anatole France, commis-bibliothécaire au Sénat," *Revue de Paris,* CLXXXV (Dec. 1, 1924), 481–90.

Bouvard, Jean. "Les Souvenirs inédits du médecin d'Anatole France [P.-L. Couchoud]," *Le Dauphiné libéré* (Grenoble), Mar. 24, 1954, p. 3.

Braun, Sidney D. "Péguy and Bernard Lazare: A Common Mystique," *Symposium,* IV (May, 1950), 131–40.

Brunetière, Ferdinand. "Revue littéraire: À propos du *Disciple*," *Revue des deux mondes,* CCII (July 1, 1889), 214–26.

———. "Revue littéraire: Question de morale," *Revue des deux mondes,* CCIII (Sept. 1, 1889), 212–26.

Crucy, François. "Anatole France," *Floréal,* I (Sept. 18, 1920), 757–58.

Doumic, René. "M. Anatole France chez les Pingouins," *Revue des deux mondes,* XLVIII (Nov. 15, 1908), 446–53.

[Gohier, Urbain.] "Anatole France ou 'Monsieur Rance,' " *La Vieille-France*, No. 366 (May 1, 1924), 1–3.

Huard, Georges. "Le Père d'Anatole France, François-Noël Thibault, libraire et editeur (1805–1890)," *Bulletin du Bibliophile*, new series, 4th year (Mar. 1, 1925), 121–39.

"Le Jubilé d'Anatole France: Prenons nos distances," *Clarté*, new series, 3d year (May 1, 1924), 197–98.

Lemaître, Jules. "Anatole France," *Revue politique et littéraire*, 3d series, X (Sept. 12, 1885), 322–30.

Monod, Gabriel. Review of *Monsieur Bergeret à Paris*, *Revue historique*, LXXVI (July–Aug., 1901), 379.

Palante, G. "Anatole France, peintre social," *La Revue socialiste*, XXXIII (Apr., 1901), 442–52.

Ricard, L.-X. de. "Anatole France et le Parnasse contemporain," *La Revue*, XL (Feb. 1, 1902), 301–19.

———. "Petites Mémoires d'un Parnassien," *Le Temps*, Dec. 7, 1898.

Rouveyre, Andrè. "Brandès parmi nous," *Mercure de France*, CXCIV (Mar. 15, 1927), 568–88.

Suffel, Jacques. "Anatole France, maître d'école," *Le Soir* (Brussels), Sept. 2, 1950.

———. "Autour d'Anatole France: Documents inédits," *Mercure de France*, CCCX (Oct. 1, 1950), 248–65.

Vaillant-Couturier, Paul. "How Anatole France Turned Against the War," *The Nation*, CXX (Apr. 15, 1925), 406–07.

Vogt, Blanche. "Un Jaurès inconnu," *Les Œuvres libres*, No. 140 (Feb., 1933), 295–336.

The following periodicals, not listed above or under France's works, also have been cited (published in Paris unless otherwise noted):

L'Action française, *Bulletin officiel de la Ligue des Droits de l'Homme*, *Cahiers de la Quinzaine*, *Crapouillet*, *Le Cri des jeunes* (Montpellier), *La Croix*, *L'Echo de Paris* (Bordeaux edition), *L'Homme libre* (Bordeaux), *La Liberté*, *Le Lys rouge*, *Les Maîtres de la plume*, *Le Matin*, *Paris-Soir*, *Le Petit Journal*, *La Petite République*, *Le Socialiste*, *La Vie ouvrière*.

Index

Abbaye, L', 167
Académie Français, 22, 53, 88, 163
Action française, l', 190, 218
Adam, Juliette, 25, 40
Agadir, 178–79, 183
Albert, François, Sen., 234–35
Algeciras, 139, 178–79
Allemane, Jean, 69, 188–89
America, 153, 200, 215–16
Amis du Peuple Russe, Les, 142–43
anarchism, anarchists: in 1890s, 68, 70–72; in Les Opinions de Jérôme Coignard, 83; in Le Puits de Sainte Claire, 85–86; in Histoire contemporaine, 105; Tailhade episode, 140; in L'Île des pingouins, 155; in Switzerland, 160; and war, 175; Sacco-Vanzetti case, 215
André, Louis, Gen., 130, 133
Angell, Norman, 184, 196; The Great Illusion, 184
anticlericalism, 20, 98, 122, 126–32 passim, 174, 228; see also Catholicism, clericalism
antimilitarism, 174–85, 223–24; see also militarism

anti-Semitism, 95, 99, 101, 133, 136–37; see also Jews, pogroms
Arcos, René, 167
Armenia, Armenians: and Turks, 90, 135–36, 160; and Russia, 142; and Quillard, 187
army: virtues of, 31–32; and aristocracy, 96–97; A.F. on, 101; and militia plan, 112; and proletariat, 143; and socialism, 188; see also antimilitarism, militarism
Association Générale des Etudiants de Paris, 168
Assumptionists, 98
Aubernon, Mme Lydie, 25, 26, 40
Aulard, François-Alphonse, 234
Aurore, L', 100, 101, 141
Austria, 165, 194
Avanti, 222

Babeuf, François-Emile dit Gracchus, 116
Balzac, Honoré de, 10, 35
Barbusse, Henri: organizes Clarté, 195–96; and 1919 election, 206; and Latzko, 208; and press laws,

Barbusse, Henri (*cont.*)
214; and Latin America, 215;
on A.F., 267
Barrès, Maurice: on A.F., 37; and
Boulanger, 47; and Mme de
Caillavet, 54; *L'Ennemi des lois,*
75–76; and tradition, 93, 94, 114;
and nationalism, 168; and
Renan, 228, 229; Communists
and, 233
Barthou, Louis, 180
Bataille syndicaliste, La, 185
Béchellerie, La, 200, 203
Belgians, Belgium, 89, 139
Béraud, Jean, 69
Bibliothèque Nationale, 6
Bibliothèque Socialiste, 116
Bismarck, Otto von, Prince, 16,
45, 140
Bloc des gauches, 124–25, 151
Bloc national, 205, 207
Blum, Léon, 211, 218
Boisdeffre, Raoul Françoise de,
Gen., 106
Bölöni, Mme Georges (Sándor
Kémeri), 165
Bolsheviks, bolshevism: in 1905,
141; and 1917 Revolution, 199,
223; fear of, 205; and A.F., 210;
and International, 211; and Al-
lies, 218; and Social Revolution-
aries, 219
Bonaparte, Mathilde, Princesse,
25, 40
Bonapartists, 98
Boulanger, Georges, Gen.: in poli-
tics, 44–51, 78, 174; and A.F., 56,
62–64, 73, 249; and nationalism,
97, 99; and Déroulède, 107
Boulangism, Boulangists, 45–50
passim, 76, 98
bourgeois, bourgeoisie, 84, 111,
222; and intellectuals, 35; and

education, 43; and workers, 69,
146; and usury, 83; and army,
97; and Dreyfus Affair, 100; and
nationalism, 110, 142; and jus-
tice, 113; and revolution, 210;
and government, 214; and war,
229; of the Left, 235
Bourgeois, Emile, 131
Bourget, Paul, 56–58, 93, 94; *Le
Disciple,* 56–58
Bracke (Alexandre Desrousse-
aux), 188
Braibant, Charles, 50–51, 83
Brandes, Georg, 165
Brazza, Pierre Savorgan de, 135–
36
Breton, Jules, 24–25
Briand, Aristide, 152, 180, 194
Brochard, Victor, 40–41
Brousson, Jean-Jacques, 167, 244
Brunetière, Ferdinand, 51, 58–59,
94, 114, 238
Buisson, Ferdinand, 188
*Bulletin de la Ligue des Droits de
l'Homme,* 131, 133
Burtsev, Vladimir, 198, 199
Byron, George Gordon, sixth
baron, 9

Cachin, Marcel, 187, 240
Cahiers de la Quinzaine, 126, 127
Caillaux, Joseph, 196, 216, 218
Caillavet, Albert Arman de, 26,
54
Caillavet, Gaston Arman de, 27,
40, 48
Caillavet, Mme Albert Arman de
(née Léontine Lippmann):
meets A.F., 26–27; and A.F.'s
career, 38, 54–55, 84, 162, 167;
begins liaison with A.F., 40–42,
43; and Boulanger, 47–50, 249–
50; and *Thaïs,* 51–52; salon, 53,

115; and *Le Lys rouge*, 86; and Academy, 88–89; and Dreyfus Affair, 102, 114; and Combes, 129; and Italy, 149; death, 163–66, 168, 173
Calmann-Lévy, Gaston, 54
Calmettes, Fernand, 14, 16, 18
Capian, 26, 27, 40, 41, 44
capitalism, capitalists: development of, 113, 155; and *Crainquebille*, 116; and socialism, 117, 120, 150, 158; and imperialism, 138, 157; and internationalism, 143; and justice, 145, 153; and government, 153, 188; and war, 157, 180, 184, 222, 229; and Russian Revolution, 208
Cartel des gauches, 232–33, 235
Catholicism, Roman: and philosophy, 7–8; and romanticism, 8; and Napoleon III, 12; and Léo Taxil, 33; Boulanger and, 50; and monarchism, 97; and Dreyfus Affair, 98; and separation fight, 122–35, 150, 151, 187; and nationalism, 143; and *Vie de Jeanne d'Arc*, 167; *see also* Christianity, clericalism, religion
Challaye, Félicien, 138–39
Chambre bleu horizon, 207
Charles X, King of France, 5
Chateaubriand, René, vicomte de, 9
Chat-Noir, 68, 71
chauvinism, 50, 76, 98; *see also* nationalism, patriotism
China, 187
Christianity, 52, 86, 93, 136; *see also* Catholicism, religion
Clarté (group), 206, 214, 215, 233
Clarté, 214, 215, 216, 233
classicism, 7–9, 17

Clemenceau, Georges: and Mme de Caillavet, 54; and Panama, 78; and Dreyfus Affair, 100; premier, 151, 152, 185; and A.F., 190, 197
clericalism: republicans and, 32; Boulanger and, 49; Joan of Arc and, 65; and Dreyfus Affair, 124; and separation fight, 127, 128; and Affaire des Fiches, 130; and conscription, 184; *see also* anticlericalism, Catholicism
Colbert, Jean-Baptiste, 35
Collège Stanislas, 5, 8, 14, 17, 51
colonialism, colonies: and reform, 135, 137–39, 145, 160; capitalism and, 157; *see also* imperialism
Combes, Emile, 125–31, 151, 187; *Une Campagne laïque*, 129
Comité Catholique pour la Défense du Droit, 126
Comité d'Action pour la Liberté d'Opinion, 186
Commune, Paris, 3, 17–19, 33–34, 225
communism, communists: A.F. and, 115, 198; *Clarté* and, 216; and Bolshevik Revolution, 223; of 1930s, 240; *see also* International, Parti Communiste français
Comte, Auguste, 12, 160–61
Confédération Générale du Travail (C.G.T.), 152, 181
Constans, Ernest, 49
Coopération des Idées, La, 148
Corday, Michel, 212, 221–22, 229; *Les Hauts fourneaux*, 221–22, 229
Corday, Mme Michel, 212
Costa de Beauregard, Charles-Albert, marquis de, 88

Couchoud, Paul-Louis, 164–65, 183, 193
Cour de Cassation, 106, 107, 108
Croix, La, 98

Dansette, Adrien, 129
Darwin, Charles, 11–12
Darwinism, social, 93
Declaration of the Rights of Man, 81
defeatism, 190, 194, 196, 216
Delcassé, Théophile, 139
democracy: and society, 15, 99; and class lines, 64; in *Les Opinions de Jérôme Coignard,* 79, 82; Russian, 141; in *L'Île des pingouins,* 153
Démocratie, La, 13
Déroulède, Paul, 45–46, 107, 109; *Chants du soldat,* 45
Desbordes-Valmore, Marceline, 90
Devoyod, Elise, 9, 21
determinism, 11, 12, 57, 93, 114
Dickens, Charles, 10
Didier, Joseph, 66, 67
Doumic, René, 94, 114, 261
Dreyfus Affair, 94–111; and A.F., 114–15, 132, 170, 175; effects of, 122, 149; and 1902 elections, 123; and church, 129; in *L'Île des pingouins,* 153
Dreyfus, Alfred, 94–111 passim, 124–27 passim, 175, 223, 232
Dreyfus, Matthieu, 95
Dreyfusards, 95–111 passim; ties between, 115, 149, 152; and anticlericalism, 122, 126–32 passim; and Ligue des Droits, 217
Drumont, Edouard, 101
Duhamel, Georges, 167
Dumas, Alexandre *fils,* 26
Dunois, Amédée, 218–19, 227, 229
Dutourd, Jean, 239

Echo de Paris, L', 74, 78, 84, 87, 96, 99, 107
education, 43, 124, 145–46, 204; *see also* schools
Edward VII, King of England, 152
Eekhoud, Georges, 139
Encyclopédie, L', 169
Engels, Friedrich, 116
England, English, 122, 179, 196, 199, 208
English Review, The, 183
Epictetus, 157
error, 29, 33, 58, 104; *see also* truth
evolution (theory), 11, 12, 119
existentialism, 240

Fabian society, 196
Faguet, Emile, 94
Falloux, 101, 124
fanaticism, fanatics: and illusions, 29; and French Revolution, 34, 170–71; and socialism, 69; and science, 147; and A.F., 161; and war, 194; zeal of, 241
Faure, Félix, President, 95, 102, 106, 107
fear, 72, 113
Fédération des Jeunesses Laïques et Républicaines, 187, 233
Ferrer, Francisco, 168
Feuille Commune, La, 206
Fiches, Affaire des, 130–34, 151
Fielding, Henry, *Tom Jones,* 8
Figaro, Le, 108, 110
Finland, Finns, 135, 142
Flammarion, Camille, 11
Flaubert, Gustave, 7, 10, 22, 217
Floréal, 209
Foucquet, Nicolas, 35
Fourier, Charles, 116
FRANCE, ANATOLE
  Life: birth, 3; childhood, 3–5; education, 5; youth, 6; early

jobs, 6–7; and Parnassians, 7; first article, 8; and republicans, 12–16; in National Guard, 16–17; and Paris Commune, 17–19; and Senate Library, 21, 37–38, 49–50; first marriage, 21; and *L'Univers illustré*, 22–23, 89–90; and *Le Temps*, 23, 78; Legion of Honor, 25; and Caillavet salon, 26–27, 53–54; begins Caillavet liaison, 41; and Boulanger, 44–50; divorce, 55; and *Le Disciple*, 56–59; Académie française, 88–89; buys Villa Saïd, 91; and Dreyfus Affair, 96–111; and Jaurès, 103, 200–01; becomes Socialist, 114–16; and antichurch struggle, 122–35; and Russia (1905), 140–44; and universités populaires, 145–49; to South America, 160–62; and death of Mme de Caillavet, 164–66; and antiwar agitation, 178–86; early war articles, 190–91; ill, 193, 209; later war writings, 194–97; second marriage, 209; "adheres" to communism, 212–13; Nobel Prize, 216; Ligue des Droits de l'Homme fête, 217; and Social Revolutionaries, 219–20; breaks with *l'Humanité*, 227; eightieth birthday, 231–34; death, 235–36

Works: Alfred de Vigny, 6; "Auguste Comte," 160–61; *Les Autels de la peur*, 23, 34–35, 69, 73; *Aux Etudiants*, 168–69; *Le Chat maigre*, 21–22; *La Comédie de celui qui épousa une femme muette*, 158–59; "Courier de Paris," 36, 39, 45–47, 49, 54, 66–68, 71; *Crainquebille*, 117, 209, 231, 232; *Le Crime de Sylvestre*

Bonnard, 22, 24, 27, 28, 37, 49; "Denys, tyran de Syracuse," 13; *Les Désirs de Jean Servien*, 18–19, 21, 27, 244; *Dialogue aux enfers*, 158; *Les Dieux ont soif*, 169, 174; *L'Eglise et la République*, 129, 132; *L'Etui de nacre*, 73; *Histoire comique*, 116, 176; *Histoire contemporaine*, 84, 87–88, 89, 90, 95–96, 103–10, 116, 136, 176; *L'Île des pingouins*, 152–57, 158, 159, 161, 169–72; *Le Jardin d'Epicure*, 84, 86; *Jocaste*, 21; "Les Légions de Varus," 13; *Le Livre de mon ami*, 22, 27; *Le Lys rouge*, 83, 84, 86–87, 163; "Napoléon III," 15–16; *Les Noces corinthiennes*, 20, 21, 53; *Les Opinions de Jérôme Coignard*, 78–84; *Opinions sociales*, 116, 136; *Le Parti noir*, 129; *Le Petit Pierre*, 3–4; "Pierre Lafitte," 160–61; *Pierre Nozière*, 3–4; *Poèmes dorés*, 10–11, 27; *Le Puits de Sainte Claire*, 84–85; "Rabelais," 160; *La Révolte des anges*, 171–72, 174; *La Rôtisserie de la Reine Pédauque*, 74–75, 78; *Les Sept Femmes de la Barbe-bleue*, 159–60; *Sur la Pierre blanche*, 117–20, 137, 150, 155, 156, 161, 173, 176; *Sur la Voie glorieuse*, 192; *Thaïs*, 51–53, 56, 58, 69, 74; "La Vie à Paris," 23; *Vie de Jeanne d'Arc*, 84, 87, 156–57, 166–67; *La Vie en fleur*, 3–4, 213–14, 222; *La Vie littéraire*, 28, 31, 39, 43, 56–59, 60, 61–62, 63, 65, 68, 78

France, Mme Anatole (née Valérie Guérin de Sauville), 21, 24–25, 39–41, 55, 163

France, Mme Anatole, *see* La-prévotte, Emma
France, Mme Noël, 4, 8, 40, 162, 164, 236
France, Noël, 4–8 passim, 17, 20, 114
France, Suzanne (A.F.'s daughter; Mme Henri Mollin, then Mme Lucien Psichari), 25, 55, 133, 166
"Franciana," 16, 212, 245
Francis, St., 85
Franco-Prussian War, 3, 16, 17, 44, 92, 98–99
Franco-Russian alliance, 140, 143
Freemasonry, Freemasons, 96, 131, 133, 226
Frossard, Ludovic-Oscar, 226

Gagnon, Paul, 95
Gagey, Laura (Mme Pierre), 165
Gambetta, Léon, 123
Gapon, 141
Garde Nationale, 16, 34
Garde Républicaine, 48
Gaullism, 239
Gazette rimée, La, 13
Germans, Germany: and Morocco, 139, 178–80 passim; and Franco-Russian alliance, 140; Clemenceau and, 152; and World War I, 183, 189–93 passim, 199, 200; and Versailles Treaty, 207, 230; proletariat of, 229; *see also* Franco-Prussian War
Girondists, 14, 17
Gobineau, Joseph-Arthur, comte de, 93
Goethe, Johann Wolfgang von, 8; *Werther,* 8
Gohier, Urbain, 176
Goldsky, Jean, 196, 216, 218
Goncourt, Edmond Huot de, 10

Goncourt, Jules, 10
Good-Will Delegation, 230
Gorki, Maxim, 141–42, 220–21, 226
Government of National Defense, 16, 17
Grand Orient, 131; *see also* freemasonry
Gregh, Fernand, 89, 102–03
Gregh, Mme Fernand, 164
Grévy, Jules, President, 46, 76
Guerre sociale, La, 190
Guesde, Jules: poetry, 69; and Dreyfus Affair, 100; and reform, 144–45, 150; and worker education, 146; and A.F., 187
Guieysse, Paul, 131
Gyp, *see* Martel, comtesse de

Hague, International Peace Conference of The, 178
Héberlin-Darcy, Edouard, 158
Hébrard, Adrien, 54
Henry, Hubert-Joseph, Col., 95, 101
Hermant, Abel, *Le Cavalier Miserey,* 32, 58
Herriot, Edouard, 146
Hervé, Gustave, 186, 190
Horace, 61
Horthy, Niklos, Adm., 208
Hugo, Victor, 9, 124
humanism, 239–41 passim
Humanité, l': and *Sur la Pierre blanche,* 117; and colonialism, 138; on A.F., 190, 209, 212–13, 216, 217, 218, 221, 227–35 passim, 240; and World War I, 194; and Jaurès memorial, 200, 202–03; and Corday review, 222; and salute to soviets, 223; and Marty protest, 224

illusions: and "poet-birds," 28–29; value of, 33, 157; of progress, 35;

sources of, 105; in Argentine speech, 161–62; and satisfaction, 214

imperialism: Russia and, 138; republicans and, 142; capitalism and, 157, 180; A.F. and, 199, 204; *see also* colonialism

individualism, 100

Institut Sigisbert Pompée, 244

intellectuals: and bourgeoisie, 35; and faith, 62; of 1890s, 92–94, 114–15; protest of, 102–03; and workers, 112, 148; and Russia, 142, 144; and Clarté, 206; of Latin America, 215; and Marty case, 224; and International, 225–26, 229; and politics, 238–42 passim

International, Second, 202–03, 211

International, Third (Communist): and French party, 211, 213, 225–27; and A.F., 220; *see also* communism, Parti Communiste français

irony, A.F. and, 24, 84, 104, 239; in *La Rôtisserie de la Reine Pédauque*, 74; and pity, 86, 113; in *Le Lys rouge*, 87; Renan and, 93; in *Histoire comique*, 117

Italy, 12, 89, 149, 165–66

Jacobins, 171

James, Henry, 35

Jarry, Alfred, *Ubu-Roi*, 93

Jaurès, Jean: and Mme de Caillavet, 54; and Dreyfus Affair, 100, 101, 107; and A.F., 103, 203; and Independent Socialists, 115; and *l'Humanité*, 117; and reforms, 121, 150; and 1902 elections, 125; and anticlericalism, 127, 131, 187; and peace, 139, 200–01; and Clemenceau, 151, 152; and *Les*

Dieux ont soif, 171–72; and conscription, 180, 182, 184; assassin's trial, 200–03, 210; Parti Communiste and, 213; Carmaux memorial, 230; and *L'Île des pingouins*, 239

Jaurès, Mme Jean, 202

Jean-Pierre, 127

Jesuit, Jesuits, 52, 71, 125

Jews: in *Histoire contemporaine*, 96, 136; and Dreyfus Affair, 98–99, 134; in *Opinions sociales*, 136–37; A.F. and, 145, 233; *see also* anti-Semitism, pogroms

Joan of Arc, 65, 167

Jouhaux, Léon, 234

Journal des Débats, Le, 23

June Days (1848), 225

jusqu'auboutisme, 192, 193, 196

justice: and moderation, 32; conception of, 56, 101, 147; social, 70, 124, 128, 142, 238; and laws, 75, 82; in *Les Opinions de Jérôme Coignard*, 80; in *Le Jardin d'Epicure*, 86; in *Histoire contemporaine*, 90–91; in Dreyfus Affair, 108, 111; bourgeois, 113, 153; triumph of, 117–18, 177; socialism and, 145, 188; a farce, 159; an illusion, 162; Dunois on, 219; Soviet, 223; Dutourd on, 239

Kémeri, Sándor (Mme Georges Bölöni), 165

Kerensky, Alexander, 219

Kropotkin, Peter, Prince, 72

La Bédoyère, Henri, comte de, 8

Labori, Fernand, 109

Lafargue, Paul, 147

Lafitte, Pierre, 160

Laprévotte, Emma, 165, 193, 209, 212

Latzko, Andreas, 208

Lazare, Bernard, 99, 126–27

Leconte de Lisle, Charles-Marie, 9–10, 14, 20, 59–60

Lefebvre, Raymond, 195, 196, 207, 267

Legion of Honor, 25, 38

Lemaître, Jules: on A.F., 37; and salons, 41, 54; and tradition, 94, 114; and Dreyfus Affair, 101

Lemerre, Alphonse, 6–7, 18, 20

Lenin, 199, 210, 217

Leo XIII, pope, 71, 93, 97, 98; *Rerum novarum,* 71

Lesseps, Charles-Aimée-Marie, comte de, 77

Lesseps, Ferdinand-Marie, vicomte de, 76–77, 89

Lettres et les arts, Les, 23

liberalism, liberals, 14, 121, 232, 239, 241

liberty: trees of, 16; and instinct, 29; moral, 57; love of, 80; possibility of, 118–19; and clericals, 124, 127, 128, 134; international of, 143; political, 147; of error, 161; and fanaticism, 170; Satan and, 173; and victory, 201

lies, 105, 106, 214; *see also* truth

Ligue de la Patrie Française, 101

Ligue des Patriotes, 107

Ligue Française d'Enseignement, 234

Ligue pour les Droits de l'Homme et du Citoyen: formed, 103; Picquart campaign, 105; and amnesty, 110; and 1902 elections, 124, 125; and Affaire des Fiches, 131; and colonialism, 138; and pogroms, 207; and Latzko, 208;

and A.F., 217–18; and communism, 218–19, 226

Lion, Jacques, 16, 212, 245

Lion, Mme Jacques, 212

Littré, Emile, 11–12

London, Jack, *The Iron Heel,* 224–25

Longuet, Jean, 196

Loti, Pierre, 54

Loubet, Emile, President, 108, 134

Louis XIV, King of France, 35

Louis XVI, King of France, 68

Loynes, Anne, comtesse de, 25, 40, 41

Loyson, Hyacinthe, 188–89

MacDonald, Ramsay, 196

Mallarmé, Stephane, 60

Malon, Benoît, *Le Socialisme intégral,* 175

Malvy, Louis-Jean, 216, 218

Marat, Jean-Louis, 81

Maritain, Jacques, 128

Maritain, Jeanne, 128

Marne, First Battle of, 197

"Marseillaise, La," 45, 140

Martel, comtesse de (Gyp), 25, 55

Marty, André, 218, 223–24, 226

Marx, Karl, 116, 200, 217, 229

Marxism, Marxists, 100, 108, 221

masses: cruelty of, 34; and faith, 62; and civilization, 63; opinions of, 65; and socialists, 71–72, 205; and Dreyfus Affair, 98; and truth, 105; discernment of, 107; and war, 120; condition of, 155; and future, 157; and government, 181; and nationalism, 184; *see also* people, proletariat

Matin, Le, 191

Maupassant, Guy de, 22

Maurras, Charles: and Mme de Caillavet, 54; and classical ren-

aissance, 93; and Col. Henry,
101; and A.F., 190, 191, 218
Mercier, Auguste, Gen., 106
Méric, Victor, 224, 225, 226
Michel, Louise, 69, 160
militarism, militarists, 32, 73, 80,
99, 174–76; *see also* antimilitarism, army
Mississippi Bubble, 78
Molière, *Le Misanthrope*, 158
Mollin, Henri, Capt., 133, 166
monarchism, 8; *see also* royalism
Monod, Gabriel, 126, 127
Montaigne, Michel Eyquem de,
239
morality: science and, 30; custom
and, 31; of adultery, 56; determinism and, 57–59; Brunetière
on, 58; and lies, 105; Christian,
129; of Eekhoud's books, 139–
40; war and, 204; laws of, 215;
subversion of, 239
Morocco, 139
Morris, William, 116
Mun, Albert, comte de, 190

Napoleon I, Emperor, 65, 175
Napoleon III, Emperor, 12–17
passim
nationalism, nationalists: and
Dreyfus Affair, 97–99, 106–10
passim; primitive, 120; and
church, 124, 125, 133; Armenian,
135; and Jews, 137; and war, 139,
145, 183; and bourgeoisie, 142–
43; and capitalism, 156–57; and
Vie de Jeanne d'Arc, 167; resurgence of, 167–68, 179–80, 183–
84; and Maurras, 190; and patriotism, 203; and schools, 204;
nature of, 222; and communism,
225; and Renan, 228; and 1924

elections, 233; *see also* chauvin-
ism, patriotism
Nations, Les, 195–96
naturalism, 22, 59–61, 62, 88
Nicolas II, Tsar, 131, 140–42, 143–
44
Nietzsche, Friedrich, 93, 155
Nobel prize, 194, 216
Nouvelle Revue, La, 22

Oliva, Domenico, 128
O'Monroy, Richard, 23
Opportunists (party), 77
optimism: in *Le Crime de Sylves-
tre Bonnard,* 27; A.F. and, 90,
156, 176, 200, 214; in *Sur la
Pierre blanche,* 119
Orléanists, 233

pacifism: and socialism, 175;
masses and, 184; *Clarté* and, 216,
233; the International and, 225;
Pioch and, 230
Panama Canal Company, 76
Panama scandal, 76–78, 89, 101
Paris-Soir, 231
Parnasse, Parnassians: A.F. and, 7,
13, 217; ideals of, 9, 59; salons of,
14, 87; decline of, 21; and republicanism, 92
Parnasse contemporain, Le, 7, 60
Parti Communiste français, 121,
211, 212, 213, 216–35 passim;
see also communism
Parti Socialiste français (Jaurès),
115
Parti Socialiste, Section française
de l'Internationale ouvrière:
and reformism, 121; and church,
133; and individual freedom,
139; and Clemenceau government, 151–54; and opportunism,
159–60; and antimilitarism, 175–

Parti Socialiste (*cont.*)
85, 223; and censorship, 185–86; and 1913 elections, 187–89; and World War I, 195–96; and 1919 election, 202–07 passim; and Russian Revolution, 208; and A.F., 209–10, 218, 240; and communism, 224–25; and 1924 elections, 232–34; *see also* socialism
patriotism, 31, 32, 65, 157, 203; *see also* chauvinism, nationalism
Paul-Boncour, Joseph, 202
peace: universal, 118–20, 161, 204–05, 234; international of, 143; A.F. and, 174–85; and socialism, 188, 206; and World War I, 199; Jaurès and, 201; and 1924 elections, 233–34, 235; *see also* war
Péguy, Charles, 126–28, 168
people, the, 110, 111, 112, 147; *see also* masses, proletariat
pessimism: in A.F.'s works, 27, 156; and modern man, 61–62; and nature of man, 85–86; and intelligence, 104; and *Aux Etudiants,* 169; and 1919 elections, 206; and *The Iron Heel,* 224
Petit Parisien, Le, 191, 193
Picquart, Marie-Georges, Col.: and Dreyfus evidence, 95; arrested, 100; trial of, 105–07; and honor, 175; and A.F., 255
Pioch, Georges, 230
Pius IX, pope, 8, 12
pogroms, 207; *see also* anti-Semitism, Jews
Poincaré, Raymond, President, 54, 186
Populaire de Paris, Le, 219, 228, 231, 234
positivism, 9, 12, 160–61

Poulaillon, Henriette, 66, 67
Pouquet, Mme Jeanne Maurice, 164
poverty, 67
press, freedom of, 108, 186
Pressensé, Francis de, 121, 131, 133
Pro-Armenia, 136, 187
progress: Spencer on, 12; rate of, 30–31, 64, 70, 75, 79, 84, 241; in morals, 59, 111–12, 169; hope for, 35, 86, 119; as faith, 92; in *L'Île des pingouins,* 155; in *Les Dieux ont soif,* 173; of proletariat, 229
Progressists (party), 100
proletariat: and Dreyfus Affair, 100; victory of, 113; and A.F., 116, 217, 219; and government, 120; international of, 143; and Russian Revolution of 1905, 144; and universités populaires, 146–47; French, 199, 208; and World War I, 204; union of, 208; world, 220; progress of, 220; German, 229; *see also* masses, people
Protestants, 96
Proust, Marcel, 54, 102–03, 167; *Les Plaisirs et les jours,* 54
Pyrrho, 28, 41

Quai d'Orsay, 139, 192
Quai Malaquais, 5
Quai Voltaire, 5
Quillard, Pierre, 187
Quotidien, Le, 227, 232, 233, 234

Rabelais, François, 31, 159, 160, 239
Racine, Jean, 9
racism, 93, 136–37; *see also* anti-Semitism
Radical party, Radicals: and Boulanger, 44–48 passim; and Drey-

fus Affair, 100; and 1902 elections, 123–25, 135, 146; and Clemenceau government, 151–52; and 1914 elections, 188–89; and 1919 elections, 205; and 1924 elections, 233
Radical-Socialists, 125, 233
Rappoport, Charles, 196, 211–12
rationalism, 11–12
Ravachol, 70–72, 238
reason: and religion, 74; and skepticism, 86; and emotion, 104; establishment of, 106, 111, 113; and liberty, 147; and socialism, 188; and fanaticism, 241
Reinach, Joseph, 131, 133
Réjane, 54
religion: and A.F. as child, 5, 7; and superstition, 29; sacredness of, 32; and illusion, 33; and masses, 62; and reason, 74; workability of, 85–86; and intellectuals, 92, 93; Renan on, 129; in L'Île des pingouins, 153
Renan, Ernest: and A.F., 11; and The Tempest, 63; and progress, 92; and intellectuals, 92–94, 114; and irony, 93; monument to, 128; and religion, 129; and history, 166; centenary of, 228–29; and humanism, 239; Drames philosophiques, 252
Renard, Georges, La Conversion d'André Savenay, 69–70
republicanism, republicans: Parnassians and, 7, 92; and Second Empire, 12–17 passim; A.F. and, 31, 65, 107, 134, 142; and clericalism, 32–33; and conservatism, 33; and Boulanger, 48; and 1893 elections, 78; Catholic, 97; and Dreyfus Affair, 108–09, 111; and 1902 elections, 124; and Affaire

des Fiches, 131; and Renan memorial, 228
Revolution, French: and Noël France, 5; A.F.'s youthful view, 14; in Les Autels de la peur, 34–35; results of, 76, 92; optimism of, 81–83; glory of, 98; and patriotism, 157; in Les Dieux ont soif, 169–72; and Soviet Revolution, 227
Revolution, Russian (1905), 141–44
Revolution, Russian (February, 1917), 198
Revolution, Russian (October, 1917), 199, 207–08, 210–13 passim, 220, 223, 227
Revue alsacienne, La, 39
Revue bleue, La, 37
Revue de Paris, La, 84
Revue des deux mondes, La, 51–52, 58, 59, 94
Revue socialiste, La, 115, 175
Ricard, Louis-Xavier de, 13
Robespierre, Maxmilien, 14, 17, 80, 171
Roland de la Platière, Jean-Marie, 17
Rolland, Romain, 194
romanticism, romantics, 4, 7–9 passim, 17, 86, 92, 217
Rouanet, Gustav, 138–39
Roujon, Jacques, 250
Rousseau, Jean-Jacques, 14, 34, 153
Rousset, Emile, 187, 264
Rouvier, Maurice, 132
royalism, royalists, 8, 45, 48, 65, 96–98 passim, 112
Royer, Mme Clémence, 11
Ruhr occupation, 230
Russia, Russians: Napoleon III and, 12; and Armenia, 135; and French alliance, 140; 1905 Revo-

Russia, Russians (*cont.*)
lution, 141–44; A.F. visits, 165;
1917 Revolutions, 197–99; Allied
invasion, 208; and revolution,
211; and World War I, 219;
see also Revolution, Russian,
U.S.S.R.
Russian Social Revolutionary
Party, 198, 219–21, 223, 226
Russo-Japanese War, 138, 141, 177

Sacco, Nicola, 215
Sacco and Vanzetti case, 215
Saint-Válery-sur-Somme, 26
Salle Graffard, 69
Sand, Georges, 20
Sandeau, Jules, 38
Sardou, Victorien, 54
Sareil, Jean, 173
Scheikévitch, Marie, 164
Scheurer-Kestner, Auguste, Sen.,
95
schools, 123, 125–26, 130; *see also*
education
science, sciences: church and, 7;
Flammarion and, 11; and super-
stition, 29; and happiness, 30,
162; and morality, 56; distrust
of, 86; Zola and, 114; and war,
118, 161; and society, 147; and
socialism, 188
Senate Library, 20–21, 37–38, 49–
50
Seneca, 157
Sévérine, 196
Shakespeare, *The Tempest*, 63
Shaw, George Bernard, 196
skepticism: A.F. and, 12, 20, 56, 59,
154, 158–59, 238–42; and politics,
15; in *Le Crime de Sylvestre
Bonnard*, 27; in *La Vie littéraire*,
28; and custom, 31; and public
taste, 37; Brochard and, 40; and

judgment, 83; in *Le Jardin
d'Epicure*, 86; in *Histoire contemporaine*, 90–91, 104; and intellectuals, 92–94; and socialism,
110–11; in *Sur la Pierre blanche*,
119–20; and nationalism, 168;
in *La Vie en fleur*, 214; Renan's,
228; *Clarté* on, 233; *l'Humanité*
on, 235
socialism, socialists: rise of, 65,
68–72; A.F. and, 75, 110–11, 115–
16, 238–39; in *Les Opinions de
Jérôme Coignard*, 81, 84; in *Le
Lys rouge*, 83, 87; and internationalism, 98; and Dreyfus Affair, 100, 108; in *Histoire contemporaine*, 116; in *Sur la Pierre
blanche*, 117–20, 174; and anticlericalism, 122–25 passim; and
anticolonialism, 135; and Russia,
141, 144; and worker education,
146–48 passim; after 1905, 150–
52; in *Les Dieux ont soif*, 152–
56, 174; in *Vie de Jeanne d'Arc*,
156–58; and Jaurès, 200–01
Socialist party, *see* Parti Socialiste,
S.F.I.O.
Socialists, Independent, 115
Social Revolutionary party, Russian, 198, 219–21, 223, 226
Sorbonne, 177, 228
Souvarine, Boris, 196, 220–21
speech, freedom of, 140, 214–15
Spencer, Herbert, 11–12
spiritualism, 11, 62
Staël, Mme de, 65
stupidity, 29
Sully Prudhomme, Armand, 54
Syllabus of 1864, 134
symbolism, 59–61, 92–94 passim
syndicalism, 185

Tailhade, Laurent, 140

Taine, Hippolyte Adolphe, 11–12, 20, 93, 94, 114
Taxil, Léo, 33
Temps, Le: and *Jocaste,* 21; A.F.'s contributions to, 23, 24, 28, 31, 39, 43, 61, 65, 68, 221; and politics, 46; and *Le Disciple,* 56, 58, 59; on Zola, 60; A.F. leaves, 78; war editorial, 191; and A.F.'s war propaganda, 192
Thibault, Anatole-François, *see* France, Anatole
Thibault, François-Noël, *see* France, Noël
thought, freedom of, 57, 59
Three-Year law, 180–89 passim
Tison-Braun, Micheline, 93, 240
toleration, 29–33 passim, 59, 61
Tolstoy, Lev Nicolaevich, count, 93, 177
Tours, Congress of, 211
Trarieux, Ludovic, 103
Tréguier, 128
Trocadéro, 234
Trotsky, Leon, 225, 229, 230
truth: knowledge of, 30, 33, 56, 104; Brunetière on, 58; power of, 111; proletariat and, 147; love of, 162, 214; Dunois and, 219
Turkey, Turks, 90, 135, 199

Union of Economic Interests, 205
Union of Soviet Socialist Republics, 210–27 passim; *see also* Russia
Univers illustré, L': A.F. and, 22, 39, 89–90; readership of, 36; on Boulanger, 45, 46, 49
universités populaires, 112, 145–49, 260

Vaillant-Couturier, Paul, 195, 196, 208, 267

Valéry, St., 33
Vanzetti, Bartolomeo, 215
Vatican, 130
Versailles, Treaty of, 206–07, 216, 228
Vie ouvrière, La, 240
Villa Saïd, 91, 167, 208, 211
violence: and Commune, 19; nature of, 32; Coignard on, 80; and democracy, 82; A.F. and, 120, 174, 175; and revolution, 171, 172; in *Les Dieux ont soif,* 173; coming of, 201; and class struggle, 206, 210
Virgil, 17
Vogüé, Eugène-Melchior, vicomte de, *Le Roman russe,* 93
Vogue parisienne, La, 15
Voltaire, 14, 59, 198, 229, 239–41 passim

Waldeck-Rousseau, René, 108–09, 123, 125, 129
Walsin-Esterhazy, Marie-Charles-Ferdinand, Maj., 95, 106
war: ending of, 117–18, 120, 161, 234; and nationalists, 139, 144, 183, 203; and capitalism, 157, 180, 184, 229; opponents of, 175; and fanaticism, 194; and Juarès, 200–01; and morality, 204; civil, 230; *see also* World War I, World War II
Wells, H. G., 196
Wilhelm II, Emperor, 140
Wilson, Daniel, 45, 46, 76
Wilson, Woodrow, President, 200
workers, 69, 112, 147–48, 201; *see also* masses, proletariat
World War I, 136, 189–200 passim, 204, 219, 222, 228
World War II, 239, 240

Wrangel, Pëtr Nicolaevich, baron, 208

youth, 62

Zola, Emile, 22, 114; *La Débâcle*, 60, 73; *Germinal,* 60; *La Terre,* 60; A.F. and, 60–61, 73, 232, 251; and Academy, 88; and Dreyfus Affair, 95, 100–03; "J'accuse," 95, 100, 101, 103; death, 127

Zurlinden, Emile, Gen., 106

About the Author

Carter Jefferson was graduated from George Washington University in 1949. After several years as a newspaperman in Texas, Colorado, and New Mexico, and a tour of duty in the Navy, he completed his graduate work at Southern Methodist University and the University of Chicago. He has taught at Wayne State University and the University of Michigan and is currently a member of the history faculty of Rutgers University. Part of the research for this book was carried out during a year's stay in France.

This book was set in Linotype Janson with Caslon
Bold display type and was printed by letterpress on
60# Mead Publishers' Imperial Text. The binding
is G.S.B. S/535 Bookcloth. The book was designed by
Adrianne Onderdonk and manufactured by H. Wolff
Book Manufacturing Co., Inc., New York.